# The Tudors

FOR

# DUMMIES®

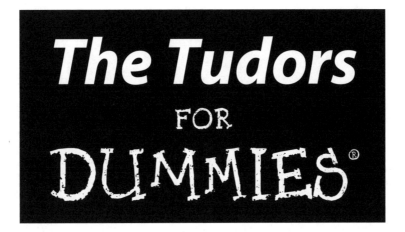

# The Tudors
## FOR
## DUMMIES®

## by David Loades and Mei Trow

## WILEY

A John Wiley and Sons, Ltd, Publication

**The Tudors For Dummies**®

Published by
**John Wiley & Sons, Ltd**
The Atrium
Southern Gate
Chichester
West Sussex
PO19 8SQ
England

E-mail (for orders and customer service enquires): cs-books@wiley.co.uk

Visit our Home Page on www.wiley.com

Copyright © 2011 John Wiley & Sons, Ltd, Chichester, West Sussex, England

Published by John Wiley & Sons, Ltd, Chichester, West Sussex

For general information on our other products and services, please contact our Customer Care Department within the U.S. at 877-762-2974, outside the U.S. at 317-572-3993, or fax 317-572-4002.

For technical support, please visit www.wiley.com/techsupport.

Wiley also publishes its books in a variety of electronic formats. Some content that appears in print may not be available in electronic books.

British Library Cataloguing in Publication Data: A catalogue record for this book is available from the British Library

ISBN: 978-0-470-68792-5 (paperback), 978-0-470-66457-5 (ebk), 978-0-470-66458-2 (ebk), 978-0-470-68804-5 (ebk)

Printed and bound in Great Britain by Bell & Bain Ltd, Glasgow

10 9 8 7 6 5 4 3 2

WILEY

# About the Authors

**Professor David Loades** studied history at Cambridge, where he researched under the great Professor Sir Geoffrey Elton, and spent his entire working life teaching history at various universities including St Andrews, Durham and North Wales. He is Professor Emeritus, University of Wales, and for the duration of his directorship of the British Academy John Foxe Project, was Research Professor at the University of Sheffield. He is currently a member of the History Faculty of the University of Oxford, a Fellow of the Society of Antiquaries and a Fellow of the Royal Historical Society. He has just completed a book on Mary Tudor and is currently writing a biography of Henry VIII, as well as a book on the mid-Tudor navy.

**Mei Trow** is an historian and criminologist who has written a number of books on the more colourful personalities from history, such as Spartacus, Vlad the Impaler, Boudicca, El Cid and Kit Marlowe. Mei is also a novelist with two crime detective series to his credit and a third in development. He regularly appears on the Discovery and History Channels as an expert and presenter.

# Authors' Acknowledgements

Writing a *For Dummies* book has been a very different experience from writing the many other books I have published, but whatever I write owes much to my pupils during a lifetime of teaching. In this instance my first debt must be to my wife, Judith, who has worked her way through each chapter.

I also thank Juliet Atkins, without whose technical skills the format would have been impossible for me. My greatest debt is to the *For Dummies* team: to Nicole Hermitage, who invited me to contribute to the series (and who must often have had second thoughts!), and to Brian who made my work more lucid. Finally, my greatest debt is to Steve Edwards who has taken this book every step of the way and who has demonstrated the patience of Job in seeing it through from start to finish!

**– David Loades**

My thanks as always to Carol, my wife, for all her hard work and technical know-how in putting *The Tudors For Dummies* together. My thanks also to Steve Edwards and his team, for their support and guidance.

**– Mei Trow**

## Publisher's Acknowledgements

We're proud of this book; please send us your comments through our Dummies online registration form located at www.dummies.com/register/.

Some of the people who helped bring this book to market include the following:

**Commissioning, Editorial, and Media Development**

**Project Editor:** Steve Edwards

**Development Editor:** Brian Kramer

**Commissioning Editor:** Nicole Hermitage

**Assistant Editor:** Ben Kemble

**Copy Editor:** Andy Finch

**Technical Editor:** Dr Janet Dickinson

**Proofreader:** Charlie Wilson

**Production Manager:** Daniel Mersey

**Cover Photos:** © The Art Gallery Collection/ Alamy

**Cartoons:** Rich Tennant (www.the5thwave.com)

**Composition Services**

**Project Coordinator:** Lynsey Stanford

**Layout and Graphics:** Carl Byers, Joyce Haughey

**Proofreader:** Rebecca Denoncour

**Indexer:** Claudia Bourbeau

**Special Help**
**Brand Reviewer:** Jennifer Bingham

**Publishing and Editorial for Consumer Dummies**

**Diane Graves Steele,** Vice President and Publisher, Consumer Dummies

**Kristin Ferguson-Wagstaffe,** Product Development Director, Consumer Dummies

**Ensley Eikenburg,** Associate Publisher, Travel

**Kelly Regan,** Editorial Director, Travel

**Publishing for Technology Dummies**

**Andy Cummings,** Vice President and Publisher, Dummies Technology/General User

**Composition Services**

**Debbie Stailey,** Director of Composition Services

# Contents at a Glance

# Table of Contents

# Introduction

· · · · · · · · · · · · · · · · · · · · · · · · · · · · · · · · · · · · · · · · · · · · · · · · · · ·

*T*he Tudors are in fashion. More than 500 years after the key events of the period, scholars, novelists and film-makers are flocking back to the 16th century. Fortunately, the Tudors left behind loads of clues as to who they were and what they wanted from life and for England. For example, in many ways the Tudor portrait painter Hans Holbein was the best publicist before Max Clifford!

The earlier, medieval rulers suffer from poor publicity, and if you want to study them, much of the research involves dry official records (accounts and grants for the most part). If you're interested in Henry VIII or Elizabeth I, however, you have stacks of correspondence – some of it official, but much of it personal. Busy secretaries and ambassadors were writing everything down. Scholars have even uncovered Henry VIII's love letters (or at least some of them). Of course, these sources didn't always get the details right, but that's where the fun begins. The official records still exist, of course, but with the Tudors you can finally get in touch with England's leaders as human beings. The Tudor monarchs made mistakes, messed up matters and came up with some very creative solutions – and you can follow all the twists and turns in this book.

Additionally, the Tudors really were important. Many buildings you visit (and perhaps live in) throughout England and Wales were built in the 16th century. Institutions that you may take for granted, such as the Church of England or Parliament, were invented or took on new importance while the Tudors were on the throne.

## About This Book

This book aims to tell the Tudor story the way it happened; not the whole story, of course – that would take a whole library of books – but enough to give you an idea of what was going on from 1485–1603. We're historians who've been writing about the Tudors for years, but we know that doesn't go for most of you and so we keep things simple (no offence!), which isn't always easy. Henry VIII's love life, for instance, defies all attempts to simplify, as does Elizabeth's on/off search for a husband. But we hope to help you understand why these events were so important and why they took up so much time and effort.

This book focuses on *English* history. Scotland was a foreign country (until King James came along), and so it appears alongside France, the Netherlands and Spain as part of English foreign policy. The Tudors and the Stuarts in Scotland were related by marriage, but that didn't make them friends. The two kingdoms were fighting each other throughout the first half of the 16th century.

Ireland, meanwhile, was a glorified English colony: it became a kingdom in its own right in 1541 but belonged to the English Crown. In fact, no English monarch visited Ireland between Richard II (1399) and William III (1689). The Tudors made a right royal mess of governing Ireland – and the after-effects still linger. Wales was ruled directly from England; the rulers and citizens may not have liked this situation, but the country received quite a fair measure of home rule after 1536. People began to talk about *Britain* (and even *Great Britain*) in the 16th century, but they meant the lands ruled by the monarch of England.

Although the Tudors are very important and fascinating for modern readers, keep in mind that they were small fry in the European political league at the time. England performed a balancing act between France and the Roman Empire in the first half of the 16th century, although Henry VIII always punched above his weight. In the second half of the century Elizabeth led (or in certain cases, didn't lead) a series of coalitions against Philip II, who ruled the Spanish Empire, the one superpower of the period.

The only European Community of the time was the Roman Catholic Church, from which England had firmly withdrawn. Elizabethan England was a sea power and traded all over the world, but its only colony at Roanoke in the Americas failed and the days of the British Empire were still 100 years in the future.

Therefore, this book provides the ingredients and recipe of half an island, lightly cooked and served (we hope) with enough relish to make it palatable.

# Conventions Used in This Book

The system of dating used throughout the Tudor period, and for a long time afterwards, was the Julian calendar, named after Julius Caesar who supposedly invented it. This old calendar was known as the *Old Style* and is important only because continental Europe adopted a *New Style* or *Gregorian* calendar from 1582. This new calendar was ten days ahead, and so the Spanish dating of the Armada, for example, was ten days later than the English version. The year also began on 25 March, so that February 1587 by modern-day reckoning would have been February 1586 by the Tudors' calendar. This situation can be confusing, and so in this book we adopt the modern convention of starting the year on 1 January: therefore, the year 1586 runs from 1 January to 31 December.

We haven't changed money at all. No paper money existed in Tudor England, and certainly no cheques or plastic! Coins included groats, angels and crowns, but the value of money has changed so much – and historians are still arguing about exactly *how* much – that we've left the original round figures with no attempt to update to today's currency values.

# Foolish Assumptions

We assume that you've heard of the Tudors and know roughly when the 16th century was – but not very much more.

Many people studied the period 1485 to 1603 at school and acquired vague impressions of Henry VIII and Elizabeth I but little understanding of the other three Tudor rulers.

You may have watched *The Tudors* series on television (in which case the facts may well surprise you), or seen David Starkey's documentary programmes that whetted your appetite to know more. David tells it like it was, but only some of it: the rest is here.

# How This Book Is Organised

The parts of the book flow chronologically, and so Part I is (mainly) about Henry VII and his origins, and Part IV focuses on Elizabeth I. Within these parts, the chapters are thematic, allowing you to pick and choose. For example, if you want to know about Henry VIII's love life, go to Part II, Chapter 5; if Elizabeth I's war with Spain grabs you, go to Part IV, Chapter 15.

## Part 1: Encountering the Early Tudors

Henry VII didn't just spring out of the grass – he had a family and background. This part looks at who he was, his Welsh roots and the civil war that gave him his opportunity. We also lead you on a quick tour of 15th-century England – its social structure, religion and beastly habits – to provide some context. The culture of the Court was a thing apart, and education struggled with an illiterate population. If you think things are bad now, look at the England of Henry VI! When the Crown was weak, the nobility dominated and fought its private quarrels under the cover of the houses of York or Lancaster. This situation created the challenge that greeted Henry VII after the Battle of Bosworth. On the whole, he made a pretty good job of getting and keeping his crown.

# Part II: Handling Henry VIII

Henry VII became monarch in 1485 and married within six months. His wife Elizabeth bore at least five children, three of whom were sons. Nevertheless, by 1502 the future Henry VIII, whom we meet in this part, was the only son left – a crisis situation. Henry VIII was brought up and educated most carefully as the heir to the throne. As a young man he was very athletic, hunting and jousting with great enthusiasm. He ran his kingdom with a light touch, preferring his hobbies, but he also yearned to prove himself by war, taking Henry V as his role model. As he aged, he became short-tempered, particularly on the subject of sex; he famously married six times and fathered one illegitimate son. His ego also developed to gigantic proportions. He eventually took on the papacy in Rome and changed the direction of English religion forever.

# Part III: Remembering the Forgotten Tudors: Edward VI and Mary

The focus in this part is on Edward and Mary, who are notoriously the two little Tudors between the two big ones. They're often passed over, particularly by popular storytellers. Nevertheless, they're both important in different ways. Edward's minority (he was a child of 9, but bright) tested two things: the Royal Supremacy and the Crown's control over the nobility. Henry VIII surrounded his son with men who turned out to be Protestants. These radical reformers converted both King Edward and the English Church, successfully sweeping away centuries of religious styles of worship. Mary is best remembered as Bloody Mary who burned Protestants, but she was far more than that. She was England's first ruling queen, and her marriage to King Philip of Spain brought up all sorts of questions about being a good sovereign and a good wife.

# Part IV: Ending with Elizabeth

Elizabeth had a different agenda to Mary but took advantage of her half-sister's reign in several ways. First, the Crown had been 'ungendered' for Mary's benefit, which gave Elizabeth a flying start. Second, she took on-board the lessons of her sister's example about how tricky marriage can be for a ruling queen. Although Elizabeth entered into several negotiations, she never tied the knot. Third, she exploited Mary's spiritual fervour and turned the whole religious settlement upside down. Although she's best remembered as Gloriana who beat the Spanish Armada, you see in this part that Elizabeth was simply a successful ruler who developed her own inimitable style and gave her kingdom status and self-respect. Having never married, sheer good luck enabled her to pass the crown to her cousin, her Protestant 'brother of Scotland' James VI, who became King James I of England in 1603.

## Part V: The Part of Tens

If you want to impress your friends with your knowledge of Tudor England, you can do worse than start at the end of this book where you find a digest of information. We supply ten crucial moves and developments, such as England's break with Rome and the start of the war with Spain. We describe ten things that link the Tudors with the present day, including the right of female succession and an independent Church of England, and highlight ten areas where the Tudors got there first. And you can tour ten surviving buildings, some of which are only partly Tudor (such as Hampton Court). The list includes places you've probably never heard of but that are well worth a visit.

# Icons Used in This Book

This book includes several icons to highlight special points and add additional layers of understanding to your reading experience.

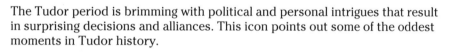

The Tudor period is brimming with political and personal intrigues that result in surprising decisions and alliances. This icon points out some of the oddest moments in Tudor history.

If you think that Henry VIII was an insatiable womaniser or Elizabeth I was a frosty virgin queen, think again! We replace commonly held beliefs with the facts.

As with all things, you can look at a problem or the importance of an event in different ways. This icon points up some of the most intriguing examples.

The Tudor legacy extends from 16th-century England to modern-day Great Britain – and beyond. We use this icon to emphasise these connections.

These paragraphs contain essential information to bear in mind when getting to grips with the Tudors.

Although everything in this book is interesting, not every single paragraph is vital. If you want to skip the more complicated stuff (or save it for later), this icon shows the way.

The events of the Tudor era have provided film makers with plenty of inspiration and have led to a number of memorable movies being made. Many of these are worth watching for an insight into Tudor times, so we highlight some of the best for you in these paragraphs.

# Where to Go from Here

At this point you can turn the page and start at the beginning of the Tudors' story. Part I gives you a snapshot overview of the period and introduces you to the first Tudor, Henry VII. Alternatively, you can jump to Parts II or IV and dive into the fascinating reigns of Henry VIII and Elizabeth I, respectively.

Each chapter of this book focuses on a specific topic or segment of Tudor history, so you can dive in anywhere. We include cross-references in each of the chapters, and so when something comes up that we mention in more detail elsewhere, you can turn to the appropriate chapter.

Whatever way you choose to enjoy this book, we hope you find the journey fun and interesting.

# Part I
# Encountering the Early Tudors

The 5th Wave                    By Rich Tennant

## In this part . . .

England was a mess before 1485. Bully boy barons with their castles and private armies had a go at each other, everybody kicked the peasants around and the Church was a law unto itself. It was a bit like Lord of the Flies – anarchy ruled until a shrewd cookie called Henry Tudor, Earl of Richmond, made his mark and kick-started modern history.

To give you some idea of how Henry changed England, this part takes you on a whirlwind tour of 15th-century England, its ups and downs, its ins and outs, and looks at the politics, religion and general skulduggery of the period.

First, though, we have a gallop through who the Tudors were and what they did in their 118 years on the throne of England. And remember, everything in their time happened at the speed of a horse or slower. Get with the rhythm.

# Chapter 1

# Touring the Time of the Tudors

*T*he old history books will tell you that 1485 was the end of the Middle Ages and the start of the modern world. It wasn't quite like that. What happened was that the last king of the Plantagenet family (Richard III) was defeated at the Battle of Bosworth by the first king of the Tudor family (Henry VII), and the rest is history.

The Tudors ruled England, Wales and Ireland for 118 years until Elizabeth I died in 1603. These years were a time of huge changes, many of them brought about by the Tudors themselves. For example:

✔ The nobility – rich, powerful, awkward – became a kind of civil service and worked for the king.

✔ Parliament got pushier.

✔ The Church changed from Catholic to Protestant.

✔ Trade took off and exploration increased.

In this chapter we take a walk through the Tudor times, from the monarchs and their Courts through to religion, education, health and the arts. So make sure your breeches and codpiece are in place or lace up your corset, and enter the world of the Tudors.

# Looking at the Tudor Kingdom

England had come to dominate the British Isles long before the Tudors arrived and, because of this, historians use the term 'England' to include Wales and from time to time, Ireland. Wales was a principality (since the 13th century, the eldest son of the king of England had always been Prince of Wales), but was regarded as part of England. Because of this, Welsh heraldry (featuring images of dragons, daffodils and so on) rarely appeared on coins.

From 1536, the various regions of Wales were turned into counties based on the English pattern. Those counties have disappeared since, though, so don't try to find the Tudor county names in Wales today – Welsh place names are used again. The Tudor county names were quite quaint though; examples include Radnorshire, Merioneth, Flintshire, Carmarthen, Caerphilly and Gwent.

Although England in the 16th century had more than its fair share of intrigue, excitement and blood and guts, across the water Ireland had plenty of drama of its own. The Tudors thought of Ireland as something that, with a bit of luck, would go away. The Irish thought equally little of their English over-lords and centuries of mistrust and misunderstanding were to lead to a running sore that only bloodletting could cure.

A lot of this book looks at events in Ireland in particular because it was a constant problem for the Tudors. Wales was quieter – perhaps because the ruler of England was Welsh!

# Getting to Know the Family

The Tudors were just like most people – proud, difficult, petty, loving, hating – but they also ran the country, and that made a big difference. You meet the Tudors all through the course of this book, but here's a quick snapshot to put them in perspective. If you've already had a sneaky look at the Cheat Sheet, this is just a reminder:

- Henry VII, born 1457 (reigned 1485–1509)
  - Married Elizabeth, daughter of Edward IV
- Henry VIII, born 1491 (reigned 1509–1547)
  - Married Catherine of Aragon (Queen 1509–1533)
  - Married Anne Boleyn (Queen 1533–1536)
  - Married Jane Seymour (Queen 1536–1537)

- • Married Anne of Cleves (Queen 1539–1540)

- • Married Catherine Howard (Queen 1540–1541)

- • Married Catherine Parr, Lady Latimer (Queen 1543–1547)

✔ Edward VI, born 1537 (reigned 1547–1553)

✔ Jane Grey, born 1537 (reigned 10–19 July, 1553)

✔ Mary I, born 1516 (reigned1553–1558)

- • Married Philip II of Spain (1554–1558)

✔ Elizabeth I, born 1533 (reigned 1558–1603)

Where did the Tudors come from? Hold on to your hats – it's complicated!

✔ Henry VII's father was Edmund Tudor, Earl of Richmond. Edmund's father was Owen Tudor, a fairly poor Welsh gentleman, and his mother was Catherine de Valois, the French widow of Henry V (reigned 1413–1422).

✔ Henry VII's mother was Margaret Beaufort, daughter of the Duke of Somerset. Margaret was a descendant of John of Gaunt, Duke of Lancaster, the son of Edward III (reigned 1327–1377).

We told you it was complicated! Thank goodness for Figure 1-1, a family tree of the families of York and Lancaster.

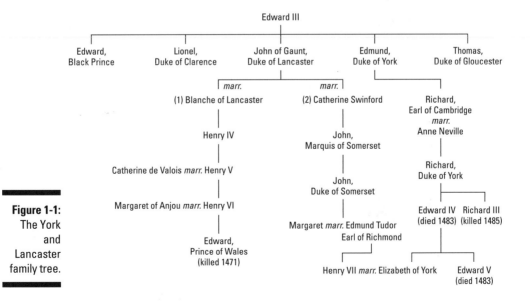

**Figure 1-1:**
The York and Lancaster family tree.

No evidence proves that Owen Tudor and Catherine de Valois ever married, which makes the Tudor line illegitimate. That wasn't much of a problem in the 15th century unless, of course, you tried to claim the English throne. Henry's claim to the throne was weak, but he got lucky at the Battle of Bosworth in August 1485 (see Chapter 2) and, with the death of Richard III, went on to become king. At that time at least 18 people had a better right to the throne than Henry, including his own wife and mother. By 1510, when his son Henry VIII was king, the figure had increased to 34! Perhaps it was this insecurity that explains much of the changes in society that happened in the Tudor period.

# Cruising the Royal Court

The *Court* was much more than a building – it was the place where the king lived with his family, where the business of government was carried out and where key decisions were made. It was always full of people, courtiers, servants, ministers, priests, entertainers and hangers-on hoping to find fame and fortune. Until 1603 the Court moved from one palace to another, taking everything but the kitchen sink with it. Henry VIII had only one set of furniture that went wherever he did!

## Mingling with the monarch

The king or queen in Tudor England *was* the government. Although the monarchs worked through Parliament to an increasing extent, all major decisions came from the top, and the king or queen had to be consulted at all times.

In theory, the monarch:

- ✔ Appointed and dismissed ministers
- ✔ Called and dismissed Parliament (in theory, the nation's representatives)
- ✔ Collected taxes
- ✔ Commanded the army and navy
- ✔ Decided on issues like war and peace
- ✔ Worked with the Church but did not run it (the Tudors soon changed that)

In practice, the monarch:

- ✔ Believed in a hotline to God as 'the Lord's anointed'
- ✔ Set the fashion in clothes, education and entertainment
- ✔ Was the chief patron, giving out lands, titles and charity

Henry VII was the first king to be called 'Your Majesty'. Before that, kings were known as 'Your Grace'. Until 1485 the king was *primus inter pares* (first among equals) but the Tudors lifted royal status much higher. The Stuart family, who followed in 1603, tried to go further still, which resulted in the Civil War (1642–1648) and the execution of Charles I (1649).

## Breaking down the Court

The Court was divided into two main parts, the Household and the Chamber, followed by various councils and a few odds and ends like the Chapel Royal, the stables, the kennels and the toils (cages for the hunting hawks).

The Tudors, like all kings before them, loved hunting (see Chapter 3), so they had a huge team of servants just to look after the wolfhounds, palfreys (saddle horses) and falcons.

### Handling the Household

The Household hadn't changed much since the 14th century. It had nearly 20 departments, handling every aspect of the royal family's lives. The lord steward ran the Household and the controller kept tabs on the running costs in the counting house (in 1545 Henry VIII's Court cost £47,500 to run – a huge sum at the time).

Think about your daily life and imagine an army of servants to doing all you chores for you. The various departments dressed and undressed the royals, provided water for washing, cleaned their rooms and made their beds. They prepared, cooked and served their meals and washed up afterwards. They lit candles and fires, looked after clothes and jewellery and emptied toilets (it was a messy job, but somebody had to do it).

Each department was run by a sergeant and most of the staff were men (the laundry was mostly female). Some staff were very specialist:

- ✔ The yeomen of the guard were the king's bodyguard (check out the beefeaters at the Tower of London – they still wear Tudor-style uniforms).
- ✔ The king's music were the royal orchestra.
- ✔ The royal confessors were the king's chaplains or priests.

In addition doctors, chemists, scholars and artists came and went, the greatest of them increasing the reputation of the Court in the eyes of the world. Hans Holbein is perhaps the best known of these great men; playwrights like William Shakespeare never got that close to the top, but Elizabeth certainly saw some of his plays.

The Tudor Court even employed pages (little boys) to take a beating rather than a naughty prince having to receive pain! They were called *whipping boys*.

Only the more senior servants were allowed to live with their wives, which made the Household a happy hunting ground for whores. Much of the lord steward's time was spent shooing harlots off the premises and preventing punch-ups between servants.

### Channelling the Chamber

The Chamber was the king's personal space. This was the centre of government and the servants there were gentlemen or even noblemen. The lord chamberlain ran the Chamber, but individual members vied with each other as royal favourites.

Having the 'ear of the king' was very important under the Tudors. Any gentleman who wanted to get on or any nobleman who had ideas he wanted carried out had to get reach the king to suggest things to him. Only the king could issue orders that would be carried out. This naturally caused rivalry and bitterness at times, but it was also a way for the monarch to keep his or her staff on their toes. In the reign of Elizabeth, for example, much of the discussion was about the queen's marriage and a number of courtiers put themselves forward as potential husbands.

Over the Tudor period, the role of the Chamber changed:

- ✔ Henry VII set up a Privy (personal) Chamber of new men – servants from relatively humble backgrounds – and dealt with his noble and gentleman attendants separately (see Chapter 2).

- ✔ Henry VIII modelled his Privy Chamber on that of the French king, Henry's rival Francis I. The men in his Chamber were his hunting and drinking cronies but he trusted them to carry out delicate diplomatic missions.

- ✔ Edward VI was too young to govern by himself and the closest advisers he had were his tutors. The Privy Chamber lost its central role.

- ✔ Mary and Elizabeth's accessions changed the whole set-up. Ladies in waiting became important, but women, apart from the queen, couldn't get involved in politics, so they tended to work on Mary and Elizabeth to get promotions and favours for their men folk.

For more on the Privy Chamber, see the nearby sidebar 'Being privy to the Privy Chamber'.

### Counting the councils

The royal Council was the fore-runner of today's Cabinet. Its members were the great secretaries of state who advised monarchs on any matter they considered important. We meet these advisers close up and personal in this book, men like . . .

> ✔ Francis Walsingham
>
> ✔ Robert Dudley
>
> ✔ Thomas Cromwell
>
> ✔ Thomas Seymour
>
> ✔ Thomas Wolsey
>
> ✔ William Cecil

. . . and many more.

But councils also existed for the North and for Wales and the West. At local level, the government was carried out by lords lieutenants of counties appointed by the monarch and landowners acting as justices of the peace. The lords lieutenants:

> ✔ Acted as judges in local cases
>
> ✔ Called out the militia (part time soldiers) in case of invasion or other emergency
>
> ✔ Collected taxes

Kings and queens weren't bound to take the advice of their councillors. As long as men like Wolsey and Cromwell got the job done for Henry VIII, they were fine. But if the advisers failed, they could not only be fired but also executed. But despite the risks of the job, some advisers were very close to their employer: Robert Dudley was Elizabeth's lover, and Francis Walsingham died bankrupt having spent so much of his own money to keep Elizabeth safe.

## Being privy to the Privy Chamber

The Privy Chamber was run by the chief gentleman or gentlewoman and was a showcase for the monarch. Under Henry VIII it was all about tournaments and lavish entertainments with French or Spanish fashions the order of the day. Under the dour Catholic Mary, it all got a bit heavy, with prayers, masses and constant discussions and gossip about the queen's two phantom pregnancies. Under Elizabeth, who worked hard to push her image as Gloriana and the virgin queen, the Chamber was for courtship, music and poetry mixed with the harder realities of exploring the world in her name and keeping her safe from assassination. Under each of the monarchs the Privy Chamber was also a marriage market and the main way for kings and queens to keep in touch with the men who actually ran the country at a local level.

# *Taking in Tudor Beliefs*

In 1500 the English had a great reputation for piety. They went to mass, which was held in Latin, visited shrines like Thomas Becket's at Canterbury Cathedral, paid priests to say prayers for the souls of the dead and, in the case of the rich, left legacies to the Church in their wills.

But some people began to doubt the power of the priests and others resented the Church's huge wealth (see later in this chapter and also Chapter 6). New ideas of the Reformation were coming from Martin Luther in Germany, and of particular interest was the concept of *solo fide* (faith alone), which was about your own beliefs in God and had nothing to do with good works.

William Tyndale's English Bible (see Chapter 6) sold in huge quantities, especially when it was backed by Henry VIII who believed everybody should read God's word.

The Tudor era was a time of great religious change:

- ✔ Henry VIII fell out with the Pope, changed the calendar and destroyed the monasteries. Henry himself stayed Catholic, but breaking up with Rome was the only way he could get a son to continue the Tudor line. So he made himself supreme head of the Church and the idea lived on after him (see Chapter 6).

- ✔ Edward VI, under advice from his Protestant uncles, changed the Latin mass to English, brought in an English prayer book and stopped individual confession. This caused confusion and dismay for many (see Chapter 7).

- ✔ When Mary became queen she brought back the Latin mass and all the traditional ceremonies, causing confusion and dismay to all those happy under Edward's arrangements. Her religious package included kowtowing to the Pope again and she burned opponents at Smithfield in London (see Chapter 10).

- ✔ Elizabeth's Church of 1559 was a *via media* (a compromise) – part Catholic and part Protestant. She made herself supreme governor and brought in a new English prayer book. Over time, her Church became less and less Catholic, but she refused to bring in yet more changes demanded by off-the-wall revolutionaries called Puritans (see Chapter 14).

England was just as Christian at the end of the Tudors' reign as it had been at the start, but some things had changed forever:

- ✔ The Pope was now the Bishop of Rome, and the Church of England was totally independent.

- ✔ Confession between priest and man had gone, as had carvings of saints, wall paintings and pilgrimages.

> ✔ Good Christians did charitable works, went to church and read their Bibles. They did not go on pilgrimages; they did not say prayers for the dead.

# Seeing How the Masses Lived

The 16th century saw a dramatic population growth. Accurate figures don't exist (the first census wasn't made until 1801), but from Church and tax records historians can work out that in 1500 about 2.5 million people lived in England and Wales (Ireland was a sort of colony and was always counted separately) and by 1600 it was about 4 million.

Farming and agriculture were by far the most common jobs and this didn't change over the Tudor period. About 90 per cent of people lived and worked on the land and most towns were very small by modern standards. London was the exception, with about 50,000 inhabitants, but that was only a quarter of the size of, say, Venice.

## Following in father's footsteps

Most boys grew up to do the job their fathers did and most girls followed their mothers. For a minority of boys (never girls), that meant becoming apprenticed to learn a trade; the training lasted seven years. At the end of that time, the apprentice made a masterpiece to prove he was competent to go it alone in the world of manufacture. Some boys entered services at all levels, running pubs, teaching, fishing along various rivers or around the coasts, or learning nasty, dangerous trades, such as working in the tanning industry, which were known as *stink jobs*. Another tiny but growing handful became merchants dealing with the European centres like Antwerp and organisations like the Hanse. The vast majority of boys, though, followed their fathers to work on the land.

## Visiting the average village

Historians know a lot about the lives of the majority of Tudor men and women from *The Book of Husbandry* written by Sir Anthony Fitzherbert in 1523 and updated throughout the century.

Early Tudor England wasn't full of downtrodden peasants longing for the Reform Act of 1832 to give them power.

The average village was made up of:

- **Yeomen:** They rented their farms from landowners, served the community as church administrators or constables (sort of policemen, but don't expect too many arrests!), paid taxes and often sent their sons to school or even university.

- **Craftsmen:** Blacksmiths, carpenters, thatchers, innkeepers and many more provided specialist services for the village.

- **A parson:** The local priest ran services, baptised newborns, married betrothed couples and buried the dead.

- **Landless labourers:** They worked for yeomen farmers and were likely to lose their jobs if land was enclosed (see the nearby sidebar 'Encountering enclosure').

It's important to bear in mind at all times the central place of religion in ordinary people's lives. Fitzherbert says the first thing people should do when they get up in the morning is say their prayers (in Latin) and ask God to 'speed the plough'. Later editions drop the Latin bit in favour of the English Lord's prayer.

The daily work was different from summer to winter, the days longer or shorter, and therefore wages differed accordingly. But no welfare state existed in the 16th century. Poor people relied on handouts from the local community, but the *sturdy beggars* (men who were perfectly fit to work) were an ongoing problem for Tudor law and order.

While their men folk toiled, women also had plenty to do. In the *Book of Husbandry* it says that a husbandman's wife must:

- Clean the house
- Feed the calves
- Feed the pigs
- Go to market if her husband isn't available
- Help her husband fill or empty the muck cart
- Know how to make hay, winnow corn and malt
- Look after the poultry and collect their eggs
- Make clothes from wool by spinning and weaving
- Make butter and cheese
- Prepare all her husband's meals
- Prepare the milk
- Supervise the servants (if she has any)
- Wake and dress the children

## Encountering enclosure

The huge death rate caused by the Black Death (bubonic plague), which reached 50 per cent in some areas, led to countryside chaos in the 1350s. Some landowners hit upon the idea of enclosing land – putting hedges or walls around fields – and turning the common land that everyone could use into sheep farms for their own benefit (sheep rearing was more profitable than growing crops). The various local rebellions by ordinary people, such as Kett's and the Oxfordshire rising (see Chapters 7 and 8), were often about this enclosure because farm labourers lost money and jobs as a result. When the population began to pick up again in the 1470s people demanded a return to crop farming to grow more food.

Sound familiar? Maybe, but these women had no birth control, no vote, only the most basic rights and no underwear worthy of the name. Women's lib was 450 years away.

# Chartering towns

The older and larger towns had charters given to them by previous kings. Smaller ones had charters from local lords. These charters allowed towns to hold fairs – like the Goose Fair in Nottingham or the Midsummer Fair in Cambridge – which were opportunities to buy, sell and have a good time.

The merchant guilds in these towns (today's chambers of commerce) were companies of skilled craftsmen, keeping out rival competition and acting as friendly societies, paying for their members' burials and looking after widows and orphans.

Councils under the mayor and aldermen ran the towns and you had to be a householder or a rich merchant to be elected. Chartered towns sent two representatives as MPs to the House of Commons in London.

# Paying the price

Inflation was running at 9 per cent in Edward VI's reign and got worse again towards the end of Elizabeth's. Wages always fell short of costs and that was the cause of much discontent in the countryside. It didn't help that various Tudor governments did their best to keep workers on the land (with the Statutes of Labourers of 1549 and 1563) and keep workers' wages low.

In 1556, historians know from John Ponet, the Protestant Bishop of Winchester, that:

✔ A pound of beef cost 4 pence.

✔ A pound of candles cost 4 pence.

✔ A pound of butter cost 4 pence.

✔ A pound of cheese cost 4 pence.

✔ A whole sheep cost £1.

✔ Two eggs cost 1 pence.

✔ A quarter (of a ton) of wheat cost 64 shillings.

✔ A quarter of malt cost 50 shillings or more.

People were so badly off that they used acorns to make bread and drank water instead of beer. Ponet put all this down to the fact that Mary had turned the country back to Catholicism.

## Trading at home and overseas

In the early Tudor period, most trade was local with village people driving their geese, cattle or sheep to market in the nearest town. Some specialist places already existed;

✔ Coventry made gloves and ribbons.

✔ Nottingham made lace.

✔ Sheffield made metal goods.

✔ Witney made blankets.

London, as the largest city, was a huge consumer market, swallowing up vast quantities of grain, cattle, cloth and sea coal. The market gardens of Essex and Kent supplied vegetables, and fish was brought up the Thames for sale at Billingsgate.

Ship yards were springing up along the coast from Newcastle in the north to Falmouth in the south west. By the 1530s Henry VIII was building ships at the Royal Docks at Deptford, 3 miles (5 kilometres) from London. Ships like this traded with the great European centres such as Antwerp and Bruges.

# Building Dream Homes

Everybody knows what a Tudor house looks like – it's black and white (half-timbered) and made a reappearance in the 1930s as 'Mock Tudor'. The royals were great builders – see Chapter 19 for ten great houses that have survived.

Throughout the period:

- ✔ Oak remained the basic building material, with infill of the framework made of *wattle and daub* (wood and clay).

- ✔ Brick began to replace wattle and daub.

- ✔ Increased prosperity meant more large houses.

- ✔ Traditionally, an Englishman's home was his E-shaped residence built around a courtyard.

  The E shape has nothing to do with Elizabeth – houses of this style were on the market long before she was born.

- ✔ Roofs were made of slate or thatch.

- ✔ Staircases replaced ladders to get from floor to floor (Amy Robsart, look out! See Chapter 12).

- ✔ Fireplaces and chimneys kept rooms largely smoke free.

- ✔ Rich people built specialist rooms in their houses – kitchens, sculleries, larders, libraries and dining rooms.

- ✔ The poor continued to live in hovels in the countryside or were crammed into tiny tenements in the towns.

- ✔ Homes didn't have bathrooms and toilets, called *privies*, were usually holes in the ground.

# Tutoring the Tudors: Education

Before the Tudors came along the Church ran all schools, as well as the two universities in England: Oxford and Cambridge. Books were expensive because they were hand-written, but the arrival of the printing press by the late 15th century changed all that.

Education was a class thing:

- ✔ The nobility learned to hunt, ride, handle weapons, dance and have good manners. In Elizabeth's reign, Sir Christopher Hatton was a member of the royal Council, but he was also the best dancer in England.

- ✔ The gentry followed the nobility and both groups could afford to hire clerks to do their writing for them.

- ✔ Merchants needed to be able to read, write and do their own book-keeping. The investor John Lok's accounts from the voyages of the explorer Martin Frobisher still survive and include everything down to the cost of nails. Grammar schools (like Henry VIII School in Coventry) taught boys to be able to go on to university or join a profession.

- ✔ Everybody else learned what they could, but most laymen were illiterate because they had no need to be anything else.

In the 1490s Henry VII made sure his sons, Arthur and Henry, got the best humanist education, which stressed knowledge of the Bible, but also the Classics and Latin and Greek culture. The universities largely opened the way to a career in the Church – although mavericks like Christopher Marlowe became playwrights and spies instead! The Inns of Court in London were training grounds for lawyers and by the end of Henry VIII's reign (1547) anybody who was anybody in the corridors of power had qualified there.

# Dying in Tudor England

The three main illnesses of the day were:

- ✔ **Influenza:** The most serious killer of the time. There was so much sickness in the army that the generals had to call off an attempt to recapture Calais in 1557–1558.

- ✔ **The Plague:** Bubonic or pneumonic, the Plague was caused by a bacillus (a type of bacteria) on a flea on a rat. No cure existed in the 16th century and outbreaks occurred from time to time. In 1603, 38,000 people died in London. 'Plague doctors' were useless. The best remedy? Travel far, travel fast and get out of town. Henry VIII always did.

- ✔ **The Sweating Sickness:** This broke out in England in 1485 and again in 1517 and 1551. It all happened quickly: men were merry at dinner and dead at supper. But the sickness wasn't always fatal. It was probably a type of flu and was called *Sudor Anglicus* because only the English were said to catch it.

Tudor medicine was dreadful. If you were sensible, you'd stay away from doctors, but check out the hilarious scene in *Shakespeare in Love* when Joseph Fiennes' Shakespeare goes to see Anthony Sher's Dr Moth because he's got writer's block (a very rare disease in any age!).

## Distaff learning

Women's education never really got off the ground under the Tudors. They had no schools of their own and couldn't join their brothers in the grammar schools. If a man was rich enough and saw any point, he might get a tutor for his daughter as well as his son; Thomas More's daughter Margaret was very well-read as a result – you can see her gabbling away in Latin to the king in the film *A Man for All Seasons*. Some highly educated women were at Court besides the queens, like Mildred Cooke, who married Elizabeth's chief minister, William Cecil.

You could get medical help (or hindrance) from four places and they were all expensive.

- **Apothecaries** handled drugs and herbs. A lot of their medicine was experimental and most of it nonsense.

- **Barber-surgeons** had their own company set up by Henry VIII and they carried out amputations on soldiers and sailors. Archaeologists have recently found the toolkit of the surgeon on board the *Mary Rose*, which sank in 1545 (see Chapter 3).

- **Physicians** believed the ideas of the ancient Greeks and still followed the Four Humours rubbish of Galen (2nd century AD). 'Cures' usually involved potions, leeches (which sucked your blood) and money.

- **Surgeons** set bones and carried out operations with no anaesthetic, so only the toughest (or luckiest) survived. Surgeons also tried to treat venereal disease, which was blamed on the French (of course).

# Coping with Crime

The growing population meant more crime and more people seeking justice. The law changed throughout the Tudor period, bringing in new offences (such as witchcraft from 1542) and setting up new courts like the Petty Sessions, which focused on the powers of the justices of the peace.

In Tudor England no police force existed. There were constables of the watch, who were a bit of a joke (see Dogberry and Verges in Shakespeare's *Much Ado About Nothing*). The local law officer in the county was the sheriff, who had powers of arrest. Nobody thought very highly of these officers – remember the 'baddie' in the Robin Hood stories is the Sheriff of Nottingham – and the chances of you getting away with your crime were huge.

Different courts tried different types of crime:

- The Manor Court sorted out country disputes over land boundaries and straying animals.

- The Archdeacon's Consistory Court handled charges of adultery. Sex crimes were regarded as sins and so the Church dealt with these. If you slept with your neighbour's wife or one of his servants, you were usually *excommunicated* (cut off from the Church) for a limited period. Most people got around this by doing some sort of penance, which involved public shaming.

- The Quarter Sessions handled theft or violence and were run by the justices of the peace with a jury of locals. You could be sent to prison, somewhere like the Fleet in London, which was dangerous and unhealthy, not to mention expensive because you had to pay for food and drink while you were inside.

- The Mayor's Court covered the breaking of town rules. The punishment was usually the pillory or stocks, wooden frames you were chained to while people hurled abuse at you as they walked past.

Spitting was in fashion during the Tudor period. You spat at people in the stocks. Women spat at touchy-feely men; churchmen spat at each other during religious arguments.

The death penalty was reserved for serious crimes, but over 200 of these crimes existed and many of them you'd find laughable today. Religious heresy (see Chapters 10 and 14) was a Church crime, but because the Church wasn't allowed to shed blood, actual punishments were passed to the secular (non-Church) courts for carrying out. Ordinary criminals were hanged with a rope over a tree branch or wooden scaffold. The nobility received the quicker 'mercy' of the axe (or in the case of Anne Boleyn, the sword – see Chapter 5).

# Acting Up

Not all the dramas of the Tudor era happened between real people at Court. Theatrical entertainment was popular among all classes. The nobility had boxes at theatres or sat on the stage to watch the action up close; the groundlings stood for the whole show. But the whole audience got the jokes!

William Shakespeare, the 'upstart crow' from Stratford, has cornered the market in Elizabethan literature today, but many others were brilliant, like Ben Jonson, Christopher Marlowe and Thomas Kyd. Comedies, tragedies and histories wowed theatre-goers up and down the country.

## Pregnant pause

Childbirth was a dangerous business in the Tudor era. Contraception was almost unknown and women became pregnant for as long as their fertility lasted. So births of ten or more children were common – check out memorial brasses on church tombs throughout the country. Three in every five children died before reaching adulthood – see the Tudor family's own body count in this respect in Chapter 5. Doctors were all men and knew little of the conception process. Midwives probably knew more, but they had no status and were the source of countless old wives' tales that did more harm than good at childbirth. Most women gave birth in a half sitting position, surrounded by people wearing their day clothes with no awareness of hygiene. For the births in important families, astrologers were consulted to foretell the child's survival likelihood from the position of the planets.

## *Pleasing the crowd*

The popular types of plays were:

- ✔ **Comic interludes:** These were sketches performed in town squares by travelling troupes, but this could land you in jail as a vagabond, so actors made sure they got powerful patrons like the Lord Chamberlain, the Earl of Leicester or Baron Hunsdon. That way, they got to perform in great houses and even at Court.

- ✔ **Mystery plays:** These were sponsored by the merchant guilds and were all about heaven and hell. These plays lost popularity by the end of the Tudor period.

 By the 1590s London had many theatres like The Bear, The Curtain and The Globe. The authorities frowned on the theatres because they encouraged fights, prostitution and theft. At times of plague, they were closed altogether and the religious extremists called Puritans wanted them shut for good. For a brilliant glimpse of Elizabeth's theatre, see the film *Shakespeare in Love*.

 Women weren't allowed to act, so all female roles were played by boys in drag. Maybe that's why even in romantic stuff like *Romeo and Juliet* the stage directions don't mention much rolling around !

## *Hum me a few bars: Tudor music*

Every film on the Tudors has got it – fantastic, thumpy tunes played on long-forgotten instruments like kits and shawms. In Henry VII's reign all official music was dirge-like and solemn, written for the Church. Under Henry VIII and even more under Elizabeth, musicians wrote bright, lively tunes for the

Court and men like Thomas Tallis and William Byrd were the Andrew Lloyd Webbers of their day. Everybody still thinks Henry VIII wrote *Greensleeves* (see Chapter 3).

It isn't true that the use of the augmented fourth musical interval in Church music could result in excommunication – although, because it's the chord used by modern composers in scary music in films, you can imagine that perhaps it wouldn't have sounded right in a solemn mass. It isn't called the 'chord of evil' for nothing!

## Strictly . . . Tudor style

Elizabeth loved dancing and many of the entertainments in her Court revolved around it.

Try this at home:

- ✔ **The Pavanne:** For the over 50s. Slow, sedate – you can wear your long gowns for this one, guys and gals!

- ✔ **The Galliard:** Getting faster. Probably best not to wear your rapiers for this one, gents!

- ✔ **The Volta:** Whoa! The rock and roll of its day. Men, lift your partner, throw her in the air (and it was a bit naughty – you got to squeeze your partner's waist!).

## Suits You, Sir

Clothes, like education, were all about class. The Tudors even passed strict rules, the Sumptuary Laws, which fined people who tried to dress above their status. The Tudors reigned for 118 years, which is a long time in the fashion business, so I'll just give you a glimpse at the start, middle and end of the era.

In 1485:

- ✔ Men dressed as they had for 300 years with shirts, *doublets* (jackets) and *hose* (tights). Genitals were covered with a triangular codpiece and shoes were pointed.

- ✔ Women wore long dresses to the ground, with tight-laced bodices and *kirtles* (petticoats) underneath. No knickers, no bra!

Throughout the period:

- ✔ Noblemen and gentlemen wore knee-length wide coats, open in front. Check out Hans Holbein's portrait of Henry VIII and his 13-year-old son Edward VI.

- ✔ The middle class man wore a robe to the knee. It was the equivalent of today's pinstripe suit. Vicars, barristers and graduates from universities wear such robes today.

- ✔ Everybody else continued to wear the basics, made of wool and leather.

- ✔ Caps and hoods changed size and shape, especially as French and Spanish fashions hit the Court and filtered down through society.

- ✔ Bright clothes were in under Henry VIII, blacks and browns under Mary, dazzling colours under Elizabeth.

In 1603:

- ✔ Breeches had replaced hose for men. The nobility and gentry wore short cloaks slung over one shoulder, a fashion called *colleywestonwise*, and carried rapiers (by law, no more than 3 feet, around 1 metre, long).

- ✔ Both sexes wore *pattens*, wooden lifts on their shoes, to raise them above the muddy streets. Shoes now had rounded toes.

- ✔ Women wore *farthingales* and *stomachers*, a pointed bodice with a framework dress that stuck out from the body.

No zips or elastic existed until the late 19th century so everything was fastened with laces, ribbons and buttons made of wood, metal or bone.

Check out the various portraits of the Tudor monarchs. With the exception of Mary they scream bling, from beautiful, huge ruffs to pearl headgear and diamonds sewn to sleeves. This was a statement – 'I dress like this because I rule one of the richest countries in the world' – what was everybody else going to do about it?

Only the lowest of the low and young girls went bareheaded. Everybody else wore headgear all the time. Men wore their hats indoors and during meals. Henry VIII was quite unusual in that he took his hat off in the presence of ladies. Both sexes even wore caps in bed.

# Chapter 2

# Starting a Dynasty: Henry VII

*I*n 1471 Henry Tudor was a 14-year-old boy living out of somebody else's pockets in Brittany, then an independent duchy (dukedom) that wasn't part of France. Fourteen years later Henry was king of England and the founder of the most flamboyant family ever to sit on the English throne.

## Becoming King

Despite his ancestry (see Chapter 1) Henry was the poor boy made good, the adventurer who risked it all and won it all.

### Escaping the fallout of the Wars of the Roses

In the Middle Ages the government was only as strong as its king. Henry VI of the House of Lancaster was weak, fond of writing poetry and giving money to the Church and titles to his favourites. But he was the grandson of Henry IV who, as Lord Bolingbroke, had grabbed the throne from Richard II and had had the rightful king murdered in 1399. Someone else with a strong claim to the throne was Richard, Duke of York, and he challenged the feeble Henry VI's right to rule. This head-on clash between the houses of York and Lancaster came to be known as the Wars of the Roses and began in 1455.

MYTH BUSTER

## What's in a name?

If you go to the Houses of Parliament in London today you'll see the brilliant painting by AH Payne showing gorgeously dressed noblemen quarrelling in a garden. One of them (York) has grabbed a white rose from a bush as his symbol; Lancaster has grabbed a red. The white rose was certainly a Yorkist badge but no evidence proves that the Lancastrians ever used a red one. The term *Wars of the Roses* was invented in the 19th century.

Henry Tudor was born in Pembroke Castle, Wales on 28 January 1457, so throughout his childhood he was living in an edgy atmosphere of civil war. Many periods of quiet occurred during the Wars of the Roses and in some areas nothing happened at all, but among the nobility the death rate in battle was huge. At Towton in Yorkshire in 1461, 28,000 men were killed; it was the bloodiest battle on English soil.

Because of the Yorkist victory at Towton, 4-year-old Henry was taken from his mother, Margaret Beaufort, and 'protected' by the Yorkist Lord Herbert.

In 1471 the Battle of Barnet was another Yorkist victory and the king, Edward IV, now considered Henry a threat because he was the only surviving male Lancastrian who might challenge his right to be king. Henry's uncle, Jasper Tudor, took the 14-year-old away to Brittany for his own safety.

## *Hanging out in France*

In Brittany Henry and his people lived for 13 years under the protection of the local duke, Francis I. Obviously, Edward IV wasn't happy about this and tried to get Francis to send the annoying boy back.

Brittany wasn't part of France then – notice in Figure 2-1 the frontier going from St Malo in the north to Poitou in the south – but Edward hoped to work on the more powerful French king to put pressure on Francis. By the terms of the Treaty of Picquigny in 1475, Edward agreed to stop pushing his claims to be king of France in exchange for Henry's return. Henry got as far as St Malo with his armed guard, en route to England, when Francis changed his mind and Henry was whisked away from Edward's ambassadors.

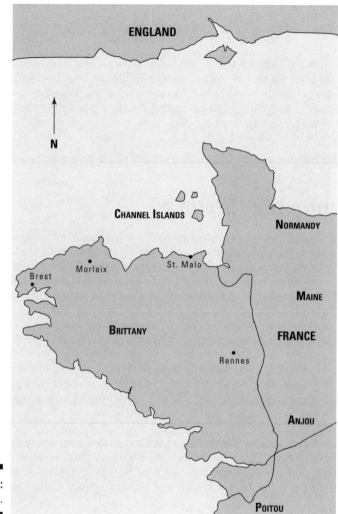

**ENGLAND**

N

**CHANNEL ISLANDS**

**NORMANDY**

• Morlaix • St. Malo

• Brest

**MAINE**

**BRITTANY**

**FRANCE**

• Rennes

**ANJOU**

**Figure 2-1:**
Brittany.

**POITOU**

I look in more detail at England's relations with France in the later section 'Pursuing peace and prosperity' and in Chapters 3, 7, 9 and 11, but when Henry became king in 1485, he called himself 'King of England and of France, Prince of Wales and Lord of Ireland'. The only bit of France the English still owned was Calais, and even that was lost under the Tudors. Even so, the title 'King of France' remained in the coronation ceremony wording until 1802 (when the British were still fighting the French, by the way!).

## Henry the Welshman

Just how Welsh was Henry Tudor? If you've seen Laurence Olivier's film *Richard III* you'll remember a blond-wigged goodie-two-shoes Stanley Baker with an over-the-top Welsh accent. Certainly, Henry spent his boyhood in Wales, but we're sure he never sounded quite like that! After he was king, however, he celebrated St David's Day (1 March), called his eldest son after the 'Welsh' King Arthur and carried the red dragon, the ancient badge of Wales, at the Battle of Bosworth and on all public occasions.

## *Securing the throne*

Events in England came to a head in 1483–1485. Edward IV's death in April 1483 (some say he was poisoned, some say he caught a cold while fishing, some say he had pleurisy or even diabetes – take your pick) meant that England once again had a boy king, the 12-year-old Edward V. His uncle, Richard of Gloucester, was supposed to protect the young king, but the prince conveniently vanished (see the nearby sidebar 'The princes in the tower'), and the whole cycle of rivalry, mistrust and open warfare began again, starting with Richard having himself proclaimed king (Richard III).

Within a month of his accession in June 1483, Richard was working on Louis XI, king of France, to override the Duke of Brittany and get Henry Tudor sent back to England. After all, Henry, the earl of Richmond, was a man now and a serious threat to Richard's hold on the country.

Next time you're touring the north of England, notice how many pubs are called the Blue Boar. These pubs were all once the White Boar, Richard's personal badge and a reminder of how popular he was in the North. In the South, however, Richard was barely known and rumours about the princes wouldn't go away.

Louis XI's death in August 1483 sidetracked the ongoing negotiations over Henry, and anyway, Richard soon had his hands full elsewhere.

## *Bucking for the throne*

The duke of Buckingham had been a staunch ally of Richard's before he became king, but now he turned against him (this is *so* typical of the nobility's reckless behaviour in the Wars of the Roses). It may be that Buckingham wanted the crown for himself (he had a vague hereditary claim to it), but in the end Henry Tudor emerged as the main contender and the whole venture was backed by the queen dowager, Elizabeth Woodville, mother of the missing Edward V. The deal was that Henry would marry Elizabeth's daughter,

Elizabeth of York, in exchange for the dowager's cash and troops to remove Richard.

Buckingham raised an army in Wales, but appalling weather and floods on the River Severn washed his men away and the duke was taken to Salisbury and beheaded in the square (check the place out when you're there next) on Richard's orders.

## Angling for French support

Henry got £3,300 out of Duke Francis, which bought him 5,000 troops and 15 ships. When he got to England, however, he found his timing was off because Buckingham was dead, and all he got from various discontented lords was a vague promise to accept him as king.

Not to be outdone, Richard was carrying out his own tricky negotiations with Duke Francis, who would clearly sell anybody for big enough bucks. But Jasper Tudor got wind of the plot and helped Henry, now back in Brittany, to get to the safety of France.

Guess what? The French had a boy king too. Charles VIII and a regency council that governed in his name (see Chapter 7 for how all this works) kept Henry dangling, making vague statements of goodwill and promising unspecified help. Talk was as cheap in the 15th century as it is today!

## The princes in the Tower

Whole books have been written on the most spectacular vanishing act of the Middle Ages. What happened was that Edward V and his 9-year-old brother Richard, the Duke of York, were taken for 'safe keeping' to the Tower of London, the huge castle which protected the city. They were seen playing happily on the battlements in the summer of 1483; then, they simply vanished.

Rumours flew that the pair had been murdered, probably on the orders of their uncle Richard. Two child skeletons were found in 1674 under a staircase in the Tower and were buried as the princes in Westminster Abbey. Archaeological work carried out on the bones in 1933 wasn't conclusive; the skeletons may have been the remains of the princes, but even so, no one knows who killed them.

History has been unkind to Richard, but it's all Shakespeare's fault. If you see the film or read the play, Shakespeare's Richard is deformed, with a hunched back, a gammy leg and one shoulder higher than the other. Not only that, he's a psychopath, a serial killer who bumps off (count them!) 11 people who stand between him and the throne. No hard evidence against Richard as the murderer of the princes exists, but he certainly had a lot to gain from their deaths. So, of course, did Henry Tudor...

## Killing a king: Bosworth Field, 1485

Henry's cause now picked up.

- ✔ John de Vere, Earl of Oxford, a very experienced soldier, deserted Richard for Henry in 1484.

- ✔ Richard's son Edward died in 1484 and his wife Anne Neville a year later. That meant that no Yorkist heirs to the throne existed, assuming the princes were dead; Richard was the last of the Plantagenets, the family that had ruled England for centuries.

- ✔ Rhys ap Thomas, a powerful Welsh landowner, told Henry that the whole of Wales would rise up on his behalf (this never quite happened).

By the end of July 1485 Henry had got together a ragbag army of 2,000 mercenaries and perhaps 500 English exiles. On 1 August he sailed for Wales. After landing at Milford Haven he marched to Haverfordwest. Then, at Newton (in today's Powys) he was met by the army of Rhys ap Thomas, which doubled the size of his force. From there he advanced to Stafford, collecting rebels as he went. Then his scouts reported that Richard was at Lichfield.

Richard didn't know exactly where Henry would strike. He sent out a proclamation on 21 June against 'Henry Tydder and other rebels' and set up his headquarters at Nottingham. As king, he could command the nobility to join him under their obligations in the feudal system – the duke of Norfolk, the earl of Northumberland and Francis, viscount Lovell, joined him with their armies at Leicester.

The two sides met on the morning of 21 August on White Moor, below the slope of Ambien Hill, in open countryside about two miles from the Leicestershire town of Market Bosworth. At a glance, Richard's looked to be the stronger side. Henry was only an average soldier, relying on de Vere and his mercenaries, and Richard outnumbered Henry two-to-one. But the king couldn't rely on the Stanleys, the earl of Derby and his brother, who seem to have watched on the sidelines before defecting to Henry.

Wanting to end the battle quickly, Richard led his bodyguard in a headlong charge to kill Henry. He hacked down his standard-bearer, but then Stanley's men intervened and Richard was outnumbered, encircled and killed. The legend that Richard's crown from his helmet was found in a bush on the field and handed to Henry may be true. What's certainly true is that Richard's body was slung over a horse ridden by his herald and was later displayed naked on the banks of the River Stour in Leicester. Henry later paid £10 for a suitable tomb for it.

Not only was Richard III the only English king to die in battle for a thousand years, he's the only one without a grave. During the dissolution of the monasteries (see Chapter 6), Leicester Abbey was smashed up and the king's body thrown into the river.

# Making a Fresh Start

It was new broom time when Henry became king. He had to get used – and quickly – to running a country that had been torn apart by on/off civil war for the past 30 years. Yet he had never even lived in England and had spent half his life in Brittany.

## Reckoning Henry

The new king was 27, far more capable than most kings of England had been and he had a natural flair for organisation. Today, he'd be a fat cat managing director of a huge multinational, teeming with ideas to make money and gain status. His first language was English, he was fluent in French and he could get by in Latin.

Henry was clean-shaven, with long brown hair that got thinner as he got older. Some of his teeth fell out in the last years of his life, giving an image (a false one, as you'll see) of a tight-lipped old skinflint. He was careful, aloof and naturally suspicious, but with an upbringing like his, who wouldn't be?

## Air-brushing history: The Rous roll

John Rous was a chantry priest at Guy's Cliffe in Warwick. He was also a genealogist, unofficial herald and a pretty good artist. While Richard was king Rous painted his famous roll, showing Richard and his family as thoroughly nice people. As soon as he was dead, Rous changed his tune, calling Richard a 'monster and tyrant, born under a hostile star and perishing like Antichrist'. Then he started painting double roses all over the place and generally sucking up to the Tudors.

# Reckoning England

Henry had only ever handled a small household before and now he had a kingdom of 2.5 million people. In Chapter 1 we look at a snapshot of life during the reign of the Tudors. Here's what the kingdom was like in 1485:

✔ Most people lived and worked on the land in villages and hamlets.

✔ Towns were small and scattered, run by the mayor and the merchant guilds.

✔ Trade mostly involved raw wool, woollen cloth and manufactured articles.

✔ Serfdom had virtually disappeared, so most men were free. They leased their strips of land from the local landlord who was usually a knight or a squire.

✔ In country areas:

- Everyone used the common land to graze animals.

- People used the woodland for building-timber and fuel for fires.

- Arable fields were planted in a crop rotation cycle – wheat, oats, barley, beans or peas. One third was left fallow (unplanted) to allow the nutrients in the soil to replenish themselves. This system had been going on for seven centuries.

✔ The Church was all-powerful with monasteries, convents, abbeys and chapels dotted all over the place.

The new king, of course, had little direct link with any of this. Henry's first job was to underline his claim to the throne – God had chosen him because of his victory at Bosworth, so he could play down his own shaky hereditary claim and he didn't have to go cap-in-hand to Parliament.

Henry had to prioritise. He needed to:

✔ Get himself proclaimed as king in London (he did this on 26 August and entered the city in triumph on 3 September)

✔ Get himself crowned

✔ Choose advisers he could trust

✔ Remove anybody he couldn't trust

✔ Marry to make sure the Tudor line continued (see Henry VIII's ongoing problems on that score in Chapter 5)

## Law and order

Any king must sort out his own power and that of his government quickly or chaos will occur. After Henry came to power he called as many justices of the peace as possible to a meeting at Blackfriars in London and told them to come up with ideas for statutes (laws). All new office holders took a binding personal oath (swearing by the saints) to serve the king faithfully. They needed constant reminders, but by and large the Tudors' servants were very loyal to them.

# Removing everything to do with Richard . . .

By pre-dating his reign to the day *before* the Battle of Bosworth, Henry could claim all those who'd supported Richard there were traitors. Henry executed the ex-king's top men like William Catesby and had Richard's nephew Edward, the earl of Warwick, thrown into the Tower. When he tried to escape in 1499, Henry had Edward executed.

Henry was very keen on heraldry and deliberately chose the double rose (red and white) to make the point that everything in the garden was lovely now that York and Lancaster had kissed and made up. Richard's last supporter, viscount Lovell, was killed at the Battle of Stoke in 1487 (see the later section 'Rousting the rebels').

# Handing out the honours

Reconciliation was the name of the game. Just before his coronation, Henry gave out new titles and quietly, without fuss, began the Tudor policy of giving a career leg-up to new men of humble origin (see the later section 'Choosing the right men'). Whatever else happened, there must be no return of the anarchy of the Roses.

Henry appointed experienced men who'd served Richard's elder brother Edward IV – Thomas Rotheram got his old job back as archbishop of Canterbury; and John Alcock, bishop of Worcester, became lord chancellor, a position similar to today's prime minister.

# Positioning Parliament

Later monarchs, especially the Stuarts (see *British History for Dummies* by Sean Lang, published by Wiley), could learn a lot from the way Henry VII ran his government. He got Parliament to choose a speaker (chairman) who was actually his choice and to agree that he (Henry) was king by divine right (God's will) and not by act of Parliament.

Here are some bits of business for 1485:

- ✔ Parliament set aside £14,000 a year for the king's Household expenditure. In time this grew and became the Civil List, which the present royal family still live on.
- ✔ Many people were restored to their legal rights, having lost land and titles in the chaos of the Wars of the Roses.
- ✔ The Act of Resumption returned a lot of land to the crown, increasing Henry's income through rents almost overnight. The duchies of Lancaster and Cornwall became Henry's.

Since that time, the prince of Wales has always been the duke of Cornwall. The present prince of Wales, Charles, gets all his income from rents from the county. To see where he gets the rest of his money from, check out his Duchy Originals!

As his reign went on, Henry used Parliament less and less. The Wars of the Roses had, of course, decimated the lords and the politicians in the Commons still did as they were told. In a 24-year-reign Parliament sat for only ten months.

It was Henry VIII's problems with the pope (see Chapters 5 and 6) that finally brought Parliament back into the political limelight.

---

# Breaking down Parliament

Parliament (from the French *parler*, to speak) supposedly represented England. Actually, it didn't. The upper chamber (the House of Lords) was made up of dukes, earls, viscounts, marquises and barons – the people who owned huge estates, had private armies and had been happily massacring each other for 30 years.

The lower chamber (House of Commons) was made up of the *knights of the shire* – men who owned less land and had the title of 'Sir' – and the burgesses (or citizens) of the towns.

Nobody represented the ordinary man (*commons* is a very misleading word) and there wasn't a woman in sight.

## The royal Council

There was no Cabinet or prime minister in Tudor times. The king made the decisions and to advise him was the Council, 40 or so men who had no collective responsibility – they just worked for the king. About half were churchmen, a quarter nobles and the rest lawyers and Household administrators. An inner core of about a dozen carried out all the business of government on the king's behalf.

One of the most infamous parts of the Council's work was the Court of Star Chamber, named after a room in which it met, which had stars painted on the ceiling. It dealt with great men who'd broken the law but who could ride roughshod over the local courts. Star Chamber has developed an undeserved reputation of being somewhere where justice wasn't available, but was just the king getting heavy and ignoring the law.

## Getting married

Henry had promised, in the run-up to the Bosworth campaign, to marry Elizabeth Woodville's daughter, Elizabeth of York. She was 19 in 1485 and Henry had never seen her. Parliament reminded the new king of his promise to marry but the snag was, the pair were distant cousins. In the Catholic Church only one man in the world could get round this usually prohibited match and that was the pope, God's vicar (number two) on earth. This permission came through on 2 March 1486. Anybody who opposed Henry and his new bride would now face *excommunication* (being cut off from the Church and heaven) as well as Henry's axe if the attempt went pear-shaped.

We know virtually nothing about the wedding, except that Archbishop Bourchier probably did the honours.

The marriage united the houses of York and Lancaster forever, but it was probably sheer exhaustion and lack of leaders that stopped a continuation of the fighting.

# Ruling the Kingdom

Some people expected the new king to make sweeping changes, but in fact Henry much preferred to operate within existing systems and was very good at making the best of an average job, turning a small kingdom on the edge of Europe into a powerful country that nobody could ignore.

## Choosing the right men

Henry deliberately picked men who relied on him for their income and success. Some were churchmen like John Morton and Richard Fox; others were gentlemen like Reginald Bray and Edmund Dudley. These 'new men' were very much the hallmark of the Tudor period and when it came to serious trouble against the royals – as in the Rising of the North and the rebellion of the earl of Essex under Elizabeth – it was the nobility who were still at it, with ideas above their station.

## Rousting the rebels: Lambert Simnel and Perkin Warbeck

Henry faced opposition in the first half of his reign. In 1486 viscount Lovell and the Stafford brothers tried to stir up discontent against Henry in Yorkshire and Worcestershire.

In the same year Lambert Simnel (impostors have to have cool names) claimed to be Edward, Earl of Warwick, which was ridiculous as Henry had the real guy safely in prison. Simnel was set up by Richard Simons, a priest, and he was actually the son of a carpenter from Oxford. The pretender got across to France, got the backing of one of Warwick's aunts (Margaret of Burgundy, who'd never seen the real Warwick) and went to Ireland, from where he intended to invade. There he was welcomed with open arms and crowned Edward VI (don't confuse him with the *real* Edward VI – see Chapters 7 and 8) on 24 May 1487.

Landing in Lancashire with about 4,000 Irish and German mercenaries, Simnel and the earl of Lincoln were decisively beaten at Stoke on 16 June. This, not Bosworth, was really the last battle of the Wars of the Roses. Richard Simons was imprisoned for life and Simnel put to work as a scullion (dogsbody) in the royal kitchens.

Then, in 1491, Perkin Warbeck (see what we mean about cool names?) turned up as another threat to Henry. He was actually the son of a boatman from Tournai, but he looked so like Edward IV that rumours spread he was Richard of York, the younger of the vanished princes (see the earlier sidebar 'The princes in the Tower'. Others took up the idea and tried to launch another invasion from Ireland, but since the Irish had been thrashed at Stoke, they weren't interested in getting involved again.

Warbeck went to France, cashing in on a temporary period of hostility between Henry VII and Charles VIII (see the following section), but when that came to nothing he latched on to Margaret of Burgundy, who hated Henry. She fed Warbeck enough information on the real Richard to make his claim seem genuine. Henry's spy network monitored Warbeck's every move, however, and when he tried to land in Kent in July 1495 with a small force he was easily beaten back.

Next Warbeck tried Scotland and was backed by King James IV, who believed every word the impostor said. He even offered Warbeck his kinswoman Katherine Gordon in marriage. The Scots invasion was feeble, however (see Chapter 7 for one that was far more serious), and it petered out. More trouble came from Cornwall where resentment against Henry's taxation (see 'Figuring out finances', later in this chapter) was the cause of open rebellion. Warbeck joined the rebels there but was chased around the country and taken prisoner.

When Warbeck tried to do a runner, it was obvious that Henry couldn't trust him and he was hanged on 29 November 1499.

The threats to Henry's throne were over.

## Pursuing peace and prosperity

Henry's main aim in foreign policy was to get other countries to recognise his dynasty and to remain on friendly terms with them. War cost money and you might not win.

### Wales

Being Welsh was a huge advantage for Henry and he cashed in on it. Wales wasn't technically a separate country, but even so it was useful to keep the Welsh on-side. So Henry made his eldest son, Prince Arthur, prince of Wales in November 1489. Arthur ran (in theory anyway because he was still a child) the royal Council that governed Wales and controlled the marcher lordships (the rich families who owned the castles along the English border). This situation would eventually lead to Wales being governed totally by England by 1536 (although the Welsh were given some rights for behaving themselves). Figure 2-2 shows the situation in 1536 – the western areas were the principality of Wales and the eastern areas were the marcher lordships.

### Ireland

The English had occupied a narrow strip of land around Dublin since the 12th century and had built castles and garrisoned them with troops to keep the natives in their place. England had been too busy during the Wars of the Roses to bother much about Ireland and most people, of all classes, regarded the Irish with contempt. Long after the word vanished from England, the majority of Irish men and women were *peasants*, desperately poor and wholly reliant on the harvest.

Figure 2-3 outlines the lay of the land in Tudor times.

- The *Pale* was the bit around Dublin, run by a governor or lieutenant appointed by the king. Outside this were marcher lordships where lords lived in their castles and often fought each other without very much reason.

- The *Obedient Lands* – the earldoms of Desmond, Ormond and Kildare – were the places run by Englishmen whose families had been in Ireland for years. The Crown could largely trust these Englishmen.

- The *English Plantations* were areas of land that the English had confiscated from the Irish and populated with their own colonisers, or *planters*.

- The *Wild Lands* were Gaelic Ireland (and led to the phrase *beyond the pale*, meaning hopeless). The Irish tribes like the O'Donnells, Maquires and O'Connells ran the Wild Lands.

The whole country was lawless with battles and skirmishes beyond the Pale and no overall control existed. The vast majority of people spoke Gaelic and wore woven kilts and plaids like the Scottish clans.

Religion was complicated in Ireland, but it wasn't a problem until the rise of Protestantism under Edward VI (see Chapter 8).

Henry had been concerned about Ireland for some time. The place was like sand, constantly slipping through his fingers, and lawlessness, squabbling and violence were rife. He was determined to get a firm grip on the situation, especially as in the late 1520s thousands of Irish people emigrated to Wales, tired of the endless fighting and the protection money they had to pay for peace and quiet.

The leading figures in Irish politics were:

- The Earl of Kildare
- The Earl of Ossory
- William Skeffington
- John Alen, archbishop of Dublin

Henry was dealing with all these men as their individual power and support came and went. When Thomas Cromwell replaced Wolsey as chief councillor for the lordship of Ireland in 1532, the job of sorting out the wayward country fell to him.

In September 1533 Cromwell ordered Kildare and other leaders to London for top level talks. Kildare didn't like the sound of that because he valued his independence too much. He started moving cannon out of Dublin Castle to his own estates, but he did finally go to London in February 1534, leaving his son, Thomas Fitzgerald, Lord Offaly, as governor.

Henry, via Cromwell, sent Offaly orders as to how to do his job (never a path to smooth Anglo–Irish relations) and Kildare resigned the governorship in protest. That was as far as Kildare intended to go, but his son had other ideas.

### Revolting with Silken Thomas

Offaly, who was known as Silken Thomas because of the *mantling* (cloth decoration) he wore on his helmet, warned Henry off any more interference by cosying up to Charles V, the holy Roman emperor, for help.

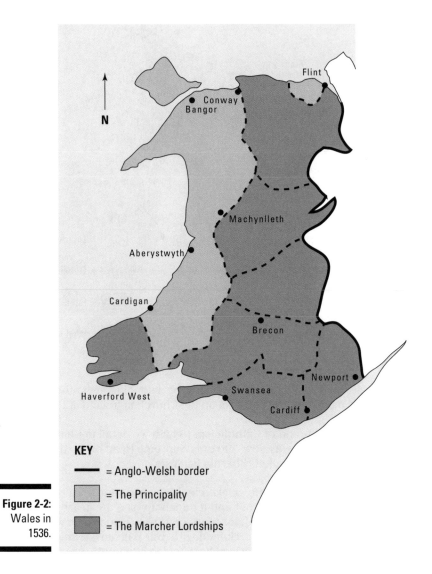

**Figure 2-2:**
Wales in
1536.

KEY

—— = Anglo-Welsh border

▦ = The Principality

▩ = The Marcher Lordships

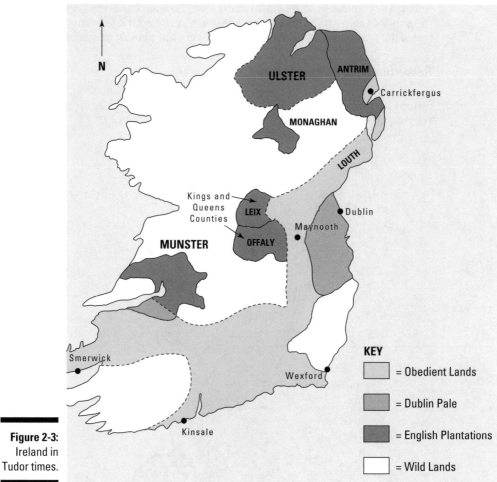

**Figure 2-3:**
Ireland in
Tudor times.

**KEY**

☐ = Obedient Lands

☐ = Dublin Pale

☐ = English Plantations

☐ = Wild Lands

Offaly was clearly trying it on. He claimed to be defending the Catholic Church, but Henry had made no direct attacks on the Church in Ireland at this stage.

In 1536 Henry's new brand of Catholicism (which we detail in Chapter 6) was accepted by Ireland. He was now 'the only Supreme Head on earth of the whole Church of Ireland called Hibernia Ecclesia'.

Offaly's troops overran the Pale, backed by Irish chieftains from the Wild Lands who saw a chance for profit and a punch-up (see the nearby sidebar 'A glimpse of 16th-century Ireland' for more on these regions). He was now the earl of Kildare and a man to be reckoned with, but William Skeffington's army brought the rebels to heel. Offaly was besieged in Maynooth, west of Dublin, and although the town surrendered he got away and continued to make a nuisance of himself, raiding far and wide.

Offaly surrendered to Henry's troops in August 1535 and was imprisoned in the Tower, dying by the axe for treason along with five uncles 18 months later. The power of the Fitzgerald family was destroyed.

### Establishing the kingdom of Ireland

Anthony St Leger became governor of Ireland in July 1540. The situation he inherited looked like this:

- The Parliament in Dublin was a rubber stamp for Henry, but it only operated in the Pale and the Obedient Lands (see the nearby sidebar 'A glimpse of 16th-centry Ireland').
- Only the monasteries (which Henry had destroyed – see Chapter 6) in the anglicised area had gone; the others were out of reach.

Henry's and St Leger's solution was to make the lordship into the kingdom of Ireland. Its status would improve and the Irish chieftains were to hand over their lands to the king, who'd then rent the lands back to them under what was left of the feudal system. This would mean that the chieftains would become lords under Henry's direct control and they could pass their lands on to their children rather than having them owned by the tribe, which was the current system.

Nobody was much fooled by Henry's olive branch and fighting broke out against those who accepted his offer. King of Ireland Henry may have been, but his new kingdom was as much trouble as ever.

### Scotland

Hostility between the English and the Scots had endured for centuries, and the way James IV welcomed Perkin Warbeck was proof the bad relations were ongoing. James had the sense, however, to drop Warbeck and instead he and Henry signed the Peace of Ayton in September of 1497. This arranged a marriage deal between James and Henry's 12-year-old daughter Margaret, which was to have huge consequences later (see Figure 2-4 and Chapter 16) because it led to the Stuarts becoming kings of England. It was the first full treaty between the two countries since 1328 and was proof was Henry's skilful diplomacy. The accord was renewed in 1499.

### France

Relations with France were fine at first (see the earlier section 'Hanging out in France), but the French king Charles VIII had plans to move in on Brittany and that put something of a spanner in the works. Charles said that Brittany belonged to France; the duke of Brittany, Francis, said it didn't. Yes it did; no it didn't – you get the picture.

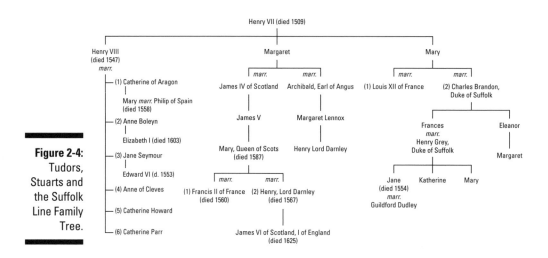

**Figure 2-4:**
Tudors,
Stuarts and
the Suffolk
Line Family
Tree.

There was a punch-up at St Aubin in the summer of 1488 in which the French thrashed the Bretons. Then Duke Francis died and his heir was a 12-year-old girl, Anne. From then on, it could have got messy. In 1489 Henry signed the Treaty of Redon with the Bretons, promising protection, and in December 1491 Charles called Henry's bluff when he claimed Anne as his ward and married her. Henry duly took an army over to France in October 1492, but the weather was awful, it wasn't the fighting season (which was May to September) and peace was in the air. So Henry and Charles signed the Treaty of Etaples, which was effectively Charles buying Henry off to the tune of £250,000. Being paid *not* to fight was brilliant and characteristic of Henry's clever diplomacy. Charles turned his attention to Italy, which resulted in over 50 years of on/off warfare.

### Spain

Nobody realised it at the time, but Spain was on its way to becoming *the* superpower of the 16th century. Henry was on the lookout for allies and 'the most Catholic of kings' Ferdinand of Aragon and his wife Isabella of Castile had a 7-year-old daughter, Catherine, who would make a suitable wife for the 3-year-old prince Arthur.

All this suited Ferdinand and Isabella, who also wanted allies, so they all signed the commercial agreement of Medina del Campo in 1489. This led to:

✔ A marriage proposal between Catherine and Arthur

✔ Acceptance of the Tudor dynasty by one of the oldest and most powerful families in Europe

✔ A further trade treaty – Magnus Intercursus – in 1496

Catherine and Arthur were married by proxy in Spain on 19 May 1499. Neither of them was present at the ceremony, underlining the fact that this was all about politics, not romance.

In October 1501 the real wedding took place when Catherine arrived in London. Everybody pulled out all the stops – Henry spent a fortune, the bells rang and all the toasts were for a long and happy life for the young couple.

But a long life together wasn't to be: Henry and Elizabeth were devastated when Arthur died, probably of tuberculosis, in April 1502. Catherine was 17, a widow in a strange land. When Elizabeth died the following spring, Henry considered marrying the girl himself, but in the end decided on passing her on to his remaining son Henry. This would mean:

- ✔ Catherine would stay in England with her considerable dowry of gold and silver.
- ✔ Catherine would one day become queen of England.
- ✔ The much dreamed of alliance between England and Spain was on after all.

But there were complications. Isabella died in November 1504 and Ferdinand couldn't inherit Castile. That went instead to the pair's daughter Joanna, who was married to Philip of Burgundy, son of the holy Roman emperor, Maximilian.

Henry now decided to throw in his lot with Joanna and Philip, who were given a slap-up welcome when they visited England in January 1506. Philip and Henry signed the treaty of Windsor in a spirit of friendship.

---

# What's love got to do with it?

Marriages between great families were arranged for political reasons. Links between England and Spain would make a huge empire encircling the always rather dodgy French. Catherine was 7 and Arthur 3 at the time of their betrothal, but don't be horrified at their ages; they didn't actually live together as man and wife, and anyway, no age of consent existed. Henry's mother, Margaret Beaufort, was only 13 when she gave birth.

That said, kings wanted to know in advance what they were getting. In Chapter 5 we explain that Henry VIII got Hans Holbein to paint a portrait of his fourth wife Anne of Cleves, so he could check her out. And when Henry VII was looking for a new wife after Elizabeth's death, he asked his ambassadors to check out the queen of Naples, paying particular attention to any facial hair she may have(!), the size and shape of her breasts, the colour of her eyes, the size of her nose and whether she had sweet breath.

## Sponsoring Cabot

Ferdinand and Isabella of Spain famously financed Columbus's trips in search of the East Indies, giving Spain a vast fortune in land and silver in the years ahead. Henry – perhaps rashly – turned Columbus down in 1489, but he did back John Cabot.

Cabot was a Venetian (Venice was one of the best known ports in the world at that time) who wanted to find a more northerly route to Cathay (China) than the one the Spaniards had opened up. London was tied up with the Antwerp trade, so Cabot operated out of Bristol.

Henry didn't give him ships or money, but he did let him have Letters Patent, the official go-ahead

empowering Cabot to claim any lands in the name of England. Because Cabot already had ships and men, this was, in a way, the icing on the cake.

Cabot reached the coast of North America in the summer of 1497 (if you're a fan of *Murder She Wrote* you'll be familiar with the mythical town of Cabot Cove on the coast of Maine) and claimed it for England.

Cabot's return voyage in May 1498 was a disaster. He vanished, presumably lost at sea, and his son Sebastian went off to seek his fortune elsewhere. But importantly, Cabot set up what was to become in time the British Colonies in America, still called New England.

Philip's sudden death in September sent Joanna off the rails and she took to carrying the embalmed body of her husband with her wherever she went. So Henry did a quick double shuffle and threw in his lot with Ferdinand again. The marriage between Catherine and prince Henry was on the front burner once more and duly went ahead (see Chapters 3, 4 and 5).

## *Figuring out finances*

We've already bust the myth about Henry's tightness, but he was very good at making money and unusually for a king – who had people for things like this – he checked the accounts himself.

Here's the lowdown on Henry's finances:

- ✔ Most cash came through the Chamber Treasury rather than the Exchequer, so that Henry could check it.

- ✔ He kept grants and payments to a minimum.

- ✔ His new men, like Reginald Bray, didn't cost as much as the nobility and the churchmen who worked for Henry were paid out of Church funds.

- ✔ He kept military expenditure down (see the earlier section 'France' for how cheap the Etaples campaign was). The exception was fitting out new warships like *Mary Rose* for £8,000 (for the end of the *Mary Rose* see Chapter 3).

- ✔ He relied heavily on customs duties (taxes) via the Port of London. These brought him in about £500,000 in 24 years.

✔ Henry set up forced loans from the rich merchants of the livery compa-nies (the equivalent of today's City brokers), especially in London. He used this money to finance the invasion of France in 1492, for example.

✔ He got cash from the rent of his lands.

✔ In the first ten years of his reign Henry made about £10,000 a year through tax. By 1504, taxation brought in £31,000.

✔ The fact that Henry only once called Parliament in the last 12 years of his reign means he was doing well financially. Later kings like the Stuarts usually only called Parliament when they were broke.

✔ Henry got good deals for his merchants wherever he could, like the pow-erful merchant venturers, who watched world exploration carefully. In the 1490s Christopher Columbus and Vasco da Gama were taking their lives in their hands sailing east and west in search of new ways to old worlds and ended up finding new worlds instead. Henry taxed the mer-chants in return, but everybody made money out of deals like Medina del Campo and Magnus Intercursus.

✔ He set up a tax on the super-rich, which the nobility resented. Yet this enabled him to control their wealth and helped give him an income of £130,000 a year. This made Henry VIII's treasury very well off.

Henry VII was the last English king to die solvent for 200 years.

# *Meeting Henry, the Human*

Henry's arranged marriage to Elizabeth of York seems to have become a love match, but luck wasn't on their side. In an age of high infant mortality, their youngest son Edmund died at just over 1 year of age in June 1500. Their eldest, Arthur, on whom Henry pinned all his hopes, died in April 1502. The following February Elizabeth died too, shortly after giving birth to a stillborn daughter. Suddenly, the 46-year-old Henry was a widower with two daugh-ters, Margaret and Mary, but only one son remaining – the 11-year-old Henry, who would become king Henry VIII (see Chapters 3 to 6).

Francis Bacon said in the 17th century: 'For [Henry VII's] pleasures, there is no news of them.' And for 300 years historians followed this idea that Henry was a grim curmudgeon with no sense of humour and a miser obsessed with counting his cash.

But historians now know that Henry loved hunting, was highly superstitious (once threatening to hang all the mastiffs in England because he believed them to be unlucky) and spent heavily on lowbrow entertainments. He once lost £40 on cards in one day, and how can we explain giving £30 to 'the damsel that danceth', about 60 times the going rate for Court entertainers? We'll leave that one up to you!

## Teaching the Tudors

Henry VII built up a royal library, adding to the one he'd 'inherited' from Richard III. We don't know its contents, but Richard was something of a scholar. Printing was still new, so it's likely that much of this library was made up of hand-written manuscripts.

The princes Arthur and Henry were brought up in the humanist tradition (see Chapter 1) by the blind poet Bernard Andre, who went on to write a biography of Henry VII. Classics were the trendy subjects of the Renaissance, which was a movement that looked back to the great days of Greece and Rome. Arthur read Homer, Vergil, Ovid, Terence, Thucydides, Caesar, Livy and Tacitus (don't knock them till you've tried them!).

Henry liked his entertainments. He never went far without his minstrels, harpists and pipers. He liked watching bear baiting and cock fighting (animal rights activists look away now) and possibly had a mild gambling addiction, betting on the outcomes of chess, archery and tennis matches. He watched plays, Morris dancers, fire eaters and stand-up comedians.

The king also gave lavish presents to people and paid good money for peculiar purposes. He bought an eagle and a leopard (for £13) for the royal zoo in the Tower. He reimbursed a peasant whose corn had been eaten by the king's deer. He rewarded harvesters. He bought gunpowder. Between 1491 and 1505 he spent over £100,000 on jewellery – it would be, after all, a portable form of wealth if he ever had to relive his early life on the run. And he ate well – eels and perch in aspic – and loved castles made from jelly. He once paid the Dutch chef John van Delf £38 1 shilling and 4 pence for garnishing a salad – none of today's celebrity chefs make money like that!

Henry also loved meeting foreigners – knights from Rhodes, a man from Constantinople (today's Istanbul), a Greek with a beard and so on.

# Passing On at the Palace

Henry's health was generally good throughout his life, but a recurring cough, especially in the spring, was almost certainly chronic tuberculosis. By the time he was 50 he'd lost many of his teeth, his hair had thinned, his eyesight had deteriorated, he was suffering from gout and he had lost weight. He died on 21 April 1509 in Richmond Palace, probably from tuberculosis, after attending the Easter service the day before.

He was buried alongside Elizabeth in a magnificent Renaissance tomb in Westminster Abbey. Next time you're there, check out Henry VII's chapel and be amazed, very amazed. You can find out more in Chapter 19 on Tudor buildings that survive today.

# Part II
# Handling Henry VIII

# In this part . . .

Think Tudors, think Bluff King Hal. Think Hal, think wives. After all these years, he still conjures up a larger-than-life image. Everything about Henry VIII was big – his body, his ambition, his ego, his palaces, his appetites. He dominated England like few kings had before and his word was law.

We meet them indoors (his better halves), his advisers, his enemies. We nod to his courtiers, kneel to his church-men, hunt with his falconers and fight with his halberdiers. We don't cross him, though. Henry VIII wasn't the monster he sometimes appears but he didn't suffer fools gladly. Best to bow pretty low and smile a lot. Oh – and don't play cards with him.

# Chapter 3

# Being Bluff King Hal: Henry VIII

*B*ecause he wasn't the eldest son, Henry VIII should never have become king. Rumours suggested he was destined for a career in the church, but the death of his elder brother Arthur in 1502 changed all that and meant that he reached pole position by accident. Henry began his reign promisingly enough as a handsome, talented Renaissance prince with a 19-inch waist, but he became a bloated monster who terrified his subjects and whose soul the pope sent to hell.

This chapter gets to the bottom of Henry's transformation, piecing together the man behind the gossipy stories and famous portraits. Unlike Henry VII, who presented a mask to the outside world, his son wore his heart on his sleeve, so we have loads of information about his inner feelings.

# Getting to Know Prince Henry

As the only son of Henry VII left standing when Arthur died, it was important that every care was taken with the little boy. This section looks at the kind of upbringing Henry had.

## Rocking round the cradle

Only two children in five lived to see their first birthday in the 15th century and mothers and the newly born faced a huge risk. Even among royals death was a constant visitor, so it was just as well that the heir (Arthur) had a spare (Henry).

The boy who would be king was born at Greenwich, east of London on 28 June 1491. In a superstitious age he was baptised quickly by Richard Fox, bishop of Exeter, because had the boy died before being 'churched' his soul couldn't go to heaven. Henry was brought up as a royal prince, loved by his doting parents, Henry VII and Elizabeth of York (see Chapter 2 for more on Henry VII).

Henry had his own servants and rockers employed to rock his cradle and lull him to sleep. For the first five years of his life he would have worn smocks and petticoats like his sisters, Mary and Margaret.

Queens didn't breastfeed their own babies so the search was on for a *wet nurse*, a local woman who'd just given birth herself. Her name was Anne Luke, and when Henry became king in 1508 he gave her a grant of £20 a year, a nice little earner and living proof that breast is best.

## Educating Henry: Tutors for Tudors

Renaissance princes had to be Renaissance Men: that is, good all-rounders. For six years (1496–1502) Henry's tutor was the Cambridge University scholar John Skelton, who taught him the all-important Classics – Latin and Greek – which were the essentials of a sophisticated education for centuries. Henry learned chunks of text by long-dead authors like Homer, Thucydides, Vergil and Livy, because all Renaissance men looked back on these works as the high point of culture and civilisation.

### Honours galore

Anybody called Henry in sixteenth century England was likely to be called Harry, or Hal, as an affectionate version of the name but, like any male royal of the day, Henry was also given a series of titles. He wasn't quite 2 when he became constable (governor) of Dover Castle in Kent and lord warden of the Cinq Ports along the south coast. At 3 he was made earl marshall of England and lieutenant of Ireland. He was duke of York by October 1494 and a knight of the bath. He was still only 4 when his father made him warden of the Scottish marches and, top of the tree in the elite stakes, knight of the Garter.

What was all this about? Well, it meant that the Tudors had a future stake in many dodgy parts of their kingdom – Ireland (under constant threat of rebellion), the Scottish Border (under constant threat of invasion), the vulnerable south coast (under constant threat) – *and* it meant that no over-mighty subject from among the barons could get his greedy hands on any of these parts. It was Tudor policy, of course, to maintain power by employing lesser men whom they could easily control. Keeping key posts in the family was another effective way of doing this.

Henry's theological education almost certainly came from his second tutor, William Hone, and such knowledge was virtually unique in a royal prince. He had a first rate grasp of the most important book of the day, the Bible (still only available then in Latin at all good bookshops). The prince also learned French, Spanish and Italian, vital in the world of power-politics he was to enter later.

As if all that knowledge wasn't enough, Henry was also an excellent horseman, huntsman, jouster, composer, musician, dancer – don't you just hate him already? Henry's dancing first came to the fore when he was 10 at Arthur's wedding in November 1501, when he won the hearts of all spectators. For more on dancing, that vital social accomplishment, see Chapter 1.

## Moving up after Arthur's death

Henry's older brother Arthur, the original heir to the throne, had only been married to the Spanish princess Catherine of Aragon for five months when he died of tuberculosis. Arthur's mother Elizabeth comforted her husband by reminding him that 'God had left him yet a fair prince, two fair princesses' and that 'God is where he was'. Henry was now catapulted into the limelight as the duke of Cornwall, and he was made prince of Wales in 1503. He was 11. For the next six years he cooled his heels with plenty of time for his favourite pastimes – hunting, jousting, eating – but he had no real work to do.

Castles in Spain were important to the Tudors. Now that Arthur was dead, Catherine *should* have gone home to Aragon and Mummy and Daddy (Isabella and Ferdinand), and taken her dowry and the all-important Spanish Alliance with her. But Henry VII's idea was to keep it all in the family by betrothing Prince Henry to his dead brother's wife. Oh dear – he should have read Leviticus (see Chapter 5).

# Seeking Riches and Power

In Chapter 2 we explain that Henry VII's reputation of being a miserly skinflint isn't quite fair, but the new king on the block, still only 18 when he was crowned after his father's death, spent money like water and had personality and courage as big as the great outdoors. Despite everything that was to happen during his reign, Henry remained amazingly popular with most of his subjects, even though they believed they were going to burn in hell's fire because of him.

Like his father, Henry VIII saw that he had two basic ways to make his kingdom rich and powerful:

✔ Go to war and grab somebody's territory (that usually meant the French at the time – everybody hated them).

✔ Arrange a Big Fat Spanish Wedding – which is exactly what Henry VII had done with Arthur and Catherine.

Henry did his duty by carrying out his father's original wish and marrying Catherine of Aragon, keeping her massive dowry and the Spanish Alliance. Now take a look at the map (see Chapter 9). He could hit France from two directions – by sea across the Channel from the North and by land, taking an army out of Spain over the Pyrenees mountain range.

## Taking on the French

One of the key things that Henry did was to renew the conflict with France which had lasted for over a hundred years. In this respect, Henry was quite backward-looking and his role model was Henry V, the all-action hero who'd trounced the French at Agincourt in 1415. Henry was clever enough to join the Holy League, a military alliance Pope Julius II had put together, so he didn't have to risk going it alone.

The only bit of France that England still owned was the town of Calais. To increase his territory, Henry sent the marquis of Dorset to grab Guyenne in south-west France. But there was no support from Henry's fellow League member and father-in-law, Ferdinand of Aragon, so the whole campaign was a disaster.

### The first wife: Catherine of Aragon

You've got to feel sorry for Catherine. The daughter of pushy parents who ruled what would become *the* superpower of the 16th century, she was a political pawn, bullied by Henry VII, deserted (although that was hardly his fault!) by Arthur and married on the realpolitik rebound to Henry, who eventually divorced her. She was six years older than Henry and produced four children in four years, all of them dying in infancy. The fifth was Mary, who was to remain staunchly loyal to her mother's religion for the rest of her life. Unable to give Henry his much-wanted son, Catherine had to step down in favour of Anne Boleyn, maintaining a dignified silence throughout. She wasn't quite such a goodie twoshoes, however, because she had an affair with a disreputable Franciscan monk who may have given her syphilis. She refused the title of princess dowager (which means pretty well *my ex*) and died in retirement in Huntingdonshire in 1536. Next time you're in Peterborough, visit her tomb and pay your respects. For more on Catherine, see Chapter 6.

## The Field of the Cloth of Gold: 1520

This was a summit conference held near Calais between Henry and Francis. The whole thing was organised by Henry's lord chancellor, Wolsey, and was a chance for both kings to show off their money, weapons and jousting ability. Mock castles were built for war games, fountains ran with wine, tents glittered in gold fabric. Both kings fought five combats on each of ten days, surprise, surprise, beating all combaters. The ostentatious declarations of affection between the two kings was only a veneer, however, and war was soon resumed.

Henry did rather better in 1513, capturing a couple of French towns and winning the Battle of the Spurs (actually, more of a skirmish). This led to a truce and Henry got the city of Tournai to keep him quiet. In exchange, he gave the elderly French king, Louis XII, his 18-year-old sister Mary in marriage. Within months Louis was dead – draw your own conclusions as to why – and Henry was faced with a far more dangerous enemy, Francis I.

## Fencing with Francis 1

The new French king invaded Italy (then just a collection of states rather than a united country) and the death of Henry's father-in-law, Ferdinand of Aragon, meant that the Spanish Alliance, which Henry might previously have counted on, would be useless against Francis.

So Henry took the advice of Thomas Wolsey, his lord chancellor and right-hand man and this led to the Treaty of London of 1518, which:

- ✔ Gave Tournai back to France
- ✔ Saved everybody's face by agreeing universal peace

The treaty was blown out of the water the following year when the top job of holy Roman emperor was up for grabs after the death of Maximilian of Austria. The three contenders were:

- ✔ Charles V of Spain (of the Habsburg family)
- ✔ Francis I of France (of the Valois family)
- ✔ Henry VIII of England (of the Tudor family)

Charles was elected because of his family connections and the fact that he had more cash than anybody else. The title gave him huge chunks of Europe and, as it turned out, bits of America. Now Charles surrounded France on three sides; Henry controlled the fourth.

# The sinking of the *Mary Rose*

The *Mary Rose* was a state-of-the-art warship but it sank in the Solent – the narrow waterway between Portsmouth and the Isle of Wight – in July 1545. We still don't know why. The French claimed (of course!) to have sunk her, but this seems unlikely given the facts. The ship's captain, just before he went down, called to another ship that his crew were 'the sort of knaves I cannot rule'. Perhaps there was some kind of mutiny on board. We know from DNA evidence from the bodies of the crew who drowned that most of them were Spanish. Henry saw it all happen, riding along the beach and muttering, 'Oh, my pretty men. Drowned like rattens!'

Check out the hull and artefacts of the *Mary Rose* in the Historic Docks in Portsmouth. The ship was raised from the sea in 1982.

# *Putting on a sideshow*

Linking with Charles V, Henry sent the duke of Suffolk to attack Paris. Charles was busy in Italy, the weather was awful and Suffolk's army became a rabble.

There was better news from Italy, where Francis I was defeated and captured by Charles's army. Even so, broke and unable to capitalise on the opportunity, Henry had to sign a humiliating peace with France in August 1525.

For a while, everything in the Tudor garden was lovely. Henry gave his 11-year-old daughter Mary (by Catherine of Aragon) as a prospective bride to Francis's son, also (confusingly!) Francis, but by 1529 Charles V and the French king were negotiating a new treaty and it looked as if Henry would find himself in a potential war with both France and Spain. It didn't help, of course, that this was the year that Henry began divorce proceedings against Catherine and she was the aunt of Charles V, whose army was surrounding the pope in Rome. The 'Ladies' Peace' was signed in the French city of Cambrai to avoid outright war.

## Fighting the French (again!)

With Charles and Francis cosying up to each other, Henry put the country on invasion alert. He built forts like Pendennis and Cowes along the south coast, demanded that local troops be mobilised and hiked taxation to pay for all his preparations.

European politics change like the wind and Charles and Francis soon fell out, so that there was now *another* two pronged attack by the emperor and Henry on France. This time – the summer of 1544 – Henry besieged Boulogne and took it, blowing up part of the town walls. Charles felt betrayed by this posturing – it wasn't part of the joint plan – and promptly defected to Francis.

The French king now launched his own two-pronged attack. One of his armies hit Boulogne and the other arrived off the south coast of England, firing on Henry's fleet off Portsmouth and attacking the Isle of Wight before being driven off.

The war ended tamely with the Treaty of Camp. Henry would keep Boulogne for a fixed period and Francis would then buy it off him.

## Making Politics Personal

One of the biggest problems that Henry faced throughout his reign was his 'great matter' – his determination to have a son to continue the Tudor line. Inevitably, this involved finding a suitable wife who would provide a male heir for him. We cover Henry's wives in more detail in Chapter 5, but we'll introduce them here, in order of their marriage to the king:

- ✔ **Catherine of Aragon** (married Henry June 1509, aged 24, separated 1531, annulled May 1533): See the earlier sidebar 'The first wife: Catherine of Aragon' for the lowdown on this sad princess.

- ✔ **Anne Boleyn** (married Henry secretly January 1533, aged 26, beheaded May 1536): Henry certainly fell for Anne, the daughter of a Kentish knight, longing, in his own words, to 'kiss her pretty dukkys' (breasts), but she was playing hard to get. Not for her was her sister's role of royal mistress (see the following section 'Playing Away from Home'); Anne wanted to be Henry's wife – oh, and queen of England too. Various foreign ministers thought her neck was too long, her mouth too wide and her 'bosom not much raised', but her long black hair was to die for and Henry was captivated. Think Genevieve Bujold in *Anne of the Thousand Days.* She bore Henry his second daughter, Elizabeth.

✔ **Jane Seymour** (married Henry 30 May 1536, aged 27, died October 1537): Even before Henry had officially tired of Anne he started flirting with Jane Seymour, who was a lady-in-waiting to both the king's first two wives. The marriage took place only 11 days after Anne's execution and Jane gave birth to Henry's much wanted son, Edward, at Hampton Court on 12 October 1537. Twelve days later she was dead from the all-too-common childbed fever and Henry, broken-hearted of course, was on the lookout for a replacement.

✔ **Anne of Cleves** (married Henry January 1540, aged 25, annulled June 1540). So far, home-grown wives like Anne and Jane hadn't proved a great success, so Henry let Thomas Cromwell suggest Anne of Cleves. This was a purely political marriage because her father John was an opponent of Charles V, the Catholic king of Spain. Cromwell and others hoped that Anne would have some influence on Henry, but they got it hopelessly wrong. She was homely to say the least – Henry called her his 'Flanders Mare' only partially because she came from that part of Europe. She had pock-marked skin and spoke virtually no English. In the *Private Lives of Henry VIII* all Charles Laughton's Henry does in bed with Anne is play cards! Henry annulled his marriage to Anne after six months.

✔ **Catherine Howard** (married Henry secretly November 1540, aged 17, beheaded 13 February 1542). Henry's fifth wife was well connected, the grand-daughter and niece of two powerful dukes of Norfolk, and she herself was a clever woman and a shrewd politician. We don't know if this marriage was ever consummated but Henry became doubtful of Catherine's fidelity and found a way to remove her for good.

✔ **Catherine Parr** (married Henry 12 July 1543, aged 31; she outlived Henry). Most of the time she acted as Henry's nurse – so, see later in this chapter.

# Playing Away from Home

The number of his wives and the size of his codpiece have led to the reputation of Henry as a stud. In 30 years he made four women pregnant and three of them were queens of England and his wives at the time.

Although Henry certainly had mistresses – it was expected of a king – he wasn't the sex god of legend and certainly *nothing* like the drooling Sid James in *Carry On Henry*!

During the Middle Ages and into the Renaissance, the nobility were obsessed with the idea of courtly love, in which men wrote poetry, women sighed and accepted presents and everybody flirted for England. In reality, marriages were dynastic, arranged by greedy fathers (like Henry VII himself) to make strong alliances and build huge power bases. What's love got to do with it?

# Playing away 1 – the other Boleyn girl

Mary was the elder daughter of Sir Thomas Boleyn of Hever Castle in Kent. The memorial brass of this social climber is still on show at St Peter's Church there, so check it out. It must be something of a record to have a king bedding both your daughters. The fact that Mary was already married to William Carey didn't bother Henry unduly – after all, the man was only a gentleman of the king's Chamber. Mary may have become pregnant by Henry, but if so it ended in a miscarriage, and the king passed on, with potentially disastrous results, to her feisty little sister Anne.

# Playing away II – Bessie Blount

Henry may have turned to Bessie Blount (pronounced Blunt) after disappointment when Catherine gave birth to Mary in 1516. Elizabeth Blount was related to the queen's chamberlain and Court gossips noted the pair together at a torchlight masque. By 1518 Bessie was pregnant and Henry Fitzroy was born at Blackmore Abbey in Essex in the spring of 1519.

Bastard sons were normally called *fitz* from the old Norman word, and even had their own badge, a bend sinister, on their coats of arms. Being illegitimate carried no shame, but a fitz couldn't legally inherit the throne. Henry Fitzroy was kept away from Court, probably because the issue of the king siring a legitimate heir became so acute in the early 1530s (see Chapter 5), and he ended up as duke of Richmond and lieutenant of the north.

# Leading an Active Life: Henry's Hobbies

Henry was between 6 foot and 6 foot 4 depending on which account you read, with powerful shoulders and legs. A typical day for him was to hunt early in the morning, often wearing out three horses in chasing stags for 30 miles. He outshot most of his bowmen at the butts (target range) and played cards and dice into the early hours. He also ate and drank an enormous amount, but still found time to attend mass five times a day.

## Jousting for boys and men

As he got older and heavier, Henry needed slower, larger horses to carry him. He was a good judge of horseflesh, even referring to his fourth wife, Anne of Cleves, as his 'Flanders Mare'.

Jousts took place in the *lists*, which were open spaces split by a wooden barrier. In tournaments two armoured knights rode at each other armed with shields and blunted lances. This was practice for actual warfare, but the object in a tournament was to unhorse your opponent by hitting his shield. This was exciting and colourful entertainment for the crowd, but it could be very dangerous. Henri II of France was killed in 1559 when a lance hit him in the sights of his visor and smashed into his brain.

Henry's first tournament as king lasted several days and he won various prizes. After all, who's going to be brave enough to knock a king off his horse? In 1524 at Greenwich tilt yard Henry took part in a war game, a mock siege of the temporary Castle of Loyaltie; his head was hit by the duke of Suffolk and his helmet was filled with lance splinters.

Many of Henry's suits of armour still survive – check them out at the Royal Armouries, Leeds and the Tower of London – and you can measure his body from them. The first suits have a 19-inch waist measurement, the later ones 54 inches. There were all sorts of sniggering comments on the size of his *codpiece* (iron jockstrap) – boasting again!

## A-hunting he would go

After the lists hunting was tame stuff, but the king and his courtiers took it very seriously, covering miles in a day with hawks and dogs. They rode *palfreys* (saddle horses) and chased deer and wild boar in the huge royal parks like Greenwich and Hampton Court (see Figure 3-1). Henry also set up hunting lodges at Langley in Oxfordshire and Sunninghill in Berkshire. The king had a reputation for being in good humour in the hunt, so if you wanted to get anything out of him, like a title, job or piece of land, raising the question while trotting alongside him was a good time to do it.

Hunting with the king was a huge honour and it was almost the last sport Henry gave up shortly before his death.

## I'll see your three castles and raise you!

Henry enjoyed many games that he made illegal for his subjects – cards and dice among them. One of the most popular card games was Cent, later called Piquet, and we know the king liked to play with Richard Hill, the sergeant of the royal cellar. Above all, Henry liked to gamble – the English vice – and, like his father, he sometimes lost heavily. Whether Hill got rich isn't recorded.

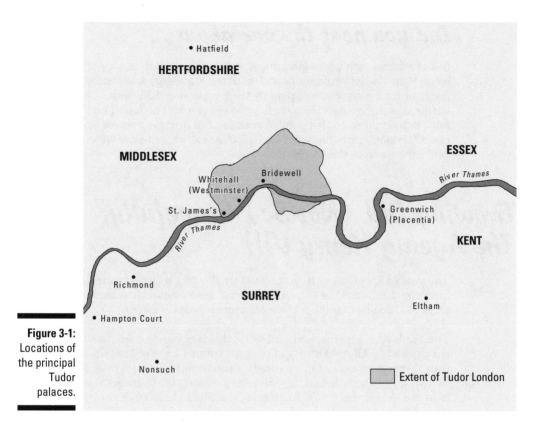

**Figure 3-1:**
Locations of
the principal
Tudor
palaces.

# 'Who but my lady greensleeves?'

Like all Renaissance princes, Henry was taught to play various instruments
as a child and he had a good singing voice. He played the lute and wrote
melodies as well as solemn dirges for the mass. Okay, so he probably didn't
write *Greensleeves*, but his love letters to Anne Boleyn suggest he had all the
talents of a born lyricist.

His Court orchestra, made up largely of French and Italian performers, played
at masques, balls and public feasts. The Bassano family provided his best
singers, and because Francis I, the king of France, was tone deaf, he couldn't
compete with Henry on that score.

Henry set up the Chapel Royal Choir – 30 men and 20 boys – who followed
the king around as he visited his various palaces – Greenwich, Nonsuch,
Whitehall, Hampton Court. The king and his chief minister, Cardinal Thomas
Wolsey, vied with each other in their choirs, sending scouts all over the
country to see whether Britain Had Talent. Dionysius Memo, the organist of
St Mark's in Venice whom Henry employed, was reckoned to be the best per-
former in Europe.

## *Did you hear the one about . . . ?*

It was a brave man who didn't laugh at the king's jokes, but for entertainment value Henry hired professionals. Top of the stand-ups was Patch, Wolsey's jester or fool, who was well paid by the king in the 1530s; but Will Somers is better known, perhaps because his glasses can still be found on the ram's horn helmet given to Henry by Maximilian I of Austria. Somers openly criticised the king's appointments and his over-eating, either of which would've sent other men to the block.

# *Growing Old (Not So) Gracefully: The Ageing Henry VIII*

The years 1527–1533 were dominated by the king's 'great matter' – his need for a son. Getting rid of Catherine, marrying Anne and clashing with the pope all led to the dissolution of the monasteries (see Chapter 6).

The 1530s didn't go too well for Henry; this was his *decadus horribilis* (horrible decade). All right, many of his misfortunes were of his own making, but they turned him into an increasingly morose and bitter old man. Anne Boleyn betrayed him, he believed, by producing a daughter (Elizabeth) when what he'd prayed for was a son. Revolting peasants in Lincolnshire objected to Henry's hike in taxation, and in the Pilgrimage of Grace in 1536 thousands of ordinary people had problems accepting Henry, not the pope, as head of the Church (see Chapter 4).

Above all, Henry felt lost. God hadn't given him a son and the pope had excommunicated him. He was halfway to hell already.

---

### Tennis, anyone?

No, not everyone. Jousting and hunting on horseback were noble pursuits – who else had the time and money? – and tennis followed suit. Henry played the game at Baynard's Castle in London and many of the nobility had tennis courts in their houses. This was 'real' or 'royal' tennis, played on semi-covered courts and using the walls rather like modern squash. You used your hands as racquets and the balls had no bounce. In 1522 Henry played doubles with Charles V against the prince of Orange and the marquis of Brandenburg. The result was a draw – 'you can't be serious' – after 11 games.

---

## Come dine with me

Henry's first meal of the day was dinner, which began at 10 a.m. or earlier. He was fond of beef, mutton, capons and pigeons. He ate wheat and rye bread and loved oysters. He was also partial to sticky puddings, pastries and biscuits, and spread honey on many of his meals. No sign of five-a-day here, even though apples, pears, strawberries, cherries, damsons, peaches, oranges, figs and grapes were available and popular.

## *Climb up on my knee, sonny boy!*

At last Henry's prayers were answered and on 12 October 1537 Jane Seymour gave birth to a boy, Edward. The sting in the tale was that she died of complications 12 days later. The boy showed promise – he was clever and bookish, inheriting the old man's academic abilities, and Henry had plans to marry the lad off to Mary, the daughter of James V of Scotland.

## *Unwieldy lies the body that wears the crown*

Henry VIII is often listed as one of many famous people who died of syphilis. Medical experts have studied the records carefully and we can now carry out a virtual autopsy on the king.

No one had any idea about balanced diets in the 16th century and Henry enjoyed his food and drink. Banquets were huge and frequent, and meals, often taken late at night, placed a great emphasis on red wine and meat. It was treason (punishable by death) to speculate on the king's health – who'd be a royal physician?

Here's a breakdown of Henry's health over the years:

- ✔ He showed no signs of the tuberculosis that killed his father, brother and both sons.
- ✔ He had a skin rash for two months in 1514 (aged 23). He may have had secondary syphilis, but other facts imply he didn't have it – for instance, his daughter Mary, his mistress Bessie Blount and his son Henry showed no symptoms.
- ✔ He picked up malaria in 1521 (aged 30) and suffered intermittently for the rest of his life.

- He got several potentially serious knocks jousting, hunting and wrestling, one of which allegedly made Anne Boleyn miscarry from worry.

- He packed on the weight and took less exercise from about 1535 (aged 46 – middle-aged spread!).

- One of his legs (we don't know which one) became ulcerated and caused great pain and fever. This may have been caused by a jousting accident or was a sign of osteitis (bone infection), which later affects other organs.

- His mood swings increased from 1540 (aged 49 – male menopause!) and he suffered occasional lapses of memory.

- By 1546, with less than a year left, the king's servants had to move him from room to room or onto his horse using a lifting apparatus (even in the winter, in the last year of his life, he sat in the saddle of his horse, wrapped up against the cold, watching others chase the stags he'd once hunted). His eyesight was failing.

## The king is dead – long live the king

In the end, you have to feel sorry for Henry. He had no friends and a string of ghastly relationships behind him. Both his sons were to die young and he had no faith at all in daughters to carry on his dynasty. The last time a woman ruled England (Matilda in the 12th century) a civil war to get rid of her ensued.

Henry died in his own bed on 28 January 1547, probably of renal and hepatic failure. He was 56 and had reigned for 37 years.

---

### The sixth wife: Catherine Parr

Nursing the king through his last years was no job for the faint-hearted. Henry could be extreme in his temper tantrums, screaming at people with his high, reedy voice, and his ulcers smelt horrible. Catherine was a widow and the daughter of Thomas Parr of Kendal. She was intelligent and cultured and dared to talk politics to Henry in a way that no one else did. It may have been because of her that Henry's will organised the succession to the throne to include his daughters Mary and Elizabeth should Edward die childless. Prophetic or what? Catherine married again after Henry, but died in childbirth at Sudeley Castle in 1548.

# Chapter 4

# Running the Kingdom, Henry's Way

Modern politicians can learn a lot from Henry's style of government. Unlike Henry VII, who did a lot of his own accounts checking, Hal would run a mile rather than do any paperwork – after all, he had people for that sort of thing. That makes it difficult to find all the evidence we need, but Henry's actions always speak louder than words.

## Managing Like a Monarch

In the end Henry's management style was all about getting his own way. As the German religious reformer Martin Luther said of him, 'Junker Heinz [Lord Harry] will do as he pleases.' Bear that in mind as you look at what follows.

### Getting in your face

Henry worked with his advisers through cosy chats on a one-to-one basis. He took aside people he could count on for support – see the later section 'Meeting the King's Advisers'– rather than holding huge meetings of the Council, which were likely to be long-winded and nit-picking. He asked for advice but wasn't bound to take it, and he always let everybody know who was in charge.

One of Henry's first actions as king was to fire Dudley and Empson, Henry VII's financial advisers in the last years of his reign. He had these two thrown into the Tower, a hugely popular move that gave the new king street cred.

Henry was highly intelligent but his concentration span was short. Look at Chapter 3 to see how much activity he crammed into 24 hours. Clerks wrote his letters and he liked to have information in a pre-digested form. Don't be fooled, though – he wasn't a king who lived for pleasure alone. He was surprisingly well-informed on all sorts of topics.

## Who calls the shots?

With his short attention span Henry often left much routine work to ministers and servants. So historians don't always know whether a particular decision was Henry's or someone else's. The bottom line is that even if it was Thomas Wolsey who hit upon cunning plans for divorces and foreign policy or Thomas Cromwell who decided to wipe out the monasteries, the final decision was always Henry's. Nothing happened without his say-so.

## Trying to go it alone

For much of his time as king, Henry tried to go his own way without interference from the Church or Parliament. Events meant, however, that he couldn't always do this, and by the time of his death he was actually more constrained than ever.

One of Henry's first personal acts was to marry Catherine of Aragon (see Chapters 3 and 5). Most people at Court had advised against the union but here was Henry surprising them all with his tough insistence. Yet the move was potentially brilliant – the Spanish Alliance was still on and the couple's children would rule over a huge Anglo–Spanish empire.

---

### Surprise, surprise!

Henry was unpredictable. After 1540 he had mental mood swings anyway because of various medical ailments (see Chapter 3), but even before that he could turn on a sixpence (or groat, to use a coin of the time) and many was the adviser who fell because of that. Thomas Cromwell in particular (see the later section 'Meeting the King's Advisers') thought he could read Henry's mind and lost his head as a result. Henry often let ministers – and wives – run on a loose rein only to pull them up short suddenly.

---

### Introducing the 'great matter'

Henry's 'great matter' was his desperate desire to have a legitimate son who would take over after his death. When it was obvious that Catherine could no longer have children, he tried to get the pope to annul the marriage. For political reasons, the pope refused (see Chapter 6).

Henry's secret marriage to Anne Boleyn in 1533 didn't cause a break with Rome – it was a symptom of it. The king was so determined to get his own way that he took control of the Church in England away from the pope and refused to go back on that even though the pope told him he would burn in hell as a result.

### Playing up Parliament

Going his own way was one thing, but taking on the pope, the hugely powerful Catholic Church and God was an enormous step and a pretty lonely road to walk. So Henry not only got his advisers on side – the ruthless Thomas Cromwell in particular – but Parliament too.

In theory, Parliament declared the Royal Supremacy (Henry's control of the Church), which gave the body a power it had never had before and one which Henry certainly never intended. The power of Parliament increased in the next three reigns because Edward VI was a child and his sisters Mary and Elizabeth 'only' women. Parliament was on the (admittedly rocky) road to the almost total power it has over the monarchy today.

### Sorting the Scots

In Chapter 3 we have a look at Henry's foreign policy, where he was playing with the big boys, the king of France and the holy Roman emperor. But the French had an understanding with the Scots, called the Auld Alliance, and English relations with Scotland had always been difficult. Even though the Scottish king, James IV, was married to Henry's sister Margaret (she was 14 at the time), no love was lost between the two countries and the border lands had a history of rape and pillage.

Henry claimed to be overlord for Scotland (which wasn't actually legal or true), and not unnaturally, the Scots resented it. Taking his opportunity, James invaded England while Henry was winning the Battle of the Spurs across the Channel (see Chapter 3), but was decisively beaten when Queen Catherine sent an English army north. The Scots king was killed at Flodden in Northumberland and his body much hacked about. Catherine sent his blood-soaked shirt to Henry as proof of the victory. An archbishop, a bishop, two abbots, nine earls and 14 lords were killed along with the king, all their bodies stripped by camp followers on the field.

James was under excommunication from the pope for having broken a peace treaty with Henry so his body couldn't be buried in holy ground. It was left in a lead casket above ground at the monastery of Sheen in Surrey and the head was taken home by a souvenir-hunting workman at the site years later, still complete with red hair and beard. The rest of James was eventually buried in the churchyard of St Michael's, Wood Street, City of London.

# Meeting the King's Advisers

Henry only had two chief ministers during his reign – Thomas Wolsey and Thomas Cromwell. They both died in his service.

## Working with Wolsey

Thomas Wolsey was one of the last ecclesiastical statesmen in England. As a cardinal he was a potential pope, and he was for a time *legate a latere*, the pope's man on the spot. As lord chancellor for Henry, he 'had the ear' of the king.

### Rising through the ranks

Typical of the new men of humble origins the Tudors employed, Wolsey was born the son of a butcher in Ipswich, Suffolk. In 1483 (when he was about 12) he went to Magdalen (pronounced Maudlin) College, Oxford.

Oxford was the oldest university in the country and students were generally younger than they are today. Wolsey graduated a bachelor of arts in 1486 (at the age of 16) and took his master's degree in 1497. He then became a junior fellow (tutor), which meant he had to take holy orders (become a priest); this he did in Salisbury the following year.

### Progressing with patrons

An ambitious young man like Wolsey needed a patron to get on, preferably a great lord who could open doors to a rich and important career. His first patron was Thomas Grey, marquis of Dorset, whose sons Wolsey had tutored. Dorset got Wolsey a parish in Somerset, but the marquis's death meant that Wolsey had to look elsewhere. He left Oxford in 1502 and became senior chaplain to Henry Deane, the archbishop of Canterbury (the top job in the English Church).

Clearly not cut out for the noble (if boring) life of a country priest, Wolsey became chaplain to Sir Richard Nanfan, deputy lieutenant of Calais, and this got Wolsey the all-important entry to the royal Court. By 1509 Wolsey had become a royal chaplain and he was working for the powerful bishop of Winchester. He had met Prince Henry, who was about to become king.

### Having the ear of the king

The best way to get on in the Tudor world was to be a personal buddy of the top man and Wolsey achieved this by 1512. All right, the marquis of Dorset's campaign in France hadn't gone well (see Chapter 3), but Wolsey's logistical organisation had. Henry was impressed, making him almoner, responsible for all the charitable handouts the king gave. Far more importantly, he made Wolsey a member of the Council.

### Getting rich in Church and state

Wolsey did well organising the Battle of the Spurs campaign too (see Chapter 3) and Henry made him dean of York, the second most important *see* (religious area) after Canterbury. In rapid succession, Wolsey became bishop of Lincoln, bishop of Tournai and archbishop of York.

The revenues (income) from the York job were £5,000 a year and not enough to keep up with Wolsey's lifestyle – he had servants, horses, dogs, mistresses and several illegitimate children to pay for. By 1523 he was abbot of St Albans and lord chancellor of England. He had a staff of 430 and his annual income of £30,000 was probably more than the king's. This meant he could build lavishly on a vast scale, as at Hampton Court, still one of the country's top tourist attractions (see Chapter 19 for a description of this palace).

### Wielding influence

Everybody got the message: if you wanted to get anything out of Henry – a grant, a job, some land, a title – then you had to go through Wolsey first. Naturally, this made Wolsey a lot of enemies – nobody likes a greedy, monopolistic lord chancellor, especially one who's come from nowhere, like Wolsey.

As chancellor Wolsey was the most powerful man in the country except for Henry. As long as he did the king's work – and did it well – he was fine. For the first 14 years of Henry's reign it was Wolsey who actually ran the country. Even so, he could never relax; there were always upstarts like Thomas Cromwell looking for a leg-up and Wolsey had to be constantly on his guard.

### Centralising the government

To make himself more powerful and ensure that his word was being obeyed all over his kingdom, Henry decided to centralise the government. Wolsey's men got the job done:

- The Council of the North got more power (nominally under Henry Fitzroy, Henry's illegitimate son).
- The Council of the Welsh Marches (borders) got more power (nominally under Henry's 9-year-old daughter, Mary).

Wolsey also increased the power of the Court of Chancery and in the king's Council used the Court of Star Chamber as never before.

## A duke gets done in

Henry naturally favoured the nobility – that was, after all, how it had been for centuries – but Wolsey preferred lesser men who could be controlled and who'd be totally loyal to the king. One problem was Edward Stafford, the duke of Buckingham. One of the 'old guard', Buckingham wanted the job of high constable, which actually no longer existed. It didn't help that Stafford's father had been executed for treason by Richard III and that he had a vague claim to the throne himself. Stafford detested Wolsey because of the man's common birth. So Wolsey did a hatchet job on Buckingham, finding unhappy servants who swore in a show trial that the duke had an 'ill mind' towards Henry and was planning to stab him to death. This was clearly treason. Henry fell for it and Buckingham went to the block in May 1521.

Wolsey's work in equity jurisdiction (the king's right to correct any defects in a previous legal decision) is probably his most important lasting legacy.

Star Chamber was a good idea in that it gave the government control over legal cases, but it also soon became swamped with requests. Some of Henry's Council did nothing else but sit as judges – even Wolsey did from time to time. So Wolsey expanded the business of an already existing court – the Court of Requests or Poor Men's Causes – to handle what was, in effect, pro bono work.

### Dabbling in foreign policy: the Treaty of London

Most of Wolsey's claim to fame rests in his handling of international politics.

People used to claim that Wolsey wanted to be pope; he had the chance in 1521 and again in 1523. There's only ever been one English pope, Nicholas Breakspear, aka Adrian IV (see *British History For Dummies*, Sean Lang, published by Wiley). But Wolsey always put England first and in foreign affairs only carried out Henry's wishes.

The Treaty of London of 1518 (see Chapter 3) was Wolsey's most brilliant achievement and the high-water mark in his European success. After that, it was downhill all the way.

The Field of the Cloth of Gold (see Chapter 3) was Wolsey's party – he was one of the best events managers of his day – but the main point of all the expense and glitter was to cement friendships between Henry and Francis I. That failed and the pair parted the best of enemies.

### Allying with the emperor

Charles V wanted war, especially against Francis I, and Henry did his best to keep out of it, trying to play one king off against the other and waiting for his own opportunities.

Wolsey's job was to make all this work by:

- ✔ Raising money for armies
- ✔ Trying to mediate between Charles and Francis

Neither was a great success.

### Falling from grace

The Anglo–French Treaty of Westminster, which Wolsey worked out in 1527, led to opposition from Charles V. What happened next made matters worse.

Henry's marriage to Catherine of Aragon was in meltdown. The only man in the world legally able to grant a divorce was the pope (Clement VII) and Henry gave Wolsey orders to sort it out. Wolsey was in the dark about Anne Boleyn and only heard about the affair from someone else – not exactly a sign of trust between a king and his right-hand man.

Henry expected Wolsey, as the pope's man in England, to push Clement into co-operating. Clement, however, was surrounded by Charles V's army camped outside Rome, and Charles was the nephew of the much-put-upon Catherine. So no deal. Eventually, in 1529, the problem was passed to Cardinal Lorenzo Campeggio, now the pope's official protector of England, but Campeggio was playing hardball and all attempts failed.

Henry had pinned all his hopes on the annulment and he was furious, blaming Wolsey for not managing the impossible. Henry fired him as chancellor and Wolsey died at Leicester Abbey on 29 November 1530 on his way to London to face trumped up charges of treason.

If you remember awesome Orson Welles in *A Man For All Seasons*, you might feel sorry for Wolsey, but nobody did at the time. And besides, a new chancellor, Thomas More, was lurking around the corner.

# Carrying on with Cromwell

Henry knew exactly *where* he wanted to go but not always *how* to get there. Wolsey had been very competent and hard-working and the search was on to find a successor.

### Coming from nowhere

Wolsey's successor as Henry's fixer was Thomas Cromwell. Cromwell never actually became Chancellor, but he was Privy Councillor, Chancellor of the Exchequer, Secretary of State, and Master of the Rolls. Not bad for someone whose origins were as humble as his predecessor's. He was born about 1485, probably in Putney, west of London and his father was a shearman and inn-keeper. Like Wolsey, he went to Oxford University, but, quarrelling with his father, he travelled throughout Europe, working at whatever came to hand, including military service for the French in Italy and operating as a merchant in Antwerp, then the heart of the international business community.

### Becoming a legal eagle

Back home by 1516, Cromwell was now fluent in several languages and joined Wolsey's service, teaching himself law on the way. Three years later he sat on Wolsey's Council and his law work made him so much money that he became a gentleman by 1522.

Two years later Cromwell joined Gray's Inn in London. This was one of several Inns of Court, like Furnival's and Lincoln's, which were colleges that trained the country's best lawyers. Cromwell probably taught at Gray's, where he would have rubbed shoulders with the best legal minds of his day. London had no university at this time but Gray's Inn took the place of one.

### Surviving Wolsey

When a great man falls, those around him stand a chance of falling as well. It takes someone of exceptional ability to become indispensable to the state and that's exactly what Cromwell did.

Cromwell got himself elected as an MP for Taunton in Somerset. He caught Henry's eye as a good man and a fine legal brain, and by 1531 he was a member of the king's Council.

### Coming to Henry's aid

By 1532 the king's 'great matter' had reached crisis point. Thomas More, one of the few men to stand up to Henry on moral grounds (see 'Telling Friend from Foe', later in this chapter), resigned from his job as chancellor and

Cromwell's clever actions in the months ahead meant that the job went to him. So what did he do to secure the top job?

- ✔ He drew up the Act in Restraint of Appeals, which stopped people going over the king's head to the pope (see Chapter 6). This made Henry's second marriage (to Anne Boleyn) legal.

- ✔ He turned his office of secretary into a clearing house for royal business. As with Wolsey, every request to the king now had to go through Cromwell, giving him enormous power.

- ✔ He co-ordinated all the work that the Council did, including the great laws that covered treason, the succession and the Act of Supremacy (see Chapter 6).

- ✔ He realised that knowledge was power and he set up a network of agents and informers that was better informed than Henry VII's. Elizabeth's spymaster, Francis Walsingham, carried on Cromwell's network (see Chapter 14), which was the forerunner of today's MI5 and MI6.

### Dissolving the monasteries and making money

It was probably Henry's idea to dissolve the monasteries because at a stroke he could get rid of support for the pope (always strongest in the monasteries) and get some cash (he was always strapped) into the bargain.

Cromwell's job was to make it all work and he became the most hated man in England as a result. Many believed that the master secretary was evil – check out Leo Mckern's performance in *A Man For All Seasons* to get the flavour of a thoroughly unpleasant individual.

From 1536 the smaller monasteries were shut, and from 1536 the rest followed. The land was sold off to the highest bidder and all income went to the king. By 1540 every monastery in England had gone, but their beautiful ruins are everywhere (check out Fountains, Glastonbury, Rievaulx, Jervaux and many more; see Chapter 6). We look at the dissolution in more detail in Chapter 6.

---

# Culling a queen

Cromwell got the job of removing Anne Boleyn when it turned out that she too wasn't going to give Henry a son. He'd supported Anne earlier because she was part of the whole Royal Supremacy deal, but now he worked on accusing her of adultery and witchcraft.

Laws against witchcraft appeared for the first time in Henry's reign and it was very convenient that Anne had a rudimentary sixth finger on her left hand, which was taken to be an obvious sign of sorcery. Cromwell now put about the fact that Anne had trapped Henry by bewitching him.

For more details on Anne's end, flick to Chapter 5.

### Killing Cromwell

When you're the earl of Essex, chancellor of the exchequer, secretary of state and master of the rolls, not to mention vicar general and lord privy seal, you can expect a bit of opposition, and that's exactly what Cromwell got. He was hated by:

- The nobility, especially the powerful duke of Norfolk, who regarded him as an upstart

- The Church, because he destroyed the monasteries

- Conservatives, because he introduced an English Bible and supported preachers who leaned towards Protestantism

While Henry was busy in the spring of 1540 with the shock of the arrival of Anne of Cleves (she wasn't quite the beauty he'd expected) and lusting after Catherine Howard (see Chapters 3 and 5), the arch Protestant basher Stephen Gardiner, bishop of Winchester, accused Cromwell of heresy.

The crime of heresy was a handy one to have at your disposal in the 16th century. Anyone not following the traditional religious line could be charged with heresy – and the penalty was death.

Cromwell was condemned by an Act of Attainder in July 1540, which meant no trial (if there had been, so little evidence against him existed he'd probably have got off) and he was executed on Tower Green days later. It was the hottest summer in living memory and he went well, maintaining his innocence but with the surprisingly magnanimous words, 'I am condemned by the law to die . . . I have offended my prince, for the which I ask him heartily forgiveness.'

# Telling Friend from Foe

Henry's high-handed decisions throughout his reign made him enemies. Some opposed his:

- Act of Supremacy

- Destruction of the monasteries

- Seeming over-reliance on advisers like Wolsey and Cromwell

- Wars with France, especially when taxes went up and a French fleet appeared off the south coast in 1545

And of course, there were those who loved him *because* of the above. You have to remember that the king was the Lord's anointed. Cross the king and you crossed God. Others believed that the king's decisions were always right *because* he was king; anything bad was probably the work of evil men like Cromwell.

## Offending Henry

It was always a risky business to upset the king and those who did – Wolsey, Cromwell, Buckingham, More, various wives – usually came to a sticky end.

Three who got away with it were:

- ✔ **Catherine of Aragon:** She was furious when Henry told her he didn't consider their marriage legal in the eyes of God or man – oh, and that meant Mary was illegitimate too. She kept up her opposition for ten years, yet he never took action against her.

- ✔ **Sir George Throgmorton:** He spoke out against Henry in the Commons, and when the king sent for him to explain himself he told him outright that he disapproved of his relationship with Anne Boleyn on account of the fact that the king 'had to do' with her sister and mother. 'Never with the mother,' Henry answered, and a very lucky Sir George walked away (backwards, of course, and having bowed three times).

- ✔ **Thomas Cranmer:** He was archbishop of Canterbury and he, Cromwell and Henry all sang (literally!) from the same hymn sheet until 1539. Then Henry put the brakes on religious change by bringing in the Six Articles (see Chapter 6) which underlined the basics of the Catholic Church. Cranmer quietly opposed Henry on this and lived to tell the tale. Henry also backed him over charges of heresy when the archbishop seemed to favour Protestant preachers and he turned a blind eye to the fact that Cranmer was married (all priests were supposed to be celibate).

Disagreeing with Henry was easy (there was a lot to criticise), but you had to do it in private so that people couldn't use gossip against you and you couldn't oppose the king openly in case that became rebellion. Henry took criticism, not opposition.

## Meeting Henry's enemies

There was nothing to rattle anybody's cages until 1529 and the king's 'great matter'. Buckingham had gone (see the earlier sidebar 'A duke gets done in') because he was a potential threat and no more. It was breaking with Rome that caused much of the problem.

The most prominent opposition to Henry came from:

- **Thomas More:** A family man who lived in Chelsea, west of London, More was a lawyer and scholar who served Henry faithfully under Wolsey. He didn't want to be chancellor and resigned in 1532 because he saw the way the religious wind was blowing. He refused to acknowledge Henry as head of the Church under the Royal Supremacy and was imprisoned and beheaded.

- **John Fisher:** He was chaplain to Margaret Beaufort, Henry VII's mother, and bishop of Rochester in Kent. He opposed Henry's divorce from the start and followed More's fate, but not before the pope (Paul III) made him a cardinal. Like More, Fisher became a saint in 1935, everybody having forgotten the fact that he'd been carrying on a treasonable correspondence with Charles V shortly before his arrest.

- **Reginald Pole:** A relative of the Tudors, he'd been educated at Henry's expense. He opposed the king over the 'great matter', but Henry let him go to Italy (then considered *the* centre of learning) to continue his studies. From here, Pole launched an anti-Henry book and worked with the pope to make life as difficult for the king as possible. Henry couldn't reach Pole, but he made sure Cromwell's spies watched and ultimately arrested the various members of his family left behind. Some of these were executed, including Pole's aged mother, the countess of Salisbury (cries of 'Shame!').

- **The Pilgrimage of Grace, 1536:** This became the greatest political protest of Henry's reign. What its leaders wanted was to put the clock back four years before all the upheavals with the Church began. Henry was sympathetic at first, because clearly no ill will against him personally existed. But a minor rising in Yorkshire tipped the balance and 125 ringleaders were hanged, 12 from the walls of Carlisle and 62 in surrounding villages. Churchmen weren't immune either – four canons, nine monks and an abbot all faced the rope (more cries of 'Shame!').

## Sir Thomas More – a man for all seasons

Much painted by Hans Holbein, the king's Court artist, More was a Humanist who wanted to reform the Church from within. His book *Utopia*, written in 1516, puts him right up there with the best scholars of the Renaissance. His *History of King Richard III* started the trend for modern biographies. In 1935 he was declared a saint, having performed miracles after his death as a martyr.

Robert Bolt's excellent play *A Man For All Seasons* has been filmed twice with Paul Schofield and Charlton Heston as More. Schofield in particular is brilliant, and check out the mood swings shown by Robert Shaw as Henry. Vanessa Redgrave had a bit part as Anne Boleyn in the Schofield version and played More's wife alongside Heston.

# Selling the Image

Outward show was as important to Henry's style of government as the hard work done by others behind the scenes. Henry looked every inch a king and his hearty, boisterous lifestyle (see Chapter 3) backed this up. Weddings, births of royal children and hosting important visitors were all excuses to hold a tournament, spend money and show off.

## Painting power

Check out the famous portrait by Hans Holbein. Henry has:

- ✔ Huge confidence – note the body language of hands on hips and feet planted firmly apart
- ✔ Lots of money
- ✔ Powerful legs
- ✔ Superb taste in clothes
- ✔ Very broad shoulders

But that was all front. Check out the portrait again. Henry has

- ✔ Far too much body fat (a 54-inch waist, as we explain in Chapter 3)
- ✔ Little piggy eyes that seem to trust no one
- ✔ Terrible taste in soft furnishings (see the wall behind him) – but of course, that's just our opinion!

And remember what we can't see:

- ✔ His ulcerated leg, bandaged under his hose (tights)
- ✔ His bad breath
- ✔ His near baldness (carefully hidden by the plumed hat)

We always think of Henry with short hair and a beard. In fact, he wore his hair long until the mid 1530s, and although he grew several beards during his reign he quickly got bored with them and had them shaved off (no doubt by one of his company of barber surgeons).

As you see in Chapter 16 on his daughter Elizabeth, health, strength, beauty and youth were all just smoke and mirrors.

## Reflecting greatness in buildings

To accentuate his greatness, Henry built or acquired a set of magnificent houses:

- Bridewell in London was rebuilt from decay over a seven-year period and cost Henry £20,000.

- Hampton Court had been Wolsey's place. Henry took it over after he fired the man in 1530. (For more about this palace, see Chapter 19).

- St James's Palace in Whitehall was built from scratch in the 1530s.

- Nonsuch Palace, south of London, was Henry's fantasy home. It had a park of 2,000 acres, cost £24,000 and was still unfinished at the time of Henry's death.

## Punching above his weight

Henry was colossal, but the image he projected at the time and the image we have now is even greater. His people loved him for his greatness. He stood up to the French, the pope and the holy Roman emperor.

The Reformation may have been a European development, but Henry's contribution to it – one that he never intended – was that it became peculiarly his. British historians called it the *Henrician* Reformation.

# Chapter 5

# Six Weddings and Two Funerals: Henry VIII's Wives and Girlfriends

*H*enry VIII's love life is world famous. He's the only English king to marry six different women, two of whom literally lost their heads as a result of saying *Volo* – 'I do'.

Henry's marriages are all about politics as much as sex. In the 16th century the government *was* the king and procreation was essential for a dynasty like the Tudors to survive. It was vital that a queen should be fertile.

In nearly 32 years of marriage Henry created 11 pregnancies with four different women and fathered four children who lived beyond babyhood:

✔ Mary – the future Queen Mary I

✔ Henry Fitzroy – illegitimate, the son of Bessie Blount

✔ Elizabeth – the future Queen Elizabeth I

✔ Edward – the future King Edward VI

After 1537 Henry was responsible for no more pregnancies, even though the king had three wives to go – Anne of Cleves, Catherine Howard and Catherine Parr. Catherine Parr outlived Henry and became pregnant by her next husband, so the fertility problem was probably Henry's.

Don't let Henry's track record fool you. Six wives and a couple of mistresses give the impression that Henry was a stud and womaniser. In fact, he took marriage very seriously – so seriously that he executed two of his wives for adultery.

Henry comes out of all this looking a rather sad figure. Driven by the need to produce a legitimate male heir, his frequent marriages smack of desperation. But he seems to have genuinely loved each of his wives (except Anne of Cleves, who everybody realised was a big mistake). Equally, he tired of women easily and his own monstrous ego was the real cause of all the marital breakdowns.

# Courting Catherine of Aragon

In Chapter 2 we explain that Catherine was the daughter of 'the most Catholic of kings', Ferdinand of Aragon, and Isabella of Castile.

## Joining Team Tudor

Catherine was engaged to Arthur, Henry VII's eldest son, when she was 7. Henry VII was an upstart who had, after all, taken the crown of England by force and his legal claim to it was dodgy. He knew that making an alliance with one of the oldest royal families in Europe would go a long way towards acceptance.

In 1501 the real wedding (as opposed to the proxy one – see Chapter 2) took place in England and everybody thought the couple were well matched. Both spoke fluent Latin and had been brought up good Catholics (at this stage nothing else existed in the Christian world) but with a humanist slant (see Chapter 1).

## Pretty as a picture?

It was the job of Court portrait painters to make their sitters as pretty or handsome as possible, so we can't really rely on their accuracy. Easily the best portrait painter of his generation was Hans Holbein from Augsburg in Germany, and his paintings are so good we have to believe that they're fairly accurate. Other portraits are very average and the problem is made worse by later copies and engravings, particularly by the Victorians. It doesn't help either that society's ideas of beauty have changed: in the 16th century pale skin and a high forehead in a woman was considered a sign of beauty and intelligence. We know Henry was famously deceived by Holbein's painting of Anne of Cleves, although she does look pretty plain in his miniature. Anne Boleyn has a rosebud mouth and blobby nose; Catherine of Aragon has a huge chin in all portraits except Holbein's. It's probably safest to say that the clothes are accurate but the faces aren't. If in doubt, I'd stick with Holbein.

Although Catherine had been due to marry an English prince for years and was clearly a smart girl, no one had ever taught her English, so she must have felt quite lost in her first months in the country, speaking Spanish to her ladies of the chamber only.

The newly-weds spent an extended honeymoon at Ludlow Castle on the Welsh Marches (borders) and it was here that Arthur died, probably of tuberculosis. We don't know whether the marriage was ever consummated. Very quickly, the 17-year-old princess was betrothed to Arthur's 11-year-old brother, Henry.

Church law said, based on the Bible's Book of Leviticus, that if a man married his dead brother's wife it was an unclean thing and he would be childless. The only man able to turn this ruling on its head was the pope, Julius II, who duly gave his consent.

Catherine herself was now in limbo. Ferdinand didn't want his daughter back (thanks, Dad!) because he was busy with affairs of state. So Ferdinand briefly made Catherine his ambassador, which improved her English and (uniquely at the time) gave a woman a political role in a man's world.

## Striking a match

Because of the shifts in European relations Henry VII had cooled on the Spanish Alliance marriage, but his death meant that Henry VIII could make up his own mind and the couple were married weeks later. Henry and Catherine were crowned in a joint ceremony on Midsummer's Day 1509. The streets around Westminster Abbey were hung with tapestries and gold cloth. The livery companies, all wearing their finery, lined Cheapside, the City of London's high street. Henry's horse was draped in gold damask and the king's doublet sparkled with rubies, emeralds and pearls. Catherine's litter was pulled by two snow-white horses. Over the top, or what?

Catherine swore she was still technically a virgin, despite some teenage boasting from Arthur. We're probably best off taking her word for it!

## Making babies, losing babies

Nine months after their wedding Catherine gave birth to a stillborn girl. This was very common at the time, with no scans or modern medical checkups available. It was a sign of gloom and doom to come, but Henry wasn't aware of that yet.

## Infant mortality

The reason so many children died young or were stillborn is probably down to the frequency of their mothers' pregnancies. Women's diet of grain, vegetables and honey (they didn't eat as much meat as the men) led to a low iron intake and anaemia. This left women prone to infections and gave them low resistance to illnesses. The medical practice of bleeding (cutting veins or applying blood-sucking leeches) for all sorts of illnesses made matters worse.

In January 1511 Catherine gave birth to Henry, who should have gone on to be prince of Wales and eventually Henry IX. Tournaments and feasts were held and the church bells rang out. Within weeks, however, rejoicing turned to despair; baby Henry died from what today people call sudden infant death syndrome (SIDS), and for the first time the relationship between king and queen began to deteriorate.

It was two years before Catherine was pregnant again and it ended in miscarriage. Court gossip suggested Henry was looking elsewhere for excitement, perhaps with the duke of Buckingham's sister, but the Court was always full of rumours and no doubt Catherine tried to ignore the chat.

When Henry went to war in France in 1513, he made Catherine regent in his absence, but this only papered over the cracks in their relationship.

## Hitting the rocks

Henry may have been carrying on with Bessie Blount by this time (see Chapter 3), but if so he was still persevering with Catherine. In January 1515 she miscarried again – another prince she failed to deliver. Henry was at home in England but didn't visit her or even send condolences, such was his disappointment.

Eleven months later Catherine produced the first of Henry's children who would see adulthood. The child was healthy but it was female, and a newly disappointed Henry made all the right noises about the baby, named Mary, being 'a token of hope' and 'a good beginning' (nobody knows what Catherine thought of this damning with faint praise).

Catherine was now 31 and her final pregnancy ended in miscarriage in 1518. Lives were generally shorter in the 16th century and the menopause hit Catherine at 33 or 34. She'd gone through six pregnancies and two live births and was putting on weight rapidly. By the time of the Field of the Cloth of Gold (1520; see Chapter 3) everybody accepted she was past it – a disaster for a king desperate for a son.

## Hedging his Bess

We don't know exactly when Henry bedded Bessie Blount, but it was certainly before 1519 because that was the year she gave birth to Henry Fitzroy. The birth of a healthy illegitimate son was like rubbing salt into Catherine's wounds. She became more devout than ever, either as a sign of remorse, an attempt to say sorry to God for failing Henry or even in the faint hope of reversing her body clock.

Princess Mary wasn't acceptable to Henry for political reasons. The last queen of England was Matilda in the 12th century and she'd made such a hash of it that civil war had broken out. Nobody knew exactly how having Mary as queen would work. If a woman married, the law said that all her property became her husband's, so if Mary married a foreign king, England would belong to him as the crown matrimonial. If Mary married a home-grown nobleman, that could see the dynastic squabbles of the Wars of the Roses (see Chapter 1) start all over again.

Henry married Bessie Blount off to Gilbert Tailboys and threw money and land at them both, buying her silence. He had other fish to fry.

# Getting Heady with Anne Boleyn

Henry probably had an affair with Mary Boleyn (see Chapter 3) in 1520 and this brought him into the circle of her sister, Anne. Both Boleyn girls have captivated historical novelists and film makers, always keen to have a slushy love story centre stage.

## Courting commotion

In 1513, when Anne was about 12, she was sent to the Court of Margaret of Austria who ran the Low Countries (today's Netherlands). From there she was sent to the Court of Mary (Henry VIII's sister), who was now queen of France and not much older than Anne. When Louis XII of France died Mary came home, but Anne stayed on, learning all the flirtiness and flightiness of the French Court.

---

## Artful Anne

Anne's portraits don't show her as a great beauty – and remember, they were painted to flatter the sitter! – but she was sexy, clever and witty. She knew how to waggle her assets (see Chapter 3 for details of Henry's admiration for her two biggest assets) and held out against the king's amorous advances for over five years.

---

Caught between the charm of Anne, with her razzle dazzle, and boring old Catherine, who was menopausal and increasingly judgemental, Henry decided by 1527 that his marriage was illegal because of the disclaimer in Leviticus. Catherine had to go.

Catherine, of course, had no such intention. She saw herself as queen of England and her daughter Mary as the heiress to the throne. Knowing that Henry needed the pope's permission to get the marriage annulled, she dashed off letters to her nephew, Charles V, whose army was camped outside Rome, to make sure that the pope didn't do the honours. Well served by her legal team, Catherine won every round in this royal battle.

In Chapter 4 we explain that Thomas Wolsey lost his job because of his failure to sort out the divorce. But another of Henry's advisers, Thomas Cromwell, hit upon the answer. If the pope wouldn't play ball and grant a divorce, then Henry could get Parliament to declare him head of the Church (see Chapter 6) and then the king could sort it out for himself.

## Getting his own way – to hell

Catherine refused to recognise Henry's jurisdiction. She was banished from Court and given £3,000 a year and the title dowager princess of Wales.

The pope excommunicated Henry but the verdict was a paper tiger because neither Charles V nor Francis I, the superpower leaders in Europe, paid any attention to the pope. The only people who did were goody-two-shoes like Thomas More and John Fisher who, as you see in Chapter 4, lost their heads as a result.

Now events moved quickly. Henry gave Anne Boleyn the title of marchioness of Pembroke and she went with Henry to France as the potential queen-in-waiting the next year. She conceived on this trip, and because the child had to be legitimate in the spring of 1533 Thomas Cranmer, as archbishop of Canterbury, the top churchman in the country, annulled Henry's marriage to Catherine. At the same time Parliament prevented Catherine from whingeing to the pope by passing the Act in Restraint of Appeals.

Henry and Anne were married in secret in January and then, on 1 June, she was crowned. Fifty barges, fluttering with flags and gold foil, brought the royal procession along the river Thames from Greenwich to Westminster. The lord mayor of London presented the new queen with 1,000 gold marks (like she needed it!). Some of the crowd were quite subdued, however, and some weren't very pleased at the obvious signs of pregnancy showing through Anne's robes.

Although a number of top people boycotted the ceremony, the Boleyn family were over the moon. Everybody else had the last laugh, though, because the much awaited royal son in September turned out to be another girl, Elizabeth.

## Déjà vu

While Cromwell and Parliament were busy sorting out the details of the Royal Supremacy (see Chapter 6), which would have the effect of dividing the country deeply, Anne was exerting as much influence on Henry as she could. She was pregnant again by the spring of 1534, but miscarried in July. Henry must have been distraught. He was putting his people through an unprecedented upheaval and for what? In a way, he was back to square one.

Matters were made worse in April when Elizabeth Barton, the holy maid of Kent, prophesied loudly and often that Henry would die a villain's death if he stayed married to the queen. She was hanged at Tyburn, west of London, the traditional execution place for common felons.

## Old wife's tale

During her banishment Catherine was afraid that she would be poisoned, and reportedly, she had her food cooked by her own servants over a fire in her chamber. She needn't have worried. Ruthless as he was in some ways, Henry didn't stoop to such methods. He made sure that the Oath of Supremacy, which all people in public life were supposed to take to recognise Henry as head of the Church (upon penalty of death), didn't apply to Catherine or his daughter Mary.

In any case, Catherine solved the problem for him by dying, probably of a series of heart attacks, at Buckden in January 1536.

Meanwhile, Henry's relationship with Anne was passionate and intensely physical. Anne wore her sexuality on her sleeve. She was feisty and if she didn't like what Henry was doing she told him so. They had furious fights and many make-ups, but the techniques that Anne had used during their courtship didn't work so well after marriage. Henry began to find his wife annoying.

## Falling out of love: A losing game

By the summer of 1535 Henry and Anne's marriage blew hot and cold. The death of Catherine the following year meant that Henry could never go back to her and Anne was pregnant again. Then Henry had an accident while jousting and was knocked out for several hours. So worried was Anne that she miscarried.

The story spread years later that Anne's miscarried baby was deformed. Because of that Henry became convinced that the child couldn't have been his and that Anne must be playing away from home. But this story wasn't current at the time and is probably one of those annoying bits of fiction that tend to grow up around royals in every generation.

Henry began to brood. He wondered whether the dazzling girl at his elbow had bewitched him. He watched every gesture, read another meaning into every word. The dead child wasn't his. So whose was it? How about Anne's own brother George, Lord Rochford? After all, he was hanging around her all the time. In Henry's paranoid mood, it all seemed to fit.

## Punishing Anne: Off with her head!

Henry didn't rush to judgement, but over three months in the spring of 1536 he became convinced of Anne's infidelity. Two things pushed him over the edge:

- **Thomas Cromwell changed sides.** As you see in Chapter 4, Cromwell was loyal to Henry and could pick up intuitively on the king's moods. Henry confided in him and Cromwell now used his considerable powers to remove Anne.

- **Anne made a silly remark to Sir Henry Norris.** He was a gentleman of Henry's Privy Chamber and Anne, no doubt as a joke, told him that, should anything happen to the king, she knew Norris fancied her. The malignant Cromwell made sure that Henry heard of this in the worst possible light and Anne and Norris were arrested on charges of adultery. Because Henry was king, the crime was also treason.

Anne couldn't believe this was happening. She'd done nothing except carry on in the same flirtatious way she always had. Henry had made up his mind, however, and as well as accusing the queen of witchcraft (see Chapter 4) Cromwell produced a bundle of dodgy evidence to 'prove' that Anne had slept with four men:

- ✔ Sir Henry Norris, who denied it.

- ✔ Francis Weston, who denied it.

- ✔ William Brereton, who denied it.

- ✔ Mark Smeaton, who confessed to it. He was a lowly music teacher and was almost certainly tortured.

The trial was a mockery, even by rigged Tudor standards, and on 10 May 1536 Anne and all her 'lovers' were found guilty.

Meanwhile, the archbishop of Canterbury hit upon Henry's affair with Mary Boleyn as an excuse to dissolve the royal marriage. After all, a consummated relationship outside marriage was the same as one inside (if it suited Henry's purpose).

Anne was beheaded on 17 May 1536 (see the nearby sidebar 'Losing her head, keeping her cool' for the grisly details).

## Losing her head, keeping her cool

Anne went to the block on 17 May. She was no longer queen, marchioness nor wife. Her brother died days earlier not far from her cell in the Tower of London. She walked the 50 yards to the execution place on Tower Green wearing a plain grey dress and spoke to the waiting crowd. She prayed that God would save the king, 'for a gentler, more merciful prince was there never, and to me he was ever a good, a gentle and a sovereign lord.' Her cloak and headdress were removed. She had the nerve to joke about her little neck to the specially imported, masked headsman who hacked through it with a single horizontal sweep of his two-handed sword (her choice – the cut would be cleaner).

Rumour had it that Henry waited for the cannon signal that Anne was dead before he rode out to hunt. This is faithfully shown in *Anne of the Thousand Days* and the camera lingers on little Elizabeth who, aged 3, is still learning how to walk in her heavy dresses and doesn't understand the significance of the cannon fire she hears.

# Marrying Jane Seymour

Jane Seymour, Henry's third wife, was the calm after the storm. The daughter of Sir John Seymour of Wulf Hall in Wiltshire, she was a bit dumpy and a bit plain. At 27, she was unusually old to be a virgin, especially because she'd already been knocking around the Court for a while in the entourage of Queen Anne.

This relationship was political as well as personal. By marrying an English bride, Henry was signalling loud and clear that he wouldn't hitch his star to a European alliance and have to bargain away his control of the Church.

## Plain Jane

Because she didn't live long, figuring Jane out is difficult. Here's what we know:

- She had common sense.
- She wasn't deeply religious but may have tried to persuade Henry not to destroy the monasteries.
- She came of good breeding stock – the Seymour family was huge.
- She didn't have the ambition to lead a party made up of the Seymours as earlier queens of England had done with their families.
- She got on with princess Mary (Catherine's daughter), who accepted her illegitimacy and was welcomed at Court in July 1536.

## It's a boy!

While Henry was busy sorting out the Pilgrimage of Grace (see Chapter 4), Jane's coronation was shelved because she was pregnant.

All the signs looked good. Astrologers who watched the heavens closely at auspicious times told Henry he would have a son and he even had a new stall created in the Garter Chapel at Windsor for the new prince of Wales.

The pregnancy was fine, but the labour and birth were difficult. Finally, on 12 June 1536 at Hampton Court, a boy was born, and he was christened Edward three days later. Henry is said to have cried with joy.

## Taking leave: A dying shame

Thomas Cranmer and the duke of Norfolk were the prince's godfathers and princess Mary was godmother. Jane sat up in bed in the antechapel to receive visitors. Then it all went pear-shaped. She developed septicaemia, which was then called childbed fever, and 11 days after Edward's birth she slipped into a coma, dying on the evening of 24 October. Henry went to his Palace of Westminster and 'kept himself secret a great while' and the Court wore the black of mourning until Candlemas (2 February 1538).

Jane was gentle and biddable, perhaps the nicest of all Henry's wives. Above all, she'd given him what his heart desired most – a son.

# Tripping Up with Anne of Cleves

Henry was 46 and perhaps no longer really interested in marriage. But it was a risk to pin all your hopes on one boy and the Council, urged by Cromwell, suggested a new queen. Henry had a couple of options:

- **A French princess:** That would do wonders for shaky Anglo–French relations, but Francis refused to allow a beauty parade of family talent for Henry's benefit.
- **The Duchess of Milan:** She was 16 and already a widow, but she didn't fancy following Anne Boleyn to the block.

In fact, foreign policy pushed Henry in another direction altogether. Charles V and Francis I became buddies again early in 1539, leaving England and Henry out of the loop to such an extent that the king feared invasion. To counter the Franco–Imperial alliance Henry could:

- Join forces with the Schmalkaldic League – but they were Lutheran princes and he was a Catholic.
- Work out a deal with the powerful John, duke of the German state of Cleves-Julich, one of Charles V's most bitter enemies.

Henry settled on the second option, and a double wedding to cement friendship with Cleves-Julich was arranged: when Duke John died, his son William proposed to marry Henry's daughter Mary, and Henry himself would marry William's sister, Anne.

## Making a big mistake

Anne of Cleves was probably frightened to death as she set sail for England in December 1539. The weather was terrible and she couldn't get to Dover before the 27th, leaving a fuming Henry to spend Christmas alone at Greenwich.

When Anne got to the bishop of Rochester's palace on 31 December en route to her new husband-to-be, Henry played a prank that Anne Boleyn would have loved but that terrified Anne of Cleves. In masks, the king and his gentlemen of the Chamber crashed into her bedroom, pretending to bring a token from the amorous bridegroom. It all went horribly wrong, with ghastly silences, even after Henry revealed who he was. 'I like her not,' was his muttered comment.

## Dealing with the fallout

Henry quickly realised he'd been had and Anne wouldn't make a handsome match (see the sidebar 'Not even a pretty face'). And very quickly the international scene changed so that the Cleves-Julich alliance no longer mattered. But Henry was unable to wriggle out at this late stage, despite putting the wedding off for 48 hours and hoping for a miracle. He married Anne in the private chapel at Greenwich on 6 January 1540. The wedding night was a disaster and Henry gave up trying to have sex with Anne after four nights. So much for a spare to back up the heir!

On the surface, all may have seemed well. But Henry's adviser Thomas Cromwell soon fell, partly as a result of his part in the Cleves fiasco.

---

### Not even a pretty face

In the days before easy communication and photography, royals saw the faces of prospective spouses via Court miniatures. The brilliant and ever-reliable Hans Holbein did an incredible job with Anne's portrait and Henry fell for it. Anne was a bumpkin with none of the sophistication or dazzle of previous wives. She spoke, read and wrote no language other than German and knew nothing of the facts of life. She was tall and gawky with smallpox scars.

On the other hand, she was good at needlework!

---

## Getting another divorce

As archbishop of Canterbury, Thomas Cranmer must have been quite used to marrying and divorcing on Henry's behalf (for more on Cranmer, see Chapter 6). This marriage was annulled on the grounds of non-consummation. London couldn't believe it – most ordinary people believed Henry was a stud.

Anne rolled over for Cranmer's contention (something she clearly hadn't been able to do for Henry!) and accepted the land given to her worth £3,000 a year. Because this was the same amount thrown at Catherine of Aragon, £3,000 was clearly the going rate for ex-queens in Tudor England.

Nothing further happened in the William–Mary projected marriage either and Anne stayed in England, making no attempt to return home, until her death in 1557. She never remarried and sex may well have remained a dark mystery to her until her dying day.

# Lusting After Catherine Howard

Catherine was another mistake, but a very different one from Anne of Cleves. Henry was on the rebound and very taken with the sexpot, who was actually five years younger than his eldest daughter. Catherine was one of the enormous grasping clan of the duke of Norfolk, and she was brought up in a huge family home at Horsham in Sussex by her step-grandmother. She could read and write but had no academic interests beyond that.

Catherine put herself about, probably under the influence of her older sisters, and had her first affair at 14 with her music teacher Henry Mannox. (Why is it always music teachers? See the earlier section on Anne Boleyn.) When she got bored with Mannox, Catherine popped into bed with Francis Dereham, a gentleman. Their affair lasted two years. After Anne of Cleves, Henry would probably have welcomed an experienced girl, but the fact that she had been to bed with other men would prove fatal for her.

## Falling for a temptress

Catherine joined the royal Household at about the same time that Anne of Cleves arrived. She probably learned quite quickly from Court gossip that things weren't going well for Henry in the bedroom, and the king got interested in Catherine by March or April 1540.

## Canoodling with Catherine

Henry was besotted. He showered Catherine with expensive gifts, jewellery and furs, most of which he'd got from the estate of Thomas Cromwell (Henry probably felt his adviser owed him something after the Cleves fiasco).

Catherine's motto was 'No other will but his', but Henry was 30 years older than she was and this physical fact probably became apparent pretty quickly.

Once Cranmer and the Church had annulled the Cleves marriage, Parliament petitioned the king (which was standard procedure) to find a new wife for the sake of the succession. Henry couldn't keep his hands off Catherine even in public, and they were married at Oatlands Palace in Surrey on 28 July.

By March 1541 Henry became ill (see Chapter 3 for his medical ailments). His leg ulcers became infected and he feared he may die. Far from an ardent lover, Catherine now faced life with a chronic invalid.

## Pushing the limits

There may have been no evidence against Anne Boleyn in terms of adultery, but in the case of Catherine Howard plenty of proof existed:

✔ While Henry was ill she took up with an earlier lover, Thomas Culpepper, a member of the Privy Chamber who believed the king was dying and Catherine was about to become a very rich widow. She wrote him love letters – a huge risk as privacy didn't exist in the Tudor Court. And she canoodled with Culpepper on a royal tour to York.

✔ She appointed Francis Dereham as her personal secretary.

Henry seems to have been completely in the dark about all this, but the Howards had many enemies. Cranmer was told and he felt duty bound to tell the king. Henry couldn't believe it, snarling with fury one moment and bursting into tears the next. But he couldn't ignore his wife's adultery, and Culpepper and Dereham were arrested. Catherine was confined to quarters.

## Reaching the end of the line

Cranmer interrogated Catherine at Hampton Court on 7 November 1541 in the presence of her father. She cracked and confessed everything with much screaming and wailing. A grief-stricken Henry threatened to torture the girl to death.

Culpepper and Dereham were found guilty on 1 December of 'conspiring the bodily harm of the king's consort' (having sex with Catherine). Both men were sentenced to die by the ghastly method of hanging, drawing and quartering at Tyburn. Because of Culpepper's status, Henry commuted the sentence to one of mere decapitation.

Not content with bringing Catherine down, Henry destroyed the entire Howard family and they'd never again find favour at his Court. The ex-queen wasn't tried, perhaps to spare Henry's feelings. The entire country now knew he was a *cuckold* (a man whose wife was unfaithful to him) and his embarrassment must have been acute enough. Catherine was condemned by an Act of Attainder (a parliamentary ploy to avoid a trial) on 8 February 1542 and executed five days later, this time with an axe.

Catherine was only 21 when she died and many in the country felt her punishment was too harsh. Henry hadn't had their marriage annulled but her betrayal shattered him, leaving him feeling old and full of self-pity.

# Slowing Down with Catherine Parr

The king's last marriage was unlike the other five. Henry had grown old not-so-gracefully (see Chapter 3) and Catherine Parr was 30 and had been married twice before.

## Becoming available

The new queen came from Kendal in Westmoreland and her father, Sir Thomas, was a courtier who'd been a companion-in-arms to the young Henry years before. Catherine was 17 when her first husband died and she married John Neville, Lord Latimer of Snape, who was a widower. She became a busy stepmother to his children and ran his estate in Yorkshire.

By 1543 Neville was dead. Now in their London town house, Catherine became friendly with princess Mary, who was four years her junior. The princess taught Catherine Latin, essential to cope with the snobs who hung around Court, and the newly widowed woman attracted two suitors:

- Thomas Seymour, brother of the earl of Hertford
- Henry Tudor, king of England

No contest!

## Growing up: Choosing a sensible wife

We don't know what drew Henry particularly to Catherine Parr. He sent her a present two weeks before her husband's death, so perhaps he admired the quiet way with which she coped with adversity.

It may have been Catherine's first instinct to jump into bed with Thomas Seymour. She was still a young woman, he was a handsome buck and Lord Latimer hadn't been active in the bedroom for years. By June 1543, however, Catherine was seen increasingly around the Court and she told Seymour she was going to marry Henry.

Cranmer and Co breathed sighs of relief when the wedding took place in the private chapel at Hampton Court on 12 July.

## Anything for a quiet life

Henry was well and truly past any sort of sex by now – he may not even have consummated his marriage to Catherine. She was a born manager and made sure that the king kept in touch with his children. Mary was 27 and could look after herself, but Elizabeth was only 10 and Edward was 6. It may be that the tutors Henry arranged for them, John Cheke and Richard Fox, who were quietly Protestant in their views, were Catherine's choice and not Henry's.

Catherine may have secretly converted to Protestantism before 1547 but she had to keep quiet about it. She certainly joined in theological chats that Henry had with various advisers and Stephen Gardiner, the bishop of Winchester who hated Protestants, believed the queen was a heretic. Henry actually drew up a list of accusations against her, perhaps with a view to putting her on trial.

Catherine may have got wind of this list and may even have seen the charges against her when a careless adviser dropped the list in a corridor(!) because she had a queen-to-king meeting with Henry and charmed him so much that he forgot the idea. When the lord chancellor arrived to arrest the queen, Henry sent him packing with a flea in his ear.

## Administering angel

Despite the fact that she was made regent when Henry was fighting in France in 1544, all Catherine seems to have done was to compose a prayer for the soldiers to use before battle. There was to be no sending of bloody shirts for her (check out Catherine of Aragon's actions while Henry was off fighting in Chapter 3).

Catherine's role was that of peacemaker. As Henry's physical problems grew, she nursed him, soothed him, made him laugh when she could. It can't have been easy.

When Henry knew he was dying in January 1547 he sent for Archbishop Cranmer, not his wife. She wasn't there at the end and even had to watch his funeral from behind an iron grid in the chapel.

## Surviving Henry

After Henry's death Catherine was still only 35 and Thomas Seymour wasted no time moving in. He was a councillor by now and a member of the Privy Chamber and still as handsome as ever. He was opposed, though, by his own brother, now lord protector to the new king, Edward VI. The boy king nevertheless gave Seymour his blessing and he carried off Catherine as well as her lands and the princesses Mary and Elizabeth, who'd been living with her.

Sadly, Catherine died in childbirth of puerperal fever in September 1548.

### Six wives frame by frame

In *The Private Life of Henry VIII* Jane Seymour, played by Wendy Barrie, is preparing for her wedding while Merle Oberon's Anne Boleyn is on her way to the block. Merle's headgear and dress were faithfully modelled on the best-known portrait of Anne, but she didn't have the feisty, yet fragile beauty of Genevieve Bujold in *Anne of the Thousand Days*. All the queens were played by fine British actresses in Keith Michel's *Six Wives of Henry VIII*: Annette Crosbie was Catherine of Aragon; Dorothy Tutin was Anne Boleyn; Anne Stallybrass was Jane Seymour; Elvi Hale was Anne of Cleves; Angela Pleasance was Catherine Howard; and Rosalie Crutchley was Catherine Parr. For my money, the most gorgeous queen was Genevieve Bujold and the funniest, in *The Private Life*, was Elsa Lanchester as Anne of Cleves. No film on Henry's wives can fail, if only because of the gorgeous clothes and the soap opera drama that they all lived through with Bluff King Hal. The most recent television series, *The Tudors*, had an ageless Jonathan Rhys Meyers as Henry with the wrong colour hair and not looking a pound over ten stone. The clothes were good, so was the heraldry in the Court scenes and there were lots of candles. If the king was looking down at this production, he'd no doubt have been delighted by it all!

# Chapter 6

# Building a New Church: Henry and Religion

*Y*ou can't understand Henry VIII's reign without talking about religion. The fact that the Catholic Church was a political, money-making and greedy organisation and that all Christian kings had to work with the pope because he was 'God's vicar [number two] on Earth' was bound to cause trouble in a century in which the Reformation was taking place all over Europe.

As we explain in Chapter 5, Henry's reason for breaking with Rome was simple: he wanted to divorce Catherine of Aragon so he could marry Anne Boleyn. At first, Henry saw the break as a personal spat between him and the pope – what's God got to do with it? Well, rather a lot, as it turned out.

The break with Rome didn't affect ordinary people very much at first. Church services went on as before, priests went on as before. Church buildings were brightly painted with scenes from the Bible, and the mass was in Latin. In short, same old, same old. Among educated people, though, deep divisions and real concerns existed.

## Catholic and Protestant: What's the difference?

Today's society in the Christian west is much more secular than in Tudor times, and the differences between Catholic and Protestant don't seem terribly important (although some Catholics and Protestants would no doubt disagree!). To explain the differences would take *a For Dummies* book in itself but, in a nutshell, 16th-century Catholics

✔ Believed in *transubstantiation,* the miracle of the communion bread and wine turning into the flesh and blood of Christ.

✔ Believed that the Pope, who ran the Catholic Church, was appointed by God.

✔ Believed that Heaven and Hell were real places.

✔ Believed that going on pilgrimage and suffering were vital to keep God happy.

✔ Used a Latin Bible.

✔ Held services (the Mass) in Latin.

✔ Believed that priests shouldn't marry.

Protestants in the 16th century

✔ Didn't believe in transubstantiation.

✔ Didn't accept the Pope as their boss.

✔ Believed that Heaven and Hell were real places.

✔ Didn't believe in pilgrimage or self-sacrifice.

✔ Used vernacular Bibles (for example, Bibles written in English in England, French in France, and so on).

✔ Held services in the vernacular.

✔ Were quite happy with married priests.

Bearing all these points in mind can be helpful as you tour through the chapters on religion in this book.

# Looking at Henry's Beliefs

Have a look at a modern British coin. You can see the queen's head (the idea of putting the monarch's face on coins as a regular thing dates from Henry VII, so everybody in the country knew what the king looked like). Along with the date, the coin also has a lot of initials. The initials DG sum up Henry VIII's hotline to Heaven – Deo Gratias (by the grace of God). FD means Fidei Defensor (defender of the faith) and that's a pretty strong hint about Henry's personal beliefs. It was a title given to him in 1521 by Pope Leo X, for burning the books of Martin Luther, the German monk who'd dared to attack the Catholic Church four years earlier and began what came to be known as the Reformation.

Heaven and hell were real places to the Tudors. So was purgatory, a sort of halfway house in which sinners sins were purged (painfully) before they could enter heaven. Hell was terrifying, staffed by legions of devils. And of course it was St Peter (regarded as the first pope) who held the keys to heaven.

## Shifting perspectives

At first, Henry accepted Catholic ideas fully, knowing that not to was heresy and that a heretic would be excommunicated. Henry's book *Assertio Septem Sacramentorum* (Assertion of the Seven Sacraments) was never likely to hit the bestseller lists, but it spelt out his Catholic ideas pretty clearly and the pope liked it.

Henry later came to believe in his own hotline to God and his people expected him, as king, to show the way in religious matters as in everything else.

 Henry never doubted the thinking behind Catholic ideas (except purgatory – he wasn't sure about that), but he did think that monks were a waste of time and he questioned the role of the pope. After all, the man was just another political leader (usually Italian), so Henry thought he shouldn't be seen in any special light.

---

## The seven sacraments

The Church looked after people's spiritual needs by carrying out the seven sacraments:

- Baptism: Dunking babies in holy water to make them members of the Church.

- Confession: Admitting sin to a priest with the idea of repentance and forgiveness.

- Confirmation: Confirming the promises made on your behalf by your godparents at baptism.

- Eucharist: Celebrating the mass in which you take bread and wine that become, by miracle, the flesh and blood of Christ.

- Extreme unction (last rites): Given by priests for the remission of sins and the comfort of the dying.

- Holy orders: Becoming a priest in the Catholic Church.

- Matrimony: The act of marriage.

## Read all about it

The clergy always said that only they could interpret the Bible, especially at a time when few people could read and the book was written in Latin and Greek. But Henry came up with the idea to publish an English Bible so that ordinary people could understand it themselves. The Bible came out in 1536, and after 1538 every church in the land had to have a copy available.

Henry was appalled at how casually people treated the Bible. In his last speech to Parliament in 1545, he said, 'I am very sorry to know how unreverently that most precious jewel, the Word of God [the Bible] is disputed, rhymed, sung and jangled in every ale house.' He tried to recall the Bible so that only gentlemen had access to it, but that didn't work; the Bible was everybody's.

## Getting back on track: The Act of Six Articles

Henry must have realised that in attacking the pope, breaking with Rome (see the following section) and allowing the English Bible, he was beginning to sound a little bit like Martin Luther, whom he hated. So he got Parliament to pass the Act of Six Articles in 1539, which underlined the traditional ideas of the Catholic Church:

- ✔ Chastity: All priests were to remain celibate; no hanky panky.

- ✔ Confession: Good for the soul.

- ✔ Communion: Only bread could be given to laymen; no wine.

- ✔ Private masses: Should be held for the souls of the dead.

As far as the mass went, Henry put it front and centre in the religious scheme of things.

*Transubstantiation* was the Catholic belief that at communion the bread and wine actually turned, by a miracle, into the flesh and blood of Christ. Protestants were already saying the bread and wine were only symbols. Henry tried to reverse their view.

The official title of the act was 'An act for abolishing diversity in opinions'. Big brother? You bet! Especially when Henry tried to include widows as a group forced into chastity on pain of death.

## Rewriting *The Bishops' Book*

*The Bishops' Book* was written in 1537 without Henry's authority and he wasn't happy about it. What it said about the mass in particular seemed to be far too Protestant. The First Commandment made it permissible to pray to Christ, but not God the Father. The list of 'don'ts' in the book included 'divination and palm reading, uncleanly and wanton words, tales, songs, sights, touching, wanton apparel and lascivious decking'.

So he issued his own version in 1543, stressing the importance of Bible reading and deciding that no non-priests could hold services or deliver sermons. Henry made over 100 changes to the bishops' version. On the bit about all men being equal in God's eyes, Henry said this applied to the soul only. Nobody, in 1543, was ready for democracy!

## Putting religion into practice

How did Henry run the Church after breaking with Rome? He saw himself as having *potestas iurisdictionis* (being the organisational head). He never claimed (unlike the pope) to have any priestly role, but he did call the shots as he made clear in the Articles of Visitation drawn up by Thomas Cromwell in the autumn of 1536, which decreed:

- ✔ English priests must now reject the pope. From now on, the pope was just the bishop of Rome.

- ✔ Lots of holy days (saints' days) were to be removed from the calendar.

- ✔ Worship of images was banned.

- ✔ Churches had to provide English as well as Latin Bibles.

## Laying the foundation for the Royal Supremacy

Henry believed his religious views were his own and he was answerable only to God. He listened to conflicting opinions and could argue well, but in the end his word was law.

In fact, English kings had often controlled sections of the Church before:

- ✔ They suggested bishops who the pope usually accepted.

- ✔ Henry II had gone head to head with Thomas Becket (the pope's man) in the 1160s over the issue of criminal priests.

- ✔ In 1393 the Act of Provisors and Praemunire said that no foreign priest could be appointed without the king's consent.

Henry sorted his position in relation to the Church through the sees of Canterbury or York. In Chapter 5 you see how closely he worked with Thomas Cranmer, archbishop of Canterbury, over his later wives. At other times Henry used Parliament to pass new laws (see the Cheat Sheet's notable Tudor laws).

Here's a rundown of how the king asserted his position:

- ✔ 1531: Henry accused all churchmen of having accepted the pope's supremacy in making Thomas Wolsey the pope's legate (ambassador). Essentially, this was the king throwing his weight around.

- ✔ 1532: The Supplication against the Ordinaries was a long list of grievances from Parliament about what was wrong with the Church (the list was actually written by Henry's adviser, Cromwell) and from then on all Church laws were to be shown to Henry for approval.

- ✔ 1533: The Act of Restraint in Appeals meant that nobody could appeal to Rome as a higher authority than the king.

- ✔ 1535: Canonical (Church) law was banned as a study in the universities and all reference to the pope was removed from the *liturgy* (wording of services).

# Breaking with Rome

The papacy wasn't expecting Henry's 'great matter' (his quest for a male heir; see Chapter 3) and his demand for a divorce from Catherine of Aragon.

## Petitioning the pope

As we explain in Chapter 5, Henry was desperate to annul his marriage to his wife, Catherine of Aragon, because she'd been unsuccessful in bearing him a male heir. But Henry's legal team told him that the Pope couldn't set aside God's word, and in any case, Clement VII's was in a difficult position: as we explain in Chapter 4, he was very worried about upsetting Charles V, Catherine's nephew, whose army was camped outside Rome.

So Henry sent his adviser Wolsey to France to try to get himself set up as acting pope (he was a cardinal after all). But this didn't work. So Henry sent two requests to the pope for annulment, which failed (as we explain in Chapter 5, Catherine got Charles on side, which didn't help Henry's case). Wolsey, Stephen Gardiner and Richard Fox all badgered Clement, but it was no go.

## Stepping up the action

On 18 June 1529 a court was held at Blackfriars in London to decide on the legality of the Henry–Catherine marriage. Catherine gave her point of view and then left and refused to return. Henry gave his opinion. The whole thing became bogged down in technicalities and the case was adjourned until October. The court never met again. It was now that a furious Henry sacked Wolsey (see Chapter 4).

Next, Henry decided to canvas opinion and sent out letters to the great European universities as well as to libraries and known experts in Canon Law and the Bible. The replies were published in Latin and English in November 1531.

The king also got a number of his nobles to write to Clement, urging him to get a move on with a solution.

When none of this had any effect, Henry lost his cool and called the pope a 'sinful bastard' (technically, Clement was born out of wedlock) who'd bought his position (technically, right again) and who had no right to adjudicate on Henry's marriage (ah, well, that was the whole point, wasn't it).

## Losing his patience

As we detail in Chapters 4 and 5, Henry now began to move faster.

- ✔ He threatened his clergy with the Praemunire charge (see 'Laying the foundation for the Royal Supremacy').
- ✔ Increasingly, he took the advice of his new legal eagle, Cromwell (see Chapter 4).
- ✔ He made Anne Boleyn pregnant.
- ✔ He married Anne secretly in January 1533.
- ✔ Henry's marriage to Catherine was called null and void by convocation (leading churchmen) in April.

In retaliation Clement threatened excommunication: take Catherine back or face hell's fire for eternity. Both men probably thought the other was bluffing – Henry was obstinate and opinionated; Clement was devious and evasive.

## Divorcing the Catholic Church

Henry never accepted Clement's excommunication – after all, the man was deeply flawed in every respect. What this meant was that the ideas of the new pope, Paul III (the legendary Peter O'Toole played him in *The Tudors*), which began the Catholic fightback in Europe called the Counter-Reformation, didn't affect Henry or England at all.

Pope Paul tried to patch things up with Henry in the summer of 1536 after both Catherine and Anne Boleyn were dead. By this time, however, Henry had declared himself supreme head of the Church and was about to destroy the monasteries (see 'Dissolving the monasteries', later in this chapter). He believed his own propaganda that all this was God's will and already had the scent of money in his nostrils.

# Running a New Church

As supreme head of the Church, Henry acquired new powers.

- ✔ He ran the Church's legal side.
- ✔ He appointed archbishops and bishops.
- ✔ He looked after all property (which was *huge*).
- ✔ He collected all Church taxes (such as Peter's Pence and First Fruits).
- ✔ He decided how services should be run.

## Taking the lead, bit by bit

Working out his new position took time, and Henry did it in stages;

- ✔ 1531: Henry tried to insist that pardons for offences must go through him.
- ✔ 1532: The Church passed its legal side to Henry.
- ✔ 1532: Parliament agreed to Henry getting Church taxes rather than the Pope.

✔ 1533: The Act in Restraint of Appeals severed links with Rome.

✔ 1534: The Supremacy Act said 'the king our sovereign lord, his heirs and successors kings of this realm, shall be taken, accepted and reputed the only Supreme Head in Earth of the Church in England'. Job done!

Anybody who refused to accept Henry's new position was guilty of high treason. Thomas More and John Fisher, look out! (See Chapter 4 on Henry's enemies.)

## Meeting the reformers

In Europe the Reformation, which began with the German monk Martin Luther in 1517, spread like wildfire and threw up other, ever more extremist revolutionaries – men like Melanchthon, Zwingli and Calvin.

Henry's religious beliefs changed only slightly over time, and had more to do with politics than piety. But he had some home grown reformers in England.

### Thomas Cranmer

Cranmer was a fellow (tutor) of Jesus College, Cambridge and a personal friend of Henry's. He was a serious Bible scholar and knew his stuff, but he was sent by Henry on a diplomatic mission to Germany and there he saw Lutheran worship going on for the first time. He even married a German girl while he was there and came back to England rather reluctantly. When he was made archbishop of Canterbury in March 1533 he was pretty off the wall in traditional terms, but he wasn't a Lutheran.

### William Tyndale

Tyndale was an Oxford scholar who was a humanist. He wanted to translate the Bible into English but couldn't find Church support for this in England, so he went to Hamburg, Cologne and finally Antwerp to get his project off the ground. When the book first appeared in England it was destroyed on the orders of the bishops, so Tyndale holds the record as being the first Englishman to have his book burnt in his own country.

The Lutheran propaganda Tyndale wrote from 1528 was music to Henry's ears because it said that the rulers of each state and not the pope should run their own churches and should beware of dodgy churchmen. Henry tried to use Tyndale's propaganda skills via Cromwell and his agent Stephen Vaughn, but Tyndale was arrested by Church authorities in Antwerp and burned alive (the punishment for heresy) in October 1536.

### Robert Barnes

Barnes was a Cambridge-based Austin friar who got into trouble with the university authorities in 1525 for preaching anti-Church sermons. In 1531 he went to Wittenberg in Germany and became a personal friend of Martin Luther.

Henry got Cromwell to persuade Barnes to come back to see whether he could be of use. Barnes acted as go-between in the political machinations involving the Schmalkaldic League (see Chapter 5).

Together with Thomas Garrett and William Jerome, Barnes fell foul of the arch-reactionary Stephen Gardiner, bishop of Winchester, and found himself in the Tower. Because they were all Cromwell's men and Cromwell himself was charged with heresy in 1540, all three were burned at Smithfield, London in July of that year.

There's no doubt that Protestantism was catching on in England, Wales and Scotland in the 1540s and Henry's break with Rome not only made this possible but encouraged it. All the tutors employed by Henry for his younger children – John Cheke, Richard Cox and Roger Ascham – were Protestants.

Bible reading became an important part of everyday life. Eventually, every family owned one and recorded family names in the front. The Bible became the most widely sold book in history and most people in the past learned to read from it. Today's parallel would be the use of home computers, which has revolutionised communication and information over the last 20 years: something that was once available only to the few is now available to everybody.

---

## Translating the Bible

Tyndale hadn't finished his translation when he died, and anyway, technically the man was a heretic. Miles Coverdale did a better version and this was approved by Henry, so sales soared.

In 1537 another English edition appeared, published by Grafton and Whitchurch and translated by John Rogers, who'd known Tyndale back in Antwerp. It was ready for use by Easter 1539 and ran to a second edition a year later. Because Thomas Cranmer added a preface, it became known as the *Great* or *Cranmer's* Bible. This was the edition 'jangled about' in the pubs that Henry tried to make available to gentlemen only (see the section 'Read all about it'). In fact, there weren't enough Bibles to go round – only 5,500 books and just over 8,000 parishes.

# Dissolving the monasteries

If opposition to Henry's supremacy over the Church was to exist, it would probably come from the monasteries, the centre of support for the pope. In the summer and autumn of 1534 royal commissioners toured the country, asking all abbots, abbesses, priors and prioresses (the monasteries' top men and women) to take oaths to the Acts of Supremacy and Succession.

The next year, ominously, the commissioners came back to make an inventory of Church lands, goods and wealth.

The last time a monarch had done such a thing was in 1086–1087, when William the Conqueror wanted to know exactly how much his kingdom was worth. Frightened people thought this was the Day of Judgement as prophesied in the Bible and the book that resulted was called *Domesday*.

What was Cromwell trying to do with this inventory?

- ✔ Looking for excuses to topple the monasteries by finding them rich and corrupt?

- ✔ Listening to disgruntled people's grievances, which were taken as fact?

- ✔ Choosing only certain houses (monasteries) to close down, in cases of genuine corruption?

### Finding reasons to shut down monasteries

In 1536 there seemed to be no attempt to end monastic life for the sake of it. At first, Henry and Cromwell decided to shut down monasteries with less than 12 members and an income of less than £200 a year. All lands went to Henry.

Then the process began to focus on the 'manifest sin, vicious, carnal and abominable living' that was supposed to go on in the monasteries. In the smaller houses, monks and nuns tended to come from a lower class than those in the great monasteries like Fountains and Rievaulx and their likelihood to sin was considered greater. (Figure 6-1 shows the locations of some of the better-known monasteries in England around this time.)

All those in holy orders (which, in this context, means those following a holy calling), male and female, took vows of poverty and chastity. They were supposed to be poor all their lives (Jesus's teaching told them so) and to be, in the case of nuns, 'brides of Christ'. These rules were widely flouted but probably less in the monasteries than elsewhere.

**Figure 6-1:**
Some of
the better-
known
monasteries
in England.

## The Rood of Grace

There were some genuine examples of corruption. At the Cistercian Abbey of Boxley in Kent was a rood (crucifix) in which the head of Jesus nodded, his eyes opened and his lips moved. This was just one example of the way in which the Church conned a gullible public because they charged them for the opportunity to witness this miracle. In February 1538 Cromwell's commissioners discovered that the figure was operated from behind by wires and pulleys worked by a hidden priest. For a more modern version, think *Wizard of Oz*.

Despite the Rood of Grace (see the nearby sidebar), the commissioners could find very little corruption in the smaller monasteries and some of them ended up begging Henry to keep them open. Henry refused, except for a tiny handful with which the king had personal dealings. About 290 were shut and selling off the land brought in £18,000 a year for Henry.

After the small monasteries there were about 185 bigger ones. There, most of the brothers went quietly, often under pressure from a local nobleman or gentleman who was keen to buy up the land. Many abbots and priors were probably bought off to enjoy a happy (and rich) retirement.

Cathedrals were different. Places like Canterbury, Norwich and Durham became secular (non-monastic) churches, run by deans, not priors. Most of the original priests stayed put, although some, pricked by their consciences, may have fled to Catholic Europe.

When the dust settled, over 2,000 monks were unemployed. Some took private work as curates or chantry priests (see Chapters 2 and 8). Now, Henry set up new sees at Chester, Gloucester, Bristol, Oxford and Peterborough.

### *Fighting friars without fire*

Friars were different from monks. They lived in the world and cared for the old and sick. They were generally very popular – think Friar Tuck in the Robin Hood stories – and were also usually poor, known as *mendicants* or beggars.

Even so, Cromwell took them on, backed by parish priests who resented the friars muscling in on their territory. Cromwell chose the ex-Dominican monk Richard Ingworth to sort them out and he and his agents visited 380 friaries in England and Wales, telling the friars their future. Most of the friars couldn't accept the laws Ingworth laid down for them, so they were allowed to go and their were friaries closed.

## Destroying and pillaging

Cromwell's men wreaked large scale destruction as they looked for valuables. They smashed the shrine of Thomas Becket at Canterbury (read Chaucer's *Canterbury Tales* to see how important this had been to medieval men and women). They ransacked St Swithun's tomb at Winchester and threw about the bones of various Saxon kings. They melted down gold and silver, and smashed stained glass. They broke up abbey libraries and destroyed irreplaceable manuscripts. A group of Italians led by Giovanni Portarini were brought in as demolition experts, blowing up churches with gunpowder. Some monasteries had their lead roofs removed, their stones used for local building and were allowed to rot (check out their ruins all over England today).

Both monasteries and friaries had been blown away by the Royal Supremacy and went with hardly a whimper.

### Clearing up the cash: the Court of Augmentation

The large monasteries netted Henry about £117,000 a year and the small ones £135,000 (because there were more of them). In the last year of his reign his additional income was £65,000, apart from the £2 million he made by selling off the monastic lands to the highest bidder. In total, he doubled his income as a result of destroying a way of life.

The cash was handled by a new government department set up by Cromwell – the Court of Augmentation of the King's Revenue. Because Cromwell ran this, he increased his power and patronage, lining his own pockets and choosing his own cash collectors at every level.

The total capital raised was £2,780,000, which all went on buildings like Nonsuch, fortifications like Pendennis and Cowes and on war itself. Expenditure in Henry's own household rose from £25,000 in 1538 to £45,700 in 1545. Henry believed in living life to the full!

By destroying the monasteries, and therefore the last link with the pope, Henry had ended a way of life that had dominated English history for centuries. No wonder his last words were said to be, 'Monks, monks, monks.'

# Part III
# Remembering the Forgotten Tudors: Edward VI and Mary

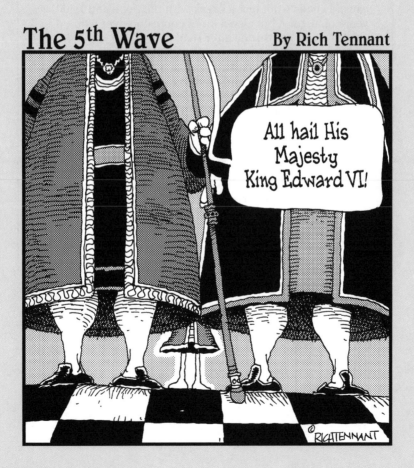

## In this part . . .

Okay, so everybody's heard of Henry VIII and his daughter Elizabeth, but he had two other children and they ruled England too. Father's many marriages caused chaos – not just a break with the pope and 1,400 years of history, but also a lot of confusion over who should sit on the throne after Henry.

Edward should've been king, and he was, but the poor boy was a sickly child and died at 15. He was replaced by his big sister, Mary, and when she died at 42 the last of the Tudors, Elizabeth, got the top job.

But it was hardly happy families. Henry had been a Catholic who'd quarrelled with the pope. Edward was brought up a Protestant (they hated the pope). Mary was a Catholic (but she didn't like the pope either!). So for 11 impossible years, the religion of England was like a yo-yo. And if you were on your way down when everyone else was going up, there was a chance you'd be burned alive at Smithfield in London.

# Chapter 7

# Ruling from the Nursery: Edward VI and His Protectors

• • • • • • • • • • • • • • • • • • • • • • • • • • • • • • • • • • • • • • • • • •

### In This Chapter

▶ Carrying out Henry VIII's will

▶ Protecting the boy king

▶ Sorting the Scots, fighting the French and dealing with English revolts

▶ Changing protectors

• • • • • • • • • • • • • • • • • • • • • • • • • • • • • • • • • • • • • • • • • •

*W*hen Henry VIII died in January 1547, growing unrest in England and Scotland meant the country needed a strong leader. But Henry's successor, his son Edward – born at Hampton Court on 12 October 1537 – was only a boy. So the new king would need a regent in place to act as his protector, particularly in maintaining the Royal Supremacy his father had instigated (see Chapter 6). As we outline in this chapter, the young king's uncle, Edward Seymour, was first in line for the job of lord protector; and hot on his heels was John Dudley, earl of Warwick.

## Setting Up a Protectorate

Princes were allowed to rule by themselves from the age of 18, but Edward was only 9. Queen Catherine (Parr) was sidelined, and the executors of Henry's will, who shared the former king's views on Church and state, worked to quickly establish a protectorate to act for the boy king.

### Crossing over from Henry

Henry's death on 28 January 1547 was kept secret while the executors decided exactly what to do. They decided:

✔ The protectorate's council must choose a leader, and that leader was Edward Seymour – the earl of Hertford and Edward's uncle – who was to be called protector of the realm and governor of the king's person.

✔ The council would be called the Privy Council and would comprise the closest advisers to the king.

Edward, who was living at Hatfield House in Hertfordshire, north of London, agreed with the Council's decisions. On 31 January, Edward Seymour took him into the City of London where he was proclaimed king.

### Burying Henry

The old king was buried at Windsor (a place that Edward came to hate) on 16 February 1547, but anybody who was anybody on the Council was too busy to go (which didn't say much for their loyalty). By tradition, Edward didn't go either and Henry's widow Catherine and daughter Mary watched from the gallery in the Chapel Royal. The chief mourner was the marquis of Dorset, who would later sit on the Council.

## The boy king

Because Edward didn't live to rule his kingdom in his own right we tend to lose sight of him a little in these chapters on his reign. He had large grey eyes and reddish gold hair like his father, and was a precocious child, rather solemn and serious.

Edward was also very intelligent. Although his father had remained a good Catholic until the day he died, Henry had known that the world had to move on, so Edward's tutors, John Cheke and Richard Cox, were reformers. Edward kept a diary that included his religious thoughts from an early age, which shows that his tutors had a big influence on him. He also recorded in his writings that what he liked most about his coronation was the acrobat performing on a rope over St Paul's churchyard.

Edward was very attached, as an infant, to his nurse, Sybil Penn, and when he became king Edward gave her an apartment in Hampton Court next to Will Somers, his father's favourite jester (see Chapter 3). His nurse was one of many staff who kept the child wrapped in cotton wool, because a boy for the Tudors was such a rare commodity. He was kept in virtual quarantine, his rooms were scrubbed twice a day, everything he handled was carefully washed and all dogs were kept out.

Even so, at Christmas 1541, the 4-year-old fell ill with what was probably a tuberculous infection, which would eventually kill him. Had he lived, he might have made a great king.

### Crowning Edward

The coronation took place in Westminster Abbey on 19 February. The service was shortened because the new king was so young (and quite small for his age according to many eyewitnesses). Archbishop Cranmer (see Chapter 6 for more on him) pushed Royal Supremacy ideas in his sermon and, as usual, several new titles were given out:

- ✔ Edward Seymour, the lord protector, became duke of Somerset.
- ✔ Thomas Seymour, already an admiral, became Lord Seymour of Sudeley.
- ✔ John Dudley, Viscount Lisle, became earl of Warwick.
- ✔ William Parr, earl of Essex, became marquis of Northampton.
- ✔ Thomas Wriothesley (pronounced Risley) became earl of Southampton.

## Taking control: The duke of Somerset

Everything should now have been plain sailing, but it soon became clear that Thomas Seymour was more than a bit annoyed at all this power going to his big brother – after all, he was Edward's uncle too. Thomas didn't help family relationships when he renewed his romance with the widow, Queen Dowager Catherine (see Chapter 5 for details of their earlier affair).

Catherine and Thomas had fancied each other for years and now that Henry was dead Thomas could move in on the rich widow. Catherine, however, as ex-queen, needed the Council's permission to marry, and Edward Seymour, duke of Somerset, got difficult. So going over his brother's head, Thomas, the well-known smooth operator, charmed the king (he got on well with kids!) and got his way. Not even Somerset dared oppose the king, especially because the decision had nothing to do with government policy.

In December 1547, for reasons that aren't quite clear, Somerset's job description changed. Rather than being protector until the king reached 18, he now only had the job 'on the king's pleasure'; so if Edward liked, he could fire him. On the other hand, Somerset didn't technically need the Council's backing for his actions while he was in post and he began to operate without the Council, telling the members about decisions afterwards. In other words, Somerset was beginning to forget he wasn't king.

### *Battling brothers*

When Catherine Seymour (previously Parr) died in childbirth in September 1548, Thomas Seymour made his moves on 14-year-old Princess Elizabeth.

By the way, check out *Young Bess.* Seymour may have been as handsome as Stewart Grainger, but I'm afraid the real Elizabeth couldn't hold a candle to Jean Simmons in the title role.

Thomas Seymour wanted to marry Elizabeth – after all, when the paper work was done, she'd be pretty rich with her own lands – but for that he needed the Council's permission and he knew he wouldn't get it. Seymour was also broke (Catherine's money went with her) so he hit upon a cunning plan. He plotted with Sir William Sharington to steal from the Bristol Mint with an armed gang, but he made so much noise about it that it looked as if he was planning a revolt. So in January 1549 Seymour was charged with treason. At the trial:

- ✔ Seymour refused to answer most questions.

- ✔ Elizabeth was questioned but the Council seemed to be more interested in her sex life (see Chapter 12).

- ✔ Catherine Ashley, Elizabeth's lady-in-waiting, was too terrified to say much at all.

Thomas Seymour was found guilty and executed in March. There were rumblings of discontent. In trying to bind the Council together against the dodgy dealings of his brother, Somerset had driven them further apart.

## *Returning to the Auld Alliance: Scotland and France*

Problems have a habit of hanging over from previous reigns, and France and Scotland were no exception at the start of Edward's reign.

### *Invading Scotland*

Henry had come up with an interesting idea to bring together England and Scotland in 1543: the Treaty of Greenwich said that Mary Queen of Scots, then an infant, would marry Edward VI of England when she was 10. The problem was, the Scottish Parliament rejected the treaty.

In the last hours of his life, Henry had told the future protector Somerset to sort the Scots out, which Somerset always intended to do, given the chance. French-backed Scottish raids on the borders had been going on for some months.

So in April 1547 Somerset got an army together, claiming (untruthfully) that the Scots were squaring up to fight. In July the Scots gave Somerset his excuse for war when the earl of Arran, backed by French warships, bombarded the pro-English castle of St Andrews into submission.

Somerset invaded Scotland in September, crossing the river Tweed with an army of 15,000 men backed by 65 warships and supplies. On the 10th of that month, at the Battle of Pinkie, near Musselburgh, the Scottish *schiltrons* (infantry spear formations) were smashed and Somerset's cavalry drove Arran's larger force from the field.

## Following up with forts

Winning a victory like Pinkie is one thing, but to hold a shaky country you have to keep men on the spot and remind people who's boss. Somerset set up garrisons at Haddington and Broughty Crag, and still more were built by English lords keen to look after their own interests.

The Scottish lords couldn't decide what to do. Most of them looked to France for support, especially to the formidably tough Mary of Guise, mother of Mary Queen of Scots and little Mary's regent in Scotland. Others leaned towards England and the Mary–Edward marriage proposed under the Treaty of Greenwich.

For the next few months a stand-off existed. The Scots had neither the men nor the equipment to attack the English forts directly, but they could make a nuisance of themselves by cutting off supplies and carrying out what today we call guerrilla warfare.

The English navy was vital. Operating from their base at Holy Island, supply ships brought essentials to the garrisons and warships patrolled the North Sea to watch out for French reinforcements.

## Allying against England

In theory, England and France were at peace because in the Treaty of Camp of 1546 Henry VIII had agreed not to fight the French unless provoked. But when Francis I died in April 1547, his son Henri II made no bones about the fact that he'd tear up the Treaty of Camp, help Scotland and smash the English garrison at Boulogne at the earliest opportunity.

Between 1546 and 1548 French *privateers* (pirates unofficially employed by the government) operated in the English Channel. The piracy didn't actually add up to outright war because if the English complained, the French would just deny all knowledge and mutter something about the state of the world today! (See Chapter 12 for more on privateers under Elizabeth I.)

Then, on 12 June 1548, a French fleet with 140 assorted ships was sighted off Dunbar. The commander of the English patrol, Vice Admiral Lord Clinton, either missed the fleet completely or thought it best not to tackle a superior force, and so 6,000 French troops landed at Leith near Edinburgh. Their attempt to hit the garrison at Broughty Crag failed, but this was potentially only the beginning.

So the Scots Government made a deal with French commander, Andre de Montalambert, whereby the 6-year-old Mary Queen of Scots would go to France to be educated and would marry the *dauphin* (heir to the French throne) Francis, son of Henri II. The score was France and Scotland, one; England, nil. The Treaty of Greenwich was dead in the water and Somerset's Scottish policy was in ruins.

Early in September, little Mary was smuggled out of Scotland to begin her new French life. Chapters 14 and 15 explain what became of Mary.

## *Pressing on in the north*

Even though there wasn't much point in carrying on in Scotland, Protector Somerset was too pig-headed to back down, or he felt he was too committed. He sent a two-pronged attack over the border.

- The earl of Shrewsbury lead 10,000 men to rescue the garrison under siege at Haddington.
- Admiral Clinton sailed into the Firth of Forth near Edinburgh to destroy the French fleet.

Shrewsbury forced Montalambert to retreat without a fight, but the fleet had long gone. In a silly cat and mouse game, after Shrewsbury's army had left Scotland the French attacked Haddington once more, only to find the garrison stronger and with plenty of supplies.

## *Upping the tempo with France*

For all his loud noises, Henri II wasn't keen on mixing with England outside Scotland. In what was still a cold war the English built up the fortifications at Boulogne, which Henri said was against the spirit of the Treaty of Camp. Both local commanders squared up to each other and fired a few shots – all pretty much handbag stuff, really.

In Chapter 3 we look at how, in the days of Henry VIII, England played France off against the holy Roman empire. That was still an option for Somerset.

The problem at first was that the emperor, Charles V, didn't rate Somerset's government or Edward's kingship. He was, after all, the cousin of Mary Tudor, Edward's big sister, and he thought that Mary, as the only legitimate child of Henry VIII, should have been queen.

When it was obvious that Mary wasn't making a fuss, Charles, always practical, set his feelings aside and did business with Somerset and his Council. He agreed to back England if Calais was attacked, but, cunning old ruler that he was, he didn't include Boulogne.

When Somerset got into difficulties with rebellion at home in 1549 (see the later section 'Facing the Many-headed Monster: Social Unrest') Henri II took advantage of the situation and declared war. But it all went pearshaped. Henri's attack on Jersey in the English-held Channel Islands was beaten back and he couldn't crack Boulogne either. His army was hit by plague and desertion.

The overthrowing of the protector in October 1549 (see 'Ousting Somerset') led to another change of direction. His replacement John Dudley, earl of Warwick, decided to cut his losses and in March 1550 he sold Boulogne back to Henri (which, as you see in Chapter 3, was the original deal).

---

## Commanding the seas

The English navy really took off under Henry VIII, reaching its high water mark under Elizabeth (see Chapter 15). In the 1540s naval battles were rare and ships were really just wooden platforms from which men fought hand to hand as if they were on land. English gunnery, however, was quickly improving and becoming feared. As long as the English fleet could supply places like Boulogne, the French could do little about it.

# Facing the Many-headed Monster: Social Unrest

In the past, what ordinary people were most afraid of was change. The speed of life was much slower in the 16th century, but the arrival of the Reformation, the huge upheavals in the Church and economic changes on the land built up to confuse and worry people. Somerset handled people's reactions to the changes badly.

## Reacting to enclosure

*Enclosure* meant enclosing land common with hedges or fences so that people could raise sheep to provide the raw material for England's all-important medieval wool trade (see the nearby sidebar 'Making enclosure happen' for more). The practice had been going on in parts of central and eastern England for years.

How did the system work?

- **Agreement of the tenants:** Everybody in an area with deeds to their land agreed via the Manor Court (see Chapter 1) to take out new leases on the enclosed land. This was almost always for pasture purposes and led to arguments among the tenants.

- **Unity of possession:** Where no Manor Court existed, the landlord could do what he liked.

The general trend was for the local lord to buy up the old arable (crop-growing) strips because he had the money to do it. Lords often overrode Manor Court decisions and the wishes of their tenants – and all this was happening at a time when the population was increasing and the demand for food was greater than ever.

How did people react?

- Poems and pamphlets appeared, talking about sheep 'eating up men' – if you mess about with a system that's been operating for 800 years, you must expect some complaints; if it ain't broke, don't fix it. William Forrest wrote, 'The world is changed from what it has been, not for the better but for the worse.' He must be about the only writer who thought that inflation was a good theme for poetry!

- Protestant preachers like Hugh Latimer backed the cause of the poor and talked about a return to the good old days of social responsibility. In March 1548 he even gave a sermon in Edward VI's private garden in the Palace of Westminster.

- Writers like Robert Crowley hammered the gentry for their enclosing ways.

Most people, as always, did nothing. But Somerset overreacted to the situation and made it worse.

## Failing to defuse the situation

The role of the king had always been to protect his people – it was part of the coronation vows. Somerset saw an opportunity to make people realise that the new religion of Protestantism was just as caring as the old. On 1 June 1548 the protector launched an inquiry into enclosures.

You know what usually happens with government inquiries? Precisely: nothing. Somerset decided that the law was fine; it just needed to be enforced properly – 'The realm must be defended with force of men . . . not flocks of sheep.'

An old saying in ancient Rome was, *Quis custodes ipsos custodebat?* (Who guards the guards?), and it was a bit like that with Somerset's inquiry. The teams looking into enclosure were the justices of the peace, the very men who wanted enclosure and who were lining their own pockets. Result? Riots.

Minor trouble broke out in the summer of 1548 with poor men roaming the streets, having lost their land and being forced to beg. By April 1549 reports of discontent reached the Privy Council and in May Somerset's Government promised to enforce the law fairly and to punish those who carried out enclosure illegally.

Nothing happened, so the riots increased. Somerset issued a general pardon to the rioters in June, but still the riots continued. Somerset didn't know what to do. Were the riots for him or against him?

There were no public opinion polls in the 16th century and no newspapers to back or oppose government policy.

Eventually, Somerset brought in martial law. The earl of Arundel did well and talked down the rebels in Sussex, but in Oxfordshire and elsewhere, rioting got out of hand. The worst affected areas were Devon and East Anglia.

## Kicking off with Kett

Most of the trouble in Devon was tied up with Edward VI's new prayer book (flip to Chapter 8 for details), but the East Anglian rising, known as Kett's Rebellion, was all about enclosure. Figure 7-1 shows the main places involved in the Rebellion.

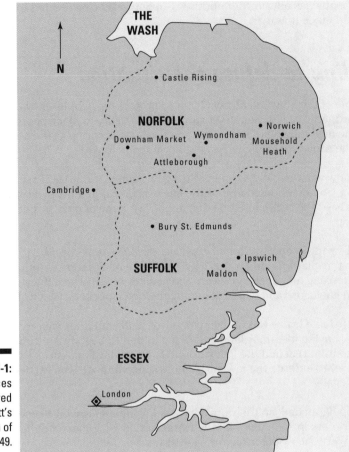

**Figure 7-1:**
Places
involved
in Kett's
Rebellion of
1549.

## Tearing the fences down

On 20 June 1549 a group of men tore down the new fences and hedges at Attleborough near Norwich and then hit nearby Wymondham. Their leader was a small-time landowner and tanner, Robert Kett, who targeted the lands of unpopular landlord Edward Flowerdew. Mobs developed all over East Anglia, as far north as Castle Rising and as far south as Ipswich.

By 12 July Kett, camped on Mousehold Heath outside Norwich, had a following of 16,000 and he demanded entry to the city. No one had any experience of handling a rising of this size and the mayor and corporation (the leading citizens of the town) didn't know what to do.

Kett presented a list of 27 demands to Somerset's Council. They covered complaints about:

- ✔ The high and rising cost of rent
- ✔ The sharp rise in inflation
- ✔ The number of sheep being raised

The demands scarcely mentioned actual enclosure.

The Council ordered Kett's mob to break up. They offered a pardon for any crimes committed up to this point but refused any other concessions. Kett and Co. stayed put.

Somerset now got heavy and sent William Parr, the marquis of Northampton, to sort Kett out. Parr had 1,800 men, mostly gentlemen and Italian mercenaries, and they marched into Norwich unopposed. The next night, however, Kett's men attacked and the totally inexperienced Parr was forced back to London with his tail between his legs.

Kett was now stymied. If he tried to march on London, his men would desert; he knew they'd never leave Norfolk in what they saw as a local fight.

### Saving the day with Dudley

Somerset couldn't afford any more mistakes, so he abandoned his Scottish plans and ordered John Dudley, earl of Warwick, south with 6,000 infantry and 1,500 cavalry. Dudley was a talented and experienced soldier. He surrounded Kett and cut off his supply lines to Norwich, sending a flag of truce to open negotiations. Kett was all for doing a deal but his more fervent followers overruled him and took Dudley on. The fight became a massacre, with Kett's followers dead all over Mousehold Heath.

Dudley hanged nearly 50 people from the town walls, but there were no more reprisals and he took his army to London, sensing he might need them again in the near future.

## In the army now

The official British Army wasn't set up until 1660 when Charles II became king. (The word 'Britain' – meaning England, Wales, Ireland, and Scotland – wasn't officially used until 1603, but there are unofficial uses of the word in Elizabeth's reign.) The Tudors used an old system called Summons of Array when they needed troops – the last workings of the now outdated medieval feudal system. Noblemen weren't allowed private armies any more, so a serious soldier shortage existed. Often Italian, German and Irish mercenaries had to be called in to make up the numbers.

# Ousting Somerset: Dudley Takes the Helm

By the autumn of 1549 the flare-ups of discontent across England were under control, but a lot of people, including members of the Council, believed that Somerset had acted too slowly and it was time for a regime change. And John Dudley, earl of Warwick, decided he was just the man for the job.

We don't know what made Dudley turn on Somerset. He may have planned a coup all along, to make himself the new protector to the young king. On the other hand, he may genuinely have believed that Somerset had blown it and that he had to go for the good of the country.

Tensions grew:

- There were rumours of a plot to make Princess Mary the regent – Dudley wasn't part of this (and neither was Princess Mary).

- Dudley appeared to join forces with religious conservatives in the Council, men like the earls of Arundel and Southampton.

- Some noblemen began to stay away from Court and collect as many armed men as they could.

## Somerset versus Dudley

Somerset, sensing unrest, ordered all loyal subjects to come, armed, to Hampton Court to protect the king from 'a most dangerous conspiracy'.

This was a fatal mistake: Somerset seemed to be calling on people to turn on their natural leaders.

Dudley and the *London Lords* (Dudley's supporters in the Council) conspired together while Somerset whisked the king to Windsor, west of London. He couldn't defend Hampton Court, which was a country house (see Chapter 19 for more on this palace), but Windsor was a medieval fortress with enormously thick walls and towers. A stand-off ensued – the London Lords virtually had the country in their power; Somerset had young Edward.

On the face of it, it looked as though the deal struck by 9 October was the work of Sir Philip Hoby, sent as a go-between to work things out between the two sides. Actually, it was probably Lord Paget, working for Somerset, and Thomas Cranmer, working for the Council who came to an understanding.

Edward was brought back to London, with a cold and a bad case of the jitters. He'd lost all faith in Somerset.

On 14 October the lord protector was sent, together with members of his family, to the Tower, where he faced 29 charges. As was usual, his supporters fell with him. Best known of Somerset's supporters were his private secretary, William Cecil (although he would bounce back – see Chapters 12 to 18) and his brother-in-law, Michael Stanhope, chief gentleman of the Privy Chamber.

## Changing the Chamber

As often happens after a palace coup, it was all change at the top:

- ✔ The Privy Council appointed six noblemen and four *principal gentlemen* (knights or squires) to be the Privy Chamber, and four of the ten had to be with the king at all times.

- ✔ The title of *protector* was quietly dropped. Because she was the king's older sister – and potentially heir to the throne if Edward should die – Mary may have been approached. If she was, she refused to get involved.

- ✔ It might have looked as though the conservative earl of Southampton was in charge, but in fact it was Dudley who was pulling the strings. Indeed, you can judge his power by the fact that at the end of November the Council met in his private rooms because he had a cold.

- ✔ New men were brought in to the Council – Nicholas Wotton, Richard Southwell, and Edmund Peckham; and Henry Grey, the marquis of Dorset and Thomas Goodrich, the Protestant bishop of Ely, who were personal buddies of Dudley.

Some people, like the holy Roman emperor's ambassador in London, expected the old faith (Catholicism) to return and couldn't understand why the pro-Protestant Cranmer was still on the Council. But it was becoming clear that Dudley wasn't really with the religious conservatives.

### Falling out, round one

By the end of November, it was obvious that everything wasn't rosy in the Council. Two groups had developed:

- ✔ Dudley, backed by Lord Paget.
- ✔ Arundel and Southampton, the religious conservatives.

The group's differences were most obvious in what to do with Somerset. Dudley wanted to let him go after a while, probably with a whacking fine. Arundel and Southampton wanted Somerset's head, and maybe Dudley's too. As Arundel put it, 'Ever we should find them traitors both and both is worthy to die.'

Some kind of plot was going on against Dudley by early December, but we don't know what because the evidence for it was 'remembered' afterwards. A lot of history is like this because history gets written by the winners. In this case, after Dudley was dead, people who were still alive could make up what they liked. Rumour and innuendo became fact and evidence.

It was the plotters' mistake, however, to make their feelings known to William Paulet, Lord St John (pronounced *Sinjun*), because he promptly went to Dudley and blabbed. Dudley set a trap to bring the plotters out into the open. He called a Council meeting at his Holborn (London) home and put Somerset's fate on the agenda. Southampton said the man should die for treason.

### Falling out, round two

On 31 December Somerset signed 31 articles of submission, a sort of confession, and now events moved quickly.

Dudley stamped out opposition in the Council:

- ✔ He kicked Richard Southwell out after dodgy rumours of 'bills of sedition written by his hand' (in other words, he had unwisely written down criticisms of Dudley). No charges were ever brought.

- ✔ Lord Paget stayed, but he and Dudley and Paget seem to have fallen out because Paget never got the lord chamberlain position he'd been hoping for.

- ✔ He removed Arundel and Southampton and had them placed under house arrest.

- ✔ He promoted the loyal St John and John Russell to earldoms.

John Dudley, earl of Warwick, now ran the country in the king's name.

# Dictating with Dudley

On 20 February 1550 Dudley became lord president of the Council and lord great master of the Household. For the rest of Edward's short life (see Chapters 8 and 9) Dudley called the shots.

Dudley sorted out trouble in the countryside by extending the laws of treason and giving more powers to local landlords and magistrates. From now on, as far as the ordinary people were concerned, it was 'them verus us'. Kett and his fellow anti-enclosure leaders were hanged.

The new ruler gave the key job of lord treasurer to the earl of Wiltshire (St John), who was one of his cronies but also an experienced figures man. He set up the reliable Protestant Thomas, Lord Wentworth, as chamberlain. As a result of this game of musical chairs, Dudley was now surrounded by men he could trust – Paulet, Wentworth, Anthony Wingfield (who became controller of the household) and Thomas Darcy (who was vice-chamberlain).

Somerset got off lightly. He was released in January 1550 and paid a £10,000 fine. He was to go nowhere near the king or Court, but he was allowed back into the Council and his daughter Anne married Dudley's eldest son. The Somerset–Dudley relationship wasn't as peachy as it seemed, however – flick to Chapter 9 to find out what happened next.

When Somerset was released, so were his people. This brought back into government circles William Cecil, who would go on to become the greatest statesman under Edward VI's sister, Elizabeth (see Chapters 12–18).

# Chapter 8

# Encouraging Protestantism

*W*hen Henry VIII died a lot of confusion over religious matters existed. The break with Rome was political and among the king's advisers were moderate, humanist reformers, some of whom were secret Protestants. Between 1547 and 1553 they 'came out' and made the Church of England Protestant.

The religious situation that the new king, Edward VI, faced looked like this:

✔ Diehard Catholics carried on worship in the old way with Latin masses and traditional types of service.

✔ Conservatives – like Arundel and Southampton, who were on the Council until Dudley axed them – despised the pope but still believed in traditional types of worship like the mass. The vast majority of people were probably conservatives.

✔ Moderate Protestants thought (like the humanists) that a lot of the Catholic services were mumbo-jumbo.

✔ Strong Protestants followed the ideas of Luther and other European reformers who believed the Catholic Church was full of idolatry and the pope was the Antichrist.

See what we mean by confusing? In this chapter we explore the bumpy ride towards Protestanism during Edward's reign.

# Choosing Reform: Gently Does It

Understanding people's motivation as far as religion goes in the 16th century is tough nowadays. People today live in a very different age when organised religion no longer has the huge hold it had in the past. Telling real religious conviction from people grabbing opportunities and paying lip service is also quite difficult, but here's a general overview:

- ✔ The reformers in Henry VIII's Council were largely a political party and they fought the conservatives tooth and nail in the last years of his reign.

- ✔ Some key people, especially Henry VIII's wife Catherine Parr (see Chapter 5) and Archbishop Cranmer (see Chapter 6), were genuine religious reformers.

- ✔ Most people in the corridors of power and elsewhere did their political sums and waited to see which way the religious wind blew before taking sides.

It may be that some people were influenced by the young king's education. After all, when he turned 18 in 1555, Edward would rule in his own right and call the religious tune.

## Sewing the seeds

Because Edward was taught by reformers – men like John Cheke – it was likely that the boy would choose a Protestant Church when he came of age. This is what Edward's protector Somerset (see Chapter 7 for more on the king's protectorate) assumed, pushing ideas of the Royal Supremacy (see Chapter 6) to remind everyone who now ran the Church.

As soon as Henry was dead, something of a floodgate opened. Reformers in London began writing Protestant pamphlets, smashing saints' statues and sticking their own heads above the religious parapet, demanding changes in all directions. Somerset's government did little to stop all this because he became convinced that Protestantism was the way forward.

As we explain in the Chapter 7, what most people in the past found difficult to accept was change. London has always been at the cutting edge of new stuff, but the farther away you went in the 16th century, the more likely you were to meet deep conservatism and mistrust of new-fangled ideas. In the West Country, Wales and parts of the North like Lancashire, people longed for the old security of the Catholic Church and had serious doubts about the Royal Supremacy.

## Testing the water with new bishops

Traditionally, when a king died royal officials' jobs ended. In practice this was rarely the case and it never affected churchmen. But when Henry VIII died, Cranmer sent out new letters of appointment to the bishops. The message was clear: Cranmer and the quietly Protestant Council were giving out the jobs.

Opposition came straight away from Stephen Gardiner, bishop of Winchester, (surprise, surprise!) because the man hated Protestants. He argued that it was the job of the supreme head of the Church to defend not undermine it, and that he held his own job by virtue of being a priest, not because the king had given it to him (although, in fact, Henry had).

In the meantime, moves towards Protestantism were happening all over the place. People sang evening prayer in English, not Latin, in the Chapel Royal; a preacher at Paul's Cross (the trendy place for far-out sermons outside the cathedral in London) said it was okay to eat meat during Lent; and smashing of statues continued.

## Moving on: Visitations and homilies

In the summer of 1547 Cranmer took two cautious steps towards reform:

- ✔ **The royal visitation:** Cranmer backed Protector Somerset in carrying out a royal visitation like the one that had destroyed the monasteries in 1538 (see Chapter 6). Objections came from Bishop Gardiner (of course) and Edmund Bonner (bishop of London), both of whom were banged up in Fleet Prison. Under the visitation, the country was divided into six areas and 30 visitors were given the job of checking out churches. They insisted that churchmen should teach and speak the Lord's Prayer in English.

- ✔ **The homilies:** Cranmer wrote 12 *homilies* (sermons) that he expected churches to use in services. The homilies were Protestant in tone but within the law of Henry VIII's Act of Six Articles (see Chapter 6), except for the one about justification through faith, which sounded horribly Lutheran in that it talked about finding salvation through faith alone and said nothing about doing good works.

Gardiner, true to form, went ballistic, claiming that Cranmer had gone too far, proving how out of touch the bishop of Winchester was with the direction in which the Church was now travelling.

Edward VI's first Parliament abolished the Act of Six Articles. Now the Church of England was in a sort of limbo – who knew exactly what to believe? In that sense, Gardiner's opinion was as good as anybody else's.

## Dissolving the chantries by law

The *chantries* were private chapels set up to pray for the souls of the dead. Some of these were cheapskate affairs, where a single priest (like John Rous at Guy's Cliffe; see Chapter 2) said mass once a month for a year or two to whole colleges of clergymen saying prayers forever. *Forever* literally meant *in perpetuity*, with younger monks taking over from older ones when they died. This process was designed to help those souls believed to be in purgatory, but for years people (Henry VIII included) had been questioning the existence of purgatory.

Parliament had voted in 1545 to shut the chantries down and give the cash to the king. This hadn't happened. So in 1547 the topic was on the front burner again. This time Parliament argued that prayers for the dead were pointless and clashed with the justification by faith ideas of the Protestants. *Justification by faith* (or *solo fide* in the original Latin) meant that all you had to do was put all your faith in God, and he would do the rest.

Result? All chantries closed, another nail in the Catholic coffin; oh, and Edward VI got land worth £600,000.

The removal of the chantries hit ordinary people in a way the destruction of the monasteries hadn't. Some of Somerset's commissioners got frosty receptions, but as usual even opponents cashed in by buying ex-Church land so they didn't feel too badly about it.

## Trying to make things clear

Without the Six Articles as a framework, extreme conservatives and extreme reformers were all trying to make headway according to their own beliefs. So the Council stepped in and said:

- ✔ Extreme Protestants must slow down.
- ✔ Everybody had to fast during Lent.
- ✔ Nobody should go it alone with new religious ideas.
- ✔ The Council knows best and is sorting it all out.

The communion service was changed by Parliament, working with Cranmer, ready for Easter 1548, and Cranmer also set up an English version of the mass – it was up to individual priests whether they used it or not.

On 11 February the Council told Cranmer to tell the bishops to scrap all saints' images from churches and chapels. Henry had made a similar effort (see the Rood of Grace in Chapter 6), but now the directive was for real. Conservatives like bishops Tunstall of Durham and Heath of Worcester did little more than pass Cranmer's word on. But by the end of 1548 the writing was on the wall. The mass was still there (just about) but more change was to come.

# Introducing the First Prayer Book

For centuries the Catholic Church had used slightly different types of Latin service depending on where you lived around the country. Archbishop Cranmer streamlined the service to a single common version in English.

## Changing content and language

In 1544 Henry VIII had let Cranmer translate the mass into English. Churchmen used the English mass now and again in the Chapel Royal, but never in the country at large.

The whole point of having the Bible and church services in English was so that everyone could understand what was going on. The Catholics didn't object to this for its own sake but they did have a problem:

- ✔ The Catholic Church did as the pope said, but Henry had brought an end to that in England.
- ✔ The Catholic Church relied on Latin as a common European language dating back to the 5th century.

Priests understood Latin (in theory!) so the congregation didn't have to. This sounds very odd today. The magic phrase *hocus pocus* comes from the people's garbled version of the communion service – *hoc est corpus* – 'This is the body [of Christ]'.

The Protestant point of view was:

- ✔ Church services should be *collective* acts of worship in a language everybody understood.
- ✔ The job of the priest was just to lead the congregation.

First, Cranmer took the most common type of mass – the Sarum (Salisbury) Use – and changed it. He shortened the rite for the dying, taking out all mention of purgatory. He also removed anything about *transubstantiation* (the idea that bread and wine taken during communion become the body and blood of Christ) and the priest's role being miraculous. God was 'real' without being physical – that put the reforming cat among the conservative pigeons. Private masses were now out – no congregation; no mass.

Next, Cranmer presented the first draft of his new prayer book – the *Book of Common Prayer* – to a church conference at Chertsey Abbey in September 1548. The attendees tinkered with the new book slightly and then passed it to the bishops for approval in October. By December, the book was part of a parliamentary bill.

The purpose of this Bill of Uniformity was to sort out the Church once and for all in a 'uniform, quiet and Godly order'. All parishes were to have the new prayer book (which they had to buy) by Whitsun (May) and churches faced punishments for not accepting the book.

In the House of Lords only two of the temporal peers voted against it but the spiritual peers (the bishops) were split ten-to-eight in favour.

Passing the Bill of Uniformity was a huge step forward for Parliament, which from now on became *the* place to decide all matters about the Church. The Church of England was accepted by law and so it remains today. The law was a step up in terms of the power of Parliament because the Commons and Lords were no longer just a rubber stamp for the king. This was to have serious repercussions for the Stuarts in the next century.

## Making enemies

Of course, not everyone welcomed Cranmer's reforms and prayer book:

- Some parish priests went on using the Latin mass until their bishops stopped them.
- Some priests ignored the bit in the prayer book about speaking with a 'clear and distinct voice' and mumbled instead. Some of their congregations probably assumed the mass was still hocus pocus.
- The king's sister, Mary, was most unimpressed (see the nearby sidebar 'Mary, Mary, quite contrary').
- Extreme Protestants didn't believe the reforms had gone far enough.

### Rebelling in the West

Most resistance to the prayer book came from farthest away from London. In Cornwall most people didn't even speak English, but had their own version of Gaelic, and they and the men of Devon rebelled. Figure 8-1 provides a general lie of the land.

Trouble first broke out on Whit Monday, 1549, in the village of Sampford Courtenay where the priest was forced to stick to the Latin mass. The area had been badly hit by the destruction of the chantries (see 'Dissolving the chantries by law', earlier in this chapter), and local land issues probably existed (this was the time of Kett's Rebellion in East Anglia; see Chapter 7).

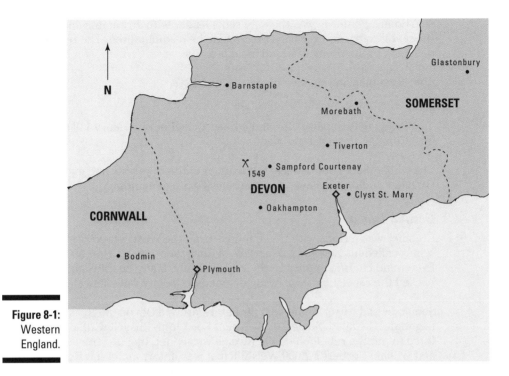

**Figure 8-1:**
Western
England.

When a local gentleman tried to talk sense to everybody a mob murdered
him on 9 June. With no strong nobleman on hand to step in (Henry VIII had
removed the Courtenay earls of Devon), mobs grew and discontent spread
from Bodmin in Cornwall. People talked of a march on London (as with the
Pilgrimage of Grace – see Chapter 6 – and Kett's Rebellion).

# Mary, Mary, quite contrary

One person seriously peeved by Cranmer's
changes was Princess Mary. A devout Catholic,
she invited anybody who wanted to go to
join her in the old Latin mass at her house in
Hunsdon, Hertfordshire at Whitsun 1548. She let
it be known that the new services would never
happen in any area she controlled.

Mary went head to head with the Council, complaining that they had no right to tinker with
religion while the king was a child. As she was

an heir to the throne, her position was acutely
embarrassing for the Council.

As always, Mary got the backing of cousin
Charles V, who said he would take action if
her right to worship was challenged again. The
Council in turn agreed that Mary could get on
with her Latin mass with a few servants only,
but she mustn't hold her mass in public. Mary
ignored them.

Sir Thomas Pomeroy was the only rebel leader with any status and he used the revolt to try and get back the fortune he'd squandered. The rebels sent 15 demands to the Council, which included:

- ✔ Scrapping all religious changes since 1547
- ✔ Reinstating the Six Articles (see Chapter 6)
- ✔ Bringing Reginald Pole, who'd been kicked out by Henry VIII (see Chapter 4), back to England

The whole thing sounded like the work of Catholic priests and even Bishop Gardiner couldn't believe what the rebels were demanding.

### Getting heavy

Cranmer was furious with the response from the West, especially when the rebels called his new form of service 'a Christmas game'. The rebels besieged Exeter and cut off supplies to the city on 2 July. Many people inside the walls backed the rebels and constantly demanded the city open its gates.

Somerset had to act, so he sent Sir Peter Carew, a Devon landowner, to negotiate. He failed. Somerset then sent Lord John Russell with a 1,400-man force to put the rebellion down. Russell was joined by Lord Grey's cavalry and William Herbert's 2,000 Welshmen. It was unfortunate that Russell didn't have enough men or clear instructions as to what to do. He clashed with the rebels at Ferry Bridges near Exeter on 27 July but the result was a draw.

Russell now marched on Exeter itself and the rebels, led by Humphrey Arundell, a Catholic landowner from Helland, near Bodmin, pulled back to the village of Clyst St Mary. After a three-day fight, losses were heavy on both sides. Arundell limped west with neither cavalry nor artillery to help him while Russell entered Exeter.

Russell at last caught the rebels at Sampford Courtenay where the whole protest had begun, and he smashed them with his Italian *harquebusiers* (musketeers). Arundell was beaten at Launceston and the ring-leaders were hanged.

This was a far more serious – and bloody – rising than Kett's and the Council dealt with it harshly.

# Taking in the refugees

As soon as word got round that England was going Protestant, refugees started to trickle in from places where the Catholic Church was all-powerful: France, Spain, Italy, the Low Countries and the Rhineland. Many of the refugees were skilled workers and they set up businesses in London, Norwich and Southampton. A load of Flemish weavers even settled in Glastonbury in Somerset.

These refugees were allowed to worship in their own way in the 'stranger churches' they set up, not bothered by the *Book of Common Prayer*. Vallerand Poullin, a famous scholar, ran the French church in London and the Polish nobleman-turned-pastor John a Lasco ran the Dutch church.

Many of these refugees were Zwinglians, following the Swiss reformer's ideas rather than those of Luther, the German monk who'd begun the Reformation. Most important was Heinrich Bullinger who had friends in high places after Bishop John Hooper, whom Henry VIII had exiled to Zurich, came back to preach to the Court in 1549 under Somerset's protection.

England wasn't open house, however. Not everyone was welcome and nobody wanted the *Anabaptists*, who believed in adult baptism, because the majority saw them as being too extreme and troublemakers.

## Continuing with Cranmer, hoping with Hooper

The fall of Somerset in October 1549 (see Chapter 7) barely broke the reformers' stride. Cranmer brought in yet more changes. Now only three holy orders existed: bishop, priest and deacon. All the others – priors, abbots, prioresses, abbesses, monks, nuns, friars, clerks, chaplains and pardoners – had gone.

---

### Countering the Counter-Reformation

A Church that had called the shots in Christendom for 1,400 years wasn't just going to roll over, and the Council of Trent (Italy), which began in 1545, marked the Catholic Church's fight back against the rise of Protestantism throughout Europe. The Council met frequently in northern Italy and elsewhere over the next few years. Leading Catholic churchmen backed the Society of Jesus and the torture of the Inquisition, denouncing the Protestant ideas wherever they existed throughout Europe.

So, Cranmer called in Protestant heavies to make England's position clear.

✔ Philip Melanchthon, leader of the Lutherans now that Luther was dead, said no when offered a post in England.

✔ Martin Bucer, one of those top scholars consulted by Henry VIII over his divorce from Catherine of Aragon, quarrelled with the Lutherans so accepted Cranmer's offer of a teaching job at Cambridge University.

✔ Peter Martyr took up Cranmer's offer of a similar job at Oxford University, but Oxford was always more right-wing than Cambridge and his fellow lecturers gave him a hard time. Martyr made suggestions for Cranmer's revised prayer book (see 'Getting Radical: The Second Prayer Book').

John Dudley, who'd taken over from Somerset (see Chapter 7), put John Hooper forward as bishop of Gloucester. Hooper came out of nowhere. An Oxford-educated Cistercian from Gloucester, he became a reformer after reading Zwingli, got out of England in 1539, married and settled in Zurich. (The Cistercians were an order of monks founded in 1098. Originally they were strict, but perhaps their involvement in agriculture and wine-making over the centuries made them more worldly!) He came back to England ten years later and became a popular London preacher.

Things were black and white to Hooper: if the Scriptures said to do something, you did it; if the Scriptures said nothing about an act, that act was forbidden.

Hooper refused to wear traditional papist robes for his consecration ceremony. In Chapter 1 we explain how clothes and status were important to the Tudors, so Hooper's protest caused a storm in the Church. Nothing new here, of course – the Catholic Church had nearly burst a blood vessel arguing, centuries earlier, about how monks should have their hair cut! The whole incident was a storm in a stirrup cup (nobody in England knew what tea was at this time!) with Dudley going head to head with the Council. Hooper ended up in prison for being difficult and eventually went through the ceremony in the clothes he hated. Who said the Tudors weren't petty?

After the robes incident, Hooper behaved himself – he worked hard, prayed, heard religious cases and visited schools. He also carried out a visitation and was horrified to find that many of his priests couldn't say the Lord's Prayer or even find it in the *Book of Common Prayer*!

John Foxe paints a pen-portrait of Hooper in his *Book of Martyrs* (1563). The bishop was extremely generous and charitable but so terrifyingly grim that people turned away rather than talk to him.

Hooper was promoted to the see of Worcester in May 1552, but as things turned out his days were numbered.

# Getting Radical: Moving on with the Second Prayer Book

As with all new ideas, the *Book of Common Prayer* went not far enough for some, but too far for others. Protestant extremists felt the book was too conservative and they didn't like the bit about the spiritual presence of God during communion. They had some heavyweight backing– in England, John Hooper, Peter Martyr (see the sidebar, 'Countering the Counter-Reformation'), Martin Bucer, Nicholas Ridley (bishop of London) and John Cheke (Edward VI's tutor); and in Europe by 1551, John Calvin, whose followers out of Geneva were becoming just as numerous as the Lutherans.

Conservative opposition was chopped in all directions. Gardiner and Bonner hadn't only lost their sees, they were in jail (see the earlier section 'Moving on: Visitations and homilies'). Cuthbert Tunstall, bishop of Durham, was framed for treason and was also removed. Anybody not going to church or still carrying out the Catholic mass was to be hit with fines or imprisonment.

Cranmer got on with the revised version of his prayer book. This time he bypassed the bishops and took his book straight to Parliament. The Act for the Uniformity of Common Prayer passed both Houses at the end of March 1552. Dudley, now promoted to be duke of Northumberland, made sure the law went through unopposed.

A French version of the prayer book was produced for the Channel Islands and European exiles in London (how 21st-century politically correct is that!). And this happened at the same time that English people treated all foreigners with suspicion and, in the worst cases, spat at foreigners in the street.

## Picking apart the revised prayer book: Noxious Knox

The *Book of Common Prayer* talked about kneeling to take communion, but some reformers thought sitting (as in the Last Supper) would be better. The abrasive John Knox – a Scotsman who was one of the king's chaplains and who'd later be a fanatical opponent of Mary Queen of Scots and women in general – made a fuss about all this. Knox was backed by Hooper, a Lasco and even Dudley in the Council.

Publication of the book was held up until 'certain faults therein be corrected'. Cranmer was furious. He'd already had his views on the sale of the chantries ignored and Parliament had turned down his ideas for changing Church law in 1552. This was the last straw.

Cranmer realised, a bit late perhaps, that the secular authorities (the Council and Parliament) were sidelining the bishops at every turn. In a way, it was his own fault because he'd missed too many crucial Council meetings (like the one over communion kneeling). Also, he'd been too keen to turn the bishops into better priests, which made them worse politicians, likely to be outmanoeuvred by everybody else.

## Defining faith

*The Augsburg Confession* was a book that explained clearly the beliefs, principles and practices of Lutheranism. Cranmer realised by the autumn of 1549 that the Church of England needed something similar so that everybody would sing from the same hymn sheet. He started working on this at once.

Bishop Hooper had the same idea, but decided to go it alone, coming up with 19 Articles in Gloucester in 1552. This kind of private enterprise would cause chaos because every bishop in England would be dreaming up any number of quite possibly conflicting Articles, so the Council gave Cranmer the go-ahead to come up with a solution. In May 1552 he produced his 42 Articles of the Faith, which became 45 by September.

The Council annoyed Cranmer again by giving the Articles to the royal chaplains – including Knox – to pick over, and the chaplains reduced the number to 42 once more. A bureaucratic delay followed, and Cranmer had to be patient because he knew he couldn't publish the Articles without the Council's say-so. On 9 June 1553 the Articles finally saw the light of day. They were a clear statement that England was now a fully Protestant country, and they included warnings about the extremism of the Anabaptists (see 'Taking in the refugees'), who were fast becoming the bogey-men lurking in the shadows.

## Reforming zeal and dodgy dealings

The real driving force behind the religious changes under Edward came not from Cranmer but from Dudley.

It was pretty obvious that by October 1549, by which time he was 12, the precocious boy king was firmly Protestant and quite keen on the Swiss school of reformers. If Dudley wanted to stay in power by becoming chief minister when Edward came of age in 1555, he needed to show some reforming zeal.

Dudley was also busy lining his pockets. He carried out shady deals selling off chantry lands to his friends and backers, and he 'unlorded' several bishops, which took away their lands and palaces and made money for the crown. Could there be a more devoted servant of his king?

### The Catholic response to the prayer book

The second prayer book didn't actually make much difference to the Catholics. After all, the things they cared about – the mass, prayers for the dead – had already gone with the first version in 1549. If Cranmer's Church was bickering among themselves, that was fine, because their actions were all heresy anyway.

The impression we get about the Reformation is that as soon as the *Book of Common Prayer* came in, Catholics in England went underground, hid priests in special hidey-holes in their houses and were all secretly hoping for an invasion from Spain. Some of this was certainly true, but not until years later under Elizabeth, as you see in Chapters 12 to 18.

---

## Clashing with Hibernia Ecclesia: The Irish Church

The Royal Supremacy (see Chapter 6) had gone down surprisingly well in Ireland because the clergy, who sat as a third house in the Dublin Parliament, saw it was a way to sort out their wayward flocks. But after that, it was downhill all the way:

✔ The Irish Parliament didn't meet at all between 1543 and 1557, so the Edwardian Reformation, including the new prayer books, was foisted on Ireland with no discussion whatsoever.

✔ Because the prayer books and services were now in English, they had no effect on the majority of Gaelic-speaking Irishmen.

✔ When bishops died, it was almost impossible to replace them.

✔ Jesuit missionary priests began to arrive in Ireland from 1541.

✔ The Pope continued to appoint Irish archbishops, like Robert Wauchop in Armagh, in defiance of Henry VIII who'd already given the job to George Dowdall in 1543.

✔ Most Irish men and women stayed loyal to the Pope, carrying out demonstrations from time to time against the Protestant faith, as when Bishop John Bale was forced out of the country in August 1553.

---

Reversions were happening all over the place, which meant that some courtiers made property killings and others got fat annuities. For example:

✔ The sees of Exeter, Coventry and Lichfield were reduced in size and the lands sold off.

✔ The new diocese of Westminster was merged with London.

✔ Parliament broke up the see of Durham in 1552.

The biggest killing came with the richest see of all – Winchester. Bishop Gardiner had clashed with the Council so often they'd fired him and the reformer John Ponet got the job instead. Ponet wasn't interested in money, so Dudley bought the see off him for an annuity of £1333. The lands were actually worth over £3,500 a year, so tens of thousands came into the Council's hands, mostly those of William Paulet, the lord treasurer.

One man who might have stopped all this racketeering was Thomas Cranmer, especially because from 1550 he and the Council were drifting seriously apart. But he'd spent a great deal of time – and his own money – in making Edward's Reformation work and he wasn't going to rock too many boats.

# *Managing Mary*

Henry VIII's eldest daughter had been horrified by religious events since her father's death. She'd refused to get involved in the regency, even when that meant plotting against Somerset, and she'd taken a personal dislike to Dudley, calling him 'the most unstable [religiously unreliable] man in England'.

Mary was concerned for her own privileges and even safety, but she had an ally: her cousin, Charles V, who, as holy Roman emperor, was the most powerful man in Europe.

## Plotting her escape

Van der Delft, Charles V's ambassador in London, was about to be recalled because of ill health, and he and Mary hatched a plot for her to go with him to the safety of the emperor. Mary would be giving up her right to the throne by doing this – leaving the country voluntarily could be taken as a sign that Mary had given up her position as Henry VIII's heir – but Edward wasn't 13 yet and that door seemed to be closed. No one expected that Edward wouldn't grow up to be king and have children of his own, so Mary was unlikely to inherit anyway.

Mary's plan was to be rowed out from Maldon in Essex to van der Delft's waiting ship. Unfortunately, food shortages and high prices had led to local rioting in Essex and government troops were watching the coast, as well as Mary's house at Woodham Walter.

Mary's Plan B (the Tudors were, after all, a pretty cunning lot!) was to steal a ship with van der Delft's secretary, Jehan Dubois. Mary had doubts – she packed and unpacked several times and dithered and delayed until Dubois had to go for fear of being caught in the plot himself (after all, a Dutchman whisking an heir to the English throne abroad raised all kinds of problems, even if it was Mary's idea).

While Mary felt abandoned and was wailing 'What is to become of me?', cousin Charles breathed a sigh of relief. It wasn't worth antagonising England over a woman who couldn't make up her mind.

## Coming to Court

Mary attended Court at Christmas 1550 to find herself under attack from the king himself. She'd always pretended that all this religious nonsense was the work of the evil advisers on the Council. Now she saw that Edward was as heretical as any of them and he seemed to know all about her plans. It must have been humiliating for the 34-year-old princess to be told off by a 13-year-old, king or no king.

Charles continued to support Mary, but Edward wouldn't back down and the emperor knew that Dudley was moving towards a French alliance. Charles couldn't afford to go to war for Mary's sake, so he told his cousin to shut up and give in gracefully – drop the public Catholic worship idea and count herself lucky. Without Charles's support, Mary had no choice.

Edward gave in slightly and the Council backed off. Mary continued with the Latin mass in private, but the public services in her chapel (which she never went to) used the *Book of Common Prayer.*

Many saw Mary as the symbolic head of the old guard. What wasn't clear was whether she was an out-and-out Catholic, like her mother, Catherine of Aragon (see Chapter 5), or whether she believed in the Six Articles as laid down by her father for his Church. Edward's death in July 1553 would throw a spotlight on Mary and perhaps stop the English Reformation in its tracks (see Chapter 9).

# Chapter 9

# Changing with the Times: Edward, John, Jane and Mary

................................................................

## In This Chapter

▶ Charting the rise and fall of John Dudley

▶ Cosying up to France

▶ Whizzing through the shortest reign in English history: Jane Grey

▶ Crowning Mary, and marrying her off

................................................................

*I*n 1552, with the capable Lord President John Dudley, earl of Warwick, in charge, and the young King Edward growing up to be a Protestant, everything seemed to be on an even keel. But in a whirlwind few months Edward died, Jane Grey became queen in a palace coup and then she lost her head to Mary, who put the religious clock back.

## Taking Over: Dudley Rules OK

John Dudley took over as lord president of the Council in February 1550 (see Chapter 7 for details) and on the surface he and his predecessor Somerset got on fine. Somerset's daughter (Anne Seymour) married John Dudley II (Warwick's son), Somerset came back onto the Council and it seemed as though the pair had buried the hatchet. But in fact:

✔ Both Dudley and Somerset were arrogant, impetuous and opinionated and didn't have much idea of co-operation.

✔ Somerset didn't like Dudley's cosying up to France or the way the religious wind was blowing under relative extremists like Hooper and Knox (see Chapter 8).

✔ Somerset thought that Dudley had handled the Western Rebellion (see Chapter 8) and other rural discontent badly. Somerset felt Dudley hadn't tried to sort out genuine grievances but had just backed the landlords.

In the summer of 1550 Council meetings were pretty interesting!

## Getting personal

At the end of June 1550 Dudley fired a warning shot. He had a quiet word in the ear of Richard Whalley, one of Somerset's agents, and said that Somerset must:

- ✔ Stop trying to get Bishop Gardiner out of jail (Chapter 8 explains how the bishop ended up incarcerated) because the Council couldn't stand Gardiner

- ✔ Not imagine the king was on his side, because he wasn't

- ✔ In future work with and through the Council and stop going it alone

Dudley's approach just made things worse.

### Plotting against the ex-protector

Somerset was trying to get some of his ideas pushed through Parliament without the Council's backing. Dudley outmanoeuvred him by not calling Parliament for two years.

Then, in September 1551, the sweating sickness hit the country again, big time (Chapter 1 explains more about this illness), starting in Shrewsbury and spreading. The 16th century being the 16th century, Protestants believed the epidemic was because of delays in religious reforms. Catholics believed the epidemic was because the reforms had gone too far. Either way, God was responsible, visiting his wrath on a misguided people (depending on your religious persuasion). Somerset caught the disease, and while he was out of action Dudley moved against him. He reported a plot to the king.

## The Catholic connection

Rumours flew – when didn't they? – that Somerset was a secret Catholic, in cahoots with Princess Mary and Bishop Gardiner who, as we explain in Chapter 8, weren't in favour of the move to Protestantism. Somerset was also supposed to be in touch with semi-Catholic lords like the earl of Derby. In fact, he just suggested tolerance (a 20th- not a 16th-century idea) and didn't like what Cranmer had done to the prayer book (see Chapter 8). But despite his misgivings, Somerset tried to support the archbishop when the Council ganged up on him. It wasn't a good idea to be too fair or too honest in Tudor England (look what happened to Thomas More in Chapter 4).

Sir Thomas Palmer, a crony of Dudley's and a shady character, swore that Somerset planned to raise a rebellion in the north, murder Dudley and take London. The rather naive Edward swallowed the lie, and on 16 October Somerset and his 'accomplices', Ralph Vane, Michael Stanhope and John Thynne, were arrested. The rumour that reached the emperor's ambassador in Rome was that Somerset and Co. were going to grab the Tower of London and have most of the Council wiped out by hitmen.

Palmer went further, telling all and sundry that Somerset planned to snatch the king himself with 2,000 rebels. People were hauled in to face accusations, both wild and trivial. But all Somerset had actually done was assemble men and not send them away when told to.

From 30 November Somerset stood trial at Westminster. The marquis of Winchester was judge and by Tudor standards the proceedings were pretty fair. The court dropped most of the over-the-top charges and acquitted Somerset on the charge of treason. The London mob went wild with excitement, which annoyed Dudley, who'd had no idea his arch-enemy was so popular.

### Punishing the ex-protector

Despite Somerset's acquittal on the charge of treason, his fans were to be disappointed. Assembling men was a hanging offence (or if you were a noble-man, an axing offence) so Somerset was still in the frame. The mob's attitude gave Dudley pause for thought, however, and he varied the fate of Somerset's cronies. Vane and Stanhope were executed but Paget was just fined and Thynne, along with lords Arundel and Strange, was released.

On 22 January Somerset was beheaded on Tower Hill. Historian John Foxe wrote that he made 'a Godly end' and the troops Dudley had got together on St James's Field meant that the usually rowdy London apprentices (the low-lifes who'd be called *Roundheads* in 1640) behaved themselves.

# Getting promotion: Warwick on the way up

On 20 October 1551 the Council made Dudley general of the marches (the Scottish Borders) and that gave him property and a power base in the North. Dudley had been busy buying and selling land all over the country but his estates, like his men, were scattered. This would now change, and he had himself made Duke of Northumberland (for the sake of clarity, though, we'll go on calling him Dudley). But despite his titles, Dudley never lived in the North, so he had no real support there when things went against him (see 'Defending Jane?', later in this chapter).

By the start of 1552 Dudley was top man but he'd made enemies:

- ✔ Lord Paget, who'd been framed on charges of embezzlement, fined and had the rank of knight of the garter taken away (you just don't do that to people!).

- ✔ The earl of Arundel was mightily miffed about his imprisonment over the Somerset affair.

- ✔ Richard Rich, the lord chancellor, was forced to resign by Dudley in 1551 (don't feel too sorry for him though: Rich was the same double-dealer who'd lied on Cromwell's behalf to topple Thomas More – see Chapter 4).

Dudley was careful not to appear a dictator, always working through the Council. That was no problem for him of course, because he'd appointed the entire Council anyway.

But opposition was growing. The powerful earls of Derby, Shrewsbury, Cumberland and Westmoreland hated Dudley, seeing him as an upstart, and they had lots of cash and large followings. Probably because of this, Dudley decided to speed up Edward VI's education, guessing that the nobility wouldn't cross their king.

---

## Financial woes

Financially, England was in a mess. Henry VIII had started debasing the silver currency to pay for his wars against France (see Chapter 3). He'd had tin added to the silver to make the coins go further. Somerset carried on the process. The result was rocketing prices and a credit crisis abroad. By 1550 the value of English currency on the Antwerp stock exchange was half what it had been in 1545 – the only good news was that English cloth cost less so more buyers existed.

In April 1551 the Council announced another 25 per cent devaluation of silver with effect from August. The result was chaos and the Council had to bring the date forward with the effect that the overseas market froze. Bales of unsold cloth piled up with no buyers and the weavers and spinners were out of work.

Dudley quickly increased the coins' silver content but people just hoarded the good stuff and he couldn't afford to issue more. Luckily, the Government had no expensive wars to fund at the time, and the brilliant financier Thomas Gresham, working in Antwerp on behalf of the Crown, brought the merchants' repayments to the Government under control.

## *Sitting on the diplomatic fence*

Trouble broke out again in September 1551 between those old sparring partners, France (led by King Henri II) and the Roman Empire (headed up by Emperor Charles V. The Roman Empire was made up of many nationalities (see Figure 9-1). This was the age of the nation state – countries like England, France and Scotland were strong because of it. Areas that were part of the Holy Roman Empire, like the Low Countries, would soon demand to be separate nations too. When Maurice, the local ruler of Saxony, signed a secret treaty with the French promising him arms and money, and this got out, the cracks began to appear.

Dudley kept up with the situation through his ambassadors in the Low Countries (Thomas Chamberlain), in France (William Pickering) and in Venice (Peter Vannes), who were well informed by a network of spies. He had nobody in Rome so papal information came through piecemeal via Vannes.

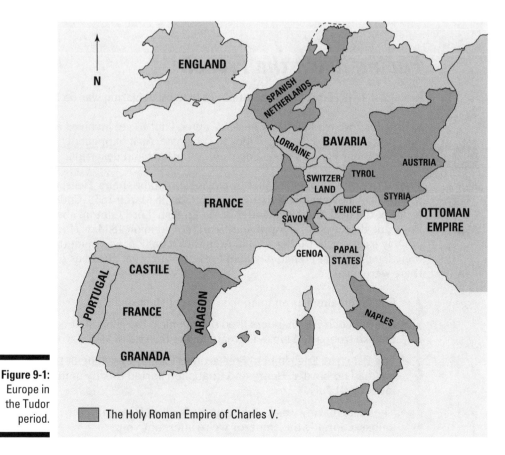

**Figure 9-1:**
Europe in
the Tudor
period.

ENGLAND

N

SPANISH NETHERLANDS

LORRAINE    BAVARIA

AUSTRIA

SWITZER-    TYROL
LAND

FRANCE    STYRIA

SAVOY    VENICE    OTTOMAN
EMPIRE

GENOA    PAPAL
STATES

PORTUGAL    CASTILE

FRANCE    ARAGON

NAPLES

GRANADA

The Holy Roman Empire of Charles V.

The news was that England wasn't in either the Roman Empire nor France's good books at the time:

- ✔ Charles V didn't approve of Dudley or his Government because of their high-handed treatment of his cousin Mary (the king's sister).

- ✔ Sir Richard Morison, the English ambassador at Charles's Court, was deeply unpopular because of his extreme Protestantism (the vast majority of Charles's subjects were, after all, Catholics).

- ✔ Information reached Charles (possibly with the help of the emperor's agents) about the English Government's dislike of the Guise party's involvement in Scotland. Mary of Guise, mother of Mary Queen of Scots, was regent there, and was anxious to cement relations between Scotland and France (see Chapter 7).

- ✔ There were rumours of a renewed French move to take back Calais.

In the face of all this, Dudley kept his power dry. Doing nothing wasn't heroic, but it kept England at peace and saved money.

## *Facing down the French*

In August 1549 Henri II proved rumours true by declaring war on England.

In Chapter 7 we explain that Charles V agreed not to get involved as long as the French confined their activities to Boulogne. As it happened, the French weren't doing very well at Boulogne, hit by plague and desertion.

The French now demanded that Boulogne should be theirs. Henri was happy to do a deal, however, and that was signed on 28 March 1550. Under the terms of the deal, the commander of the English, Lord Clinton, abandoned the Boulogne defences on 25 April and Henri moved in on 18 May. Hostages were politely exchanged, Dudley's man, Admiral Chataillon, was sumptuously entertained and the first French payment for Boulogne went ahead as planned. But there were niggles:

- ✔ Calais remained as an unspoken ghost at the feast.

- ✔ A few French commanders fired their guns in the general direction of the English troops and looked threatening at the end of May. No one was hurt.

- ✔ The Pale (the English-held area around Calais) was difficult to defend and had no border. Henry and Chataillon sorted this by mutual agreement on 21 July.

- ✔ The French army was building up – it's okay, Henri told the English ambassador; it's the emperor we're after, not you.

## Parties and honours – for nothing?

Henri II didn't have a very high opinion of England's army (he clearly didn't have much of a grasp of his own country's history either!), but he rated the English navy and realised that in a punch-up with the emperor the English could be a useful ally. So he opened up negotiations with Dudley over a marriage proposal. Edward VI was 13 in 1551; the French princess Elizabeth de Valois was 6 – perfect. Dudley's man, the marquis of Northampton, went over in person to give Henri England's highest order of chivalry, by making him a knight of the Garter.

Edward in turn was given the Order of St Michel, so it was gongs and glad-handings galore. A 400-strong French gravy train stayed in England, with the young king hunting with its leader Jacques d'Albon and enjoying his lute playing.

None of this worked, however, because Dudley stayed neutral in the war ahead. It would take more than a few supper parties to drag Dudley into somebody else's fight.

# *Priming a Prince*

Edward was 12 when Somerset was kicked out as his protector, and by now the image of the young king was changing. To some he was 'the new Josias' and the 'Godly imp' after the 8-year-old Hebrew king of the Old Testament. Edward listened to sermons, wrote essays and generally seems to have been a bookish goody-two-shoes who was pale, sickly and a bit pathetic. Some of this image, though, is based on hind-sight, because we know he died from tuberculosis. Check out Hans Holbein's portrait painted at this time. Edward hasn't got the bulk of his father, but his face is arrogant and scornful. He's holding his dagger menacingly and even his codpiece is on show!

## Edward and his twin?

*The Prince and the Pauper* is the only film featuring Edward big time. It's based on a novel by American writer Mark Twain and is a classic changing places scenario between the king when he was prince and a beggar. By an extraordinary coincidence (fiction, not fact), the

two look alike to the extent that in various films the pair are usually played by actual twins. In the Errol Flynn 1937 version the boys were Billy and Robert Mauch and in the animated version of 1990 the characters were Mickey Mouse and Prince Mickey!

## Growing up

Edward's activities were geared towards him growing into the role of king:

- Edward took part in archery contests and riding at the ring (practice for the tournament). He was excellent at tennis.

- William Thomas, clerk to the Privy Council, wrote papers on the most up-to-date political theory for the king.

- Dudley encouraged the boy to sit in on Council meetings. Dudley realised that to survive politically he also had to coach the boy himself.

- Edward's *devices* (essays) increased in number and relevance. He loved making lists and his 'reasons for establishing a mart [market]' and 'memorandum for the Council', both written in 1552, still survive (his handwriting was excellent – so was his Latin).

- Edward occasionally intervened on minor points in Government – he was impressed by Nicholas Ridley's sermon on the London poor in the spring of 1552 and worked with the lord mayor of London to turn the royal palace of Bridewell into a poor house.

Anyone wanting to influence Edward long-term would have to take the boy's ideas seriously. He was 15 in 1552 and, like his father, expected to be obeyed. Dudley did this well; the king trusted and liked him (which couldn't be said of many other people!).

## Going before his time

In April 1552 Edward got measles. Like everything else that happened to him, he wrote about his illness in his diary, but he never really got better. At the end of June a tour of the South and West took it out of him, and by Christmas, at Windsor, he was seriously ill. When Mary came to see him in February it was three days before he felt well enough to talk to her.

In March Edward opened Parliament but had to cut the ceremony short. One of his shoulders was now higher than the other and he was coughing blood. His ulcers were probably bed sores and his swollen stomach the result of tuberculous peritonitis. The young king was wracked with fever.

Dudley now had to think fast. In one of his devices, Edward had already considered the succession if he died without an heir. His father, Henry VIII's will (almost certainly prompted by his last wife, Catherine Parr) had included both Mary and Elizabeth if Edward should die before them without producing children, but times and opinions had moved on since then. Edward's own childlike ideas were limited to members of the Brandon family, who were closely connected to the Tudors (see the nearby sidebar 'What was so special about the Brandons?'), because he believed both Mary and Elizabeth were illegitimate (Henry VIII had decided his marriage to their mother, Catherine of Aragon, was illegal; see Chapter 5). At the time the Brandon option didn't make much sense – Frances, the duchess of Suffolk, was menopausal and the three nieces still unmarried teenagers.

The fact that Edward was ignoring his sisters didn't matter while he was just writing essays. As long as he was well his ideas were just cloud-cuckoo land theorising. But suddenly, by the summer of 1553, the situation of the death of an heir-less king was horribly real.

## *Making last-minute changes*

In the first week of June 1553 Jane Grey, the duke of Suffolk's daughter, married Guildford Dudley (John Dudley's son) and the king gave the marriage his blessing. Edward was too ill to go to the ceremony.

There was no time for Jane to produce a son, nor for Parliament to repeal Henry VIII's Succession Act which decreed who should follow him and in what order. The one thing that Edward himself was sure of was that Mary mustn't succeed – she was not only illegitimate, she was Catholic.

For Edward, the only rational choice successor was Jane Grey (now Dudley), and he issued a decree to that effect. When he died without direct heirs, the crown would pass to 'Lady Jane and her heirs male'. The Council were horrified but they couldn't shake Edward. No one was sure whether Edward (still a minor) could make a will that would stand up – and Parliament certainly didn't have the right to choose a new monarch.

In fact, technically, Edward's documents weren't legal because the seals were never actually attached to the *letters patent* (a document granting someone a right or privilege) that he'd drawn up.

---

## What was so special about the Brandons?

In Chapter 2 we tell you the tale of the battle of Bosworth Field. Go back to 22 August 1485 for a minute. King Richard III is thundering towards Henry Tudor, earl of Richmond, at the head of his bodyguard, the Fellowship of the White Boar. One man is standing between Richard and Henry – William Brandon, Henry's standard bearer. Richard hacks at William, and down goes Brandon, down goes the standard.

Luckily, Lord Stanley's men stop Richard before he can reach Henry.

If it weren't for William Brandon, the Tudors would never have ruled England and you wouldn't be reading this book. The Brandon family were made dukes of Suffolk by the Tudors and Henry VIII's sister Mary married one of them. It was from this family that Jane Grey came.

---

Both Mary and Elizabeth had tried to see Edward in the weeks before this decree, but a paranoid Dudley had kept them away. Charles V's ambassador got wind of it all and told the emperor that cousin Mary was being sidelined. Charles sent a special mission, ostensibly to show concern for the king's health but actually to watch out for Mary's interests. Charles's men were told, politely, to butt out.

## Passing on in a terrible storm

On 5 July a summer storm flooded whole areas and brought down trees. The lightning was frightening and the wind terrifying. In the midst of all this, his hair almost all gone, his toes and fingers gangrenous, Edward VI died. He hadn't eaten properly for three weeks.

Dudley had dismissed his doctors, insisting that the king be treated (with unknown medicine) by a 'wise gentlewoman' of his choosing. Are you thinking what we are? Although the cause of Edward's death was almost certainly pulmonary tuberculosis there were those then (as there are now) who wondered whether Dudley hadn't poisoned the boy. After all, Dudley's daughter-in-law was now queen of England.

# Reigning for Nine Days: Jane Grey

You might think that London, at the cutting edge of Protestantism, would have been delighted to have a Protestant queen as opposed to the rabid Mary. But in fact, the proclamation that Jane was queen was greeted with stony silence.

Bishop Ridley backed Jane, believing Edward's will to be valid. Bishop Hooper, however, disagreed and saw Mary as some sort of divine retribution on England for its sins: God was getting his own back.

## Manoeuvring with Mary

Always suspicious of Dudley, Mary got out of Hunsdon and fled to her Kenninghall estates in Norfolk. She proclaimed herself queen and wrote to the Council, demanding their support.

Dudley was gobsmacked. The dithery woman who hadn't fled to cousin Charles earlier now showed no intention of leaving the country, and the ships he'd sent to stop Mary going to France went over to her side; she now had cannon as well as moral support.

The Council turned Mary down and asked her politely to be a loyal subject to Jane. But in reality Mary began to gather ever more support in East Anglia, and not many people knew who Jane Grey was.

## *Defending Jane?*

The Council were actually divided over the rival queens and it didn't help that Simon Renard, Charles V's ambassador, stirred them up with gossip that Jane Grey was just a stalking horse and that the French were behind the whole thing to get Mary Queen of Scots (now 11) on the English throne. This was nonsense, but who could be sure what sort of double game Dudley was playing?

Jane Grey had married Guildford Dudley under protest. She was 15 and headstrong and fancied the earl of Hertford, but as was common for the times, politics were more important. On her wedding day Jane went home to her family rather than sleep with Guildford, and when he finally did get her into bed she went to Chelsea to get over the experience!

On 10 July she and Guildford, all dressed in white, went by river to the Tower where Jane was shown the Crown Jewels. This spooked her because reality dawned, and she absolutely refused to give Guildford the title of crown matrimonial. Duke, maybe; king, never.

Four days later Dudley realised he had to sort Mary out himself. His younger son Robert (whom appears again in Chapter 12, under Elizabeth [literally!]) hadn't managed to capture Mary and her forces were growing. But Dudley's absence left a divided Council. At Baynard's Castle in London (more or less where the Savoy Hotel now stands along the Strand) the earls of Arundel and Pembroke led most of the Council to proclaim Mary as queen. It was now 19 July, the last day of Queen Jane's nine-day reign.

Dudley's army stopped at Cambridge. Here he heard that the earl of Oxford had gone over to Mary and he waited to see what would happen. In London the duke of Suffolk told his daughter that she was no longer queen. They'd been abandoned by almost everybody.

# *Making Up With Mary*

History is all about blowing with the wind. Men who were staunchly anti-Catholic and anti-Mary now said how delighted they were that Mary was queen.

Charles V's ambassador, Simon Renard, thought that civil war would break out, but that didn't happen. He reported to Charles that a miracle had taken place in England. It must have seemed that way to Mary too, but she couldn't show her surprise. Arundel, Paget and other members of the Council went to Framlingham in Norfolk to kneel and kiss her hand.

## Checking out her team

What did the new queen – the second in ten days – do with her Government, which was full of Dudley's men?

- ✔ She put her closest supporters, Catholics Robert Rochester and Francis Englefield, into the Council, but they had no political experience. She appointed the earl of Bath, but he too was a political lightweight.

- ✔ She brought in men who'd crossed Dudley – Arundel, Paget, Rich and Thomas Wharton. She made others wait, but eventually recruited the marquis of Winchester (as lord treasurer) and the earls of Bedford, Pembroke and Shrewsbury.

Mary stayed at Framlingham until 23 July and then came south, reaching Essex by the 31st.

We're not talking huge distances here (today you can drive from Framlingham to Essex in an hour and a half), but queens travelled with everything *and* the kitchen sink, and expected gentlemen to put them up in their country houses on the way. Forced entertainment on this scale could bankrupt people.

## Stepping into power

Mary reached London on 5 August, by which time her supporters had grown to 10,000. Dudley was awaiting execution in the Tower (see the nearby sidebar 'Off with his head!') and it was there that Mary went that day. She didn't visit the ex-protector, nor Jane Grey, held across the Green from Dudley. Events now moved fast.

---

### Off with his head!

Mary's first hit was Dudley. On Tower Green on 22 August 1553 Dudley climbed the wooden scaffold and made a bold speech – 'I have done wickedly all the days of my life and most of all against the queen's highness, of whom I here ask forgiveness.' But Mary didn't buy this last minute contrition and she let him die. The imprisoned Jane Grey watched as Dudley's head rolled.

## What about Mary's sister?

We haven't mentioned Edward's other sister, Elizabeth, yet, have we? We put all that right in Chapters 12–18 of this book. Elizabeth was 19 when Mary became queen and she'd sensibly kept her head down during the crisis that had just passed. She entered London with Mary, and as long as her sister had no children, Elizabeth was the heir to the throne.

Thomas Howard, the aged duke of Norfolk who'd remained Catholic throughout, was released from prison; so was Edward Courtenay, son of the marquis of Exeter, and he was made earl of Devon. Stephen Gardiner was also released, given his old see of Winchester back and made lord chancellor. Cuthbert Tunstall, the ex-bishop of Durham, rejoined the Council having been released.

The Privy Council now had over 40 members and they were a pretty mixed bunch in terms of politics and religion.

What the crisis proved was that Parliament's power would go on. If Jane Grey had been accepted, the will of the monarch would have won the day and everything that Parliament had built up over 20 years would have counted for nothing.

Mary now faced urgent problems:

- ✔ **Her claim to the throne:** Mary was still technically illegitimate, but she could put this right via Parliament. Her coronation was more important, and the Act of Succession would cover her in the meantime. The coronation was fixed for 1 October; Parliament would be called four days later.

- ✔ **Religion:** What was going to happen? Because Mary was a devout Catholic, of course the 'old faith' would come back, but how? Would the Church of England be returned to its status under Henry VIII because all decisions made since then had been made by a child?

Parliament restored Henry VIII's marriage to Mary's mother, Catherine of Aragon (see Chapter 6), which of course made Elizabeth illegitimate, and took away all reforms in religion carried out under Edward.

Priests all over the country didn't wait for Mary to direct religious changes. They began to use the old Latin mass immediately and when Sir James Hales protested to the lord chancellor about this, Gardiner told him to shut up and obey his queen.

From 20 December 1553 Protestant services were illegal. What a miserable Christmas many of Mary's subjects must have had that year! You can read more on Mary's religious changes Chapter 10.

## Marrying Mary

Just like Henry VII when he became king (see Chapter 2), Mary needed a strong (preferably male) heir who'd live long enough to run the country. So marriage and child production were top of Mary's agenda.

Mary had a religious horror of sex (unlike Elizabeth we have no gossipy stories about girlhood flings), but she had to lie back and think of England as a matter of duty: she was 37 and her biological clock was winding down.

But who would hubby be? As an honest person who took her promises seriously, Mary remembered she'd once vowed that her cousin Charles, more of a father figure to her than bullying Henry had ever been, would make that decision for her. Charles had in fact been betrothed to Mary once himself, but he was a 53-year-old widower now and wasn't likely to jump at the idea of having Mary as his wife (have you seen the portraits of Mary?). But he had a cunning plan . . .

Mary's marital options were:

- ✔ **Charles V's son, Philip:** He was 26, a widower, a good Catholic, sexually and politically experienced and he'd one day inherit most of Europe from his father (just think – the old Anglo–Spanish alliance dreamed of by Henry VII – see Chapter 2).

- ✔ **Dom Luis:** The younger brother of the king of Portugal. But Charles didn't like him, so no go.

- ✔ **Edward Courtenay:** The earl of Devon, he had a dash of Yorkist blood and was a good Catholic. But he'd been brought up mostly in prison and couldn't really cope with the decision-making of the outside world.

No contest really – it had to be Philip.

The Mary–Philip courtship was a long distance affair, with Simon Renard as the go-between. Philip wasn't keen – in fact, in the Cate Blanchett film *Elizabeth* he's always lurking in the shadows and he doesn't have any lines to say!

When the engagement was announced on 28 October 1553 the Council and Parliament did their best not to scream in horror; a Spanish Catholic on the throne of England!

### Brokering the deal

The Council did their best but they were dealing with Charles, not Philip, and he had his own agenda. Charles wanted his successor, his younger brother Ferdinand, to become holy Roman emperor (it was an elected position) and

Philip would have the Spanish Netherlands. Philip, of course, knew nothing about this. Charles needed Philip as king of England because although the English would never give him real power, having his son as king would at least mean that the English wouldn't interfere in the emperor's ongoing war with France.

The arrangement sounded great to the English commissioners, who wrote up a treaty that was signed in January 1554. By the time Philip knew what was going on, it was too late to pull out.

### Rebelling with Wyatt

Sir Thomas Wyatt, poet, courtier and lover of Anne Boleyn (Chapter 5 gives the lowdown on Anne's flirtiness), had got off lightly under Henry VIII by being allowed to keep his head. His son wasn't so lucky.

Mary was already (with that nasty word *hindsight*) a tragic, self-deluded figure. Having seen portraits of Philip (like all Hapsburgs he had a huge chin and tiny mouth) she said she was 'half in love with him'. Oh dear!

Courtiers feared that Spaniards would take their places. Landlords were sure they'd lose their property to foreigners. All over London, anti-Spanish broadsheets and ballads appeared and it was only a matter of time before a rebellion happened.

---

## The end of Jane

There are few more tragic victims of the Tudors than Jane Grey. Rumours flew that Wyatt's Rebellion had been carried out in her name (untrue) and that as long as she lived she'd be a threat to Mary (probably untrue). Jane's husband, Guildford Dudley, was executed on Tower Hill on 12 February, and Jane saw his headless corpse in the chapel of St Peter ad Vincula before she was taken to the block on Tower Green. The lieutenant of the Tower, John Brydges, steadied her and she was accompanied by her ladies, Nurse Ellen and Mrs Tilney. Dr Feckenham, the abbot of Westminster, had been sent to convert Jane to Catholicism but that failed and the best he could do was to recite the Lord's Prayer in Latin while she said it in English. Jane made a short speech to the crowd and only panicked a little when the blindfold was put on – because she was unable to find the block – 'What shall I do? Where is it?'

The axe came down and Jane was dead. The 16-year-old was just five feet tall, so small that her body could be placed under two stones in St Peter's chapel. Alongside her lay two more Tudor victims – Anne Boleyn and Catherine Howard.

The men of Kent, the Midlands and Devon (what, again?) planned a three-pronged protest march on London to force Mary to change her mind. As it turned out, only the Kent contingent actually got there: 3,000 men under Thomas Wyatt. The only troops Mary had were the London trained militia and they didn't seem too keen to kill fellow Englishmen for the sake of a Spaniard who'd never set foot in the country. Even so, they refused to open the gates to Wyatt and after a few skirmishes the rebels were broken up and about 100 ringleaders executed, including Wyatt himself, who went to the by-now-much-used block on Tower Green.

Mary was taking no chances. She had Jane Grey put to death (see the nearby sidebar 'The end of Jane', and later that month Jane's father was also executed. Mary had heard the scuttlebutt that Edward Courtenay, the earl of Devon, was out to marry Elizabeth, and because the girl was 17 years Mary's junior, she had a lot more potential child-bearing years ahead of her. So the same day as Jane's execution, Elizabeth was arrested and held in the Tower until the Wyatt disturbances died down.

### Sorting out the pre-nup

The marriage arrangements between Mary and Philip were complicated.

Philip didn't really want to know. He daren't openly oppose his father, Charles V, but he had no intention of being bound by the restrictions to power that Mary and the Council were trying to impose on him. Mary, on the other hand, was very interested in the terms of the union, for they affected not just her but the entire future of the kingdom.

The legal position of women was peculiar:

- ✔ A woman could sue in a court of law and was answerable to the courts.

- ✔ A woman could have titles and her own land, but she couldn't carry out the military bits that went with all that, so she had to find a man to take charge of the military side for her.

- ✔ When a woman married, all her property became her husband's and she couldn't testify against him in court.

- ✔ When a woman died, her husband kept all her property and only when he died would it go to her heirs. (Are you with us so far?)

So technically, if Mary died before Philip (she did, by 40 years!) he'd be king of England in his own right and the title wouldn't pass to any child they may have until Philip died. But if Mary died before Philip, English law said he wouldn't be allowed to keep England! Nobody had ever had to face this technical problem at this high level before, and in the event of Mary's death, Philip would be bound to insist on his legal rights.

The only solution to all this was an act of Parliament. In April 1554 the law was changed, making Mary an honorary man so that Philip couldn't inherit England. So far, so peculiar, but it didn't help Mary cope with what was bound to be a difficult relationship.

Philip crossed the Channel in an appalling storm and reached Southampton on 20 July 1554. Five days later, with bells ringing and bonfires burning into the night, the couple were married in a full Catholic ceremony in the cathedral in Winchester (it must have made Bishop Stephen Gardiner's day). The slight snag was one of communication (see Chapter 10) – Mary understood but spoke no Spanish and Philip didn't speak or understand English. On the wedding night he must have rehearsed the line 'Good night, my lords all' to clear everybody but Mary out of the bedroom.

The new bride now faced the greatest test of her life; restoring the Catholic faith.

# Chapter 10

# Returning to the Old Faith: Mary I

· · · · · · · · · · · · · · · · · · · · · · · · · · · · · · · · · · · · · · · · · · · ·

*In This Chapter*

▶ Reuniting with Rome

▶ Burning the heretics

▶ Planting Englishmen in Ireland

▶ Trying for a successor with Philip of Spain

▶ Getting caught up in Philip's plans

· · · · · · · · · · · · · · · · · · · · · · · · · · · · · · · · · · · · · · · · · · · ·

*W*hen Mary became queen it was party time. In London people held street banquets, built bonfires, rang bells, threw money out of the window and hurled caps in the air. You couldn't hear what anybody was saying for the noise.

Five years later Mary died a monarch so hated that history has called her Bloody Mary. In this chapter, we look at the first years of Mary's reign, and just what she did to become so reviled.

## Reviving the Old Faith

When Mary became queen in 1553, what were her religious options?

✔ She could restore the Church to what it was when Henry VIII left it, basically his Six Articles plus an English Bible and the old mass but no monasteries (see Chapter 6).

✔ She could return completely to the old faith, kow-towing to the pope again and giving land back to the monasteries; incense, carvings of saints, pilgrimages, the whole nine yards of the medieval Catholic Church.

Pope Julius III sent Cardinal Pole to England as his right-hand man, hoping (rightly as it turned out) that he'd advise Mary closely.

The Council were in a cleft stick. No diehard Catholics were left and most of the Council had been Dudley's men, but they did like being in power and were anxious not to get chopped, either metaphorically or for real. So they probably advised Mary to proceed a step at a time and to always use Parliament.

Contrary to popular belief, Mary didn't start out bloody. She should have detested Elizabeth because she was a Protestant and a threat as long as Mary remained childless, but in fact she was very fond of her, treating her sometimes as the daughter she never had. She agonised long and hard over whether to have the ex-queen Jane Grey executed (see Chapter 9), always worked within Parliament and the law and even delayed her own wedding to sort out Christian names for a godchild.

## Making changes

Mary's first step was to bring the mass back to the Chapel Royal and other churches. The mass was popular and many people must have been happy, probably assuming the Government had gone mad over the last few years.

But ardent Protestants were less impressed:

- ✔ Protestants and Catholics clashed at Paul's Cross in London when they heard the Catholic bishop Bonner had been reinstated.
- ✔ When Archbishop Cranmer complained about the mass, he was thrown into prison.
- ✔ Peter Martyr and other leading Protestants got out of the country or went into hiding. Stephen Gardiner, as lord chancellor, promised to hunt them down.

---

### There's something about Mary

The portraits of Mary as queen don't do her justice. By then she was 40, her eyebrows had gone and her lack of teeth gave her face a hard, frosty look. But as a girl Mary had been pretty. When she was 11, she danced at a pageant at Greenwich and her father took off her cap to show the ambassadors her lovely hair – the 'silver tresses as beautiful as ever seen on human head', according to the Venetian secretary.

Mary loved dancing, spoke Greek, Latin and French and all her life she was fond of jewels, clothes and children. She was honest – unusually for a Tudor – and kind.

But Mary had been treated appallingly – her father, Henry VIII, had dumped her mother, and she'd been made a bastard and sidelined at every turn (see Chapters 5 and 9). She'd even had her darling religion – Catholicism – kicked out of the country. If it was to be payback time, nobody could be too surprised.

## Riding the whirlwind

Try to imagine an ordinary 40-year-old man, the same age as the queen, coming to terms with the changes in religion in England. When he was born, in 1514, the country was Catholic, the mass and the Bible were in Latin, the monasteries were all-powerful and the head guy, spiritually, was the pope.

Then, when he was 20, came Henry VIII's 'great matter' and the country broke with Rome. An English Bible appeared in the man's church and his priest may or may not have carried out the mass in English. If the man lived near a monastery, he'd watch the monks go to see their lands sold off and their buildings left to rot.

Through his 30s, the man would see his own church change. The mass would now always be in English, the wall paintings would be whitewashed, the carvings of saints would disappear.

Now, suddenly, it was all change again – back to the Latin mass, the wall paintings and the saints' carvings, and the bread and wine was once again the flesh and blood of Christ. Was the pope coming back again too?

Result? The average man in the English street must have encountered chaos, bewilderment and fear. Heaven and hell were still real, but how on earth did you get to one and avoid the other?

The bottom line was that most people were in the dark about what was going on and very few of them were literate enough to write their confused thoughts down. See the sidebar 'Riding the whirlwind' for how an average man may have felt.

Mary was crowned on 1 October 1553. She used 'uncontaminated' holy oil imported from the Low Countries (today's Netherlands), rather than the old stuff left lying about from Edward's coronation. Several bishops jumped ship and became Catholic again, just to keep their jobs, so we have to ask how committed they'd been to the new faith in the first place. Anybody who *did* have a conscience, like Bishop Hooper at Gloucester, lost his job – and in Hooper's case, his life.

Lord Chancellor Gardiner was keen to get England back under the pope's control *before* Mary's wedding to Philip (see Chapter 9) so that it would all look like Mary's achievement, not Philip's. Gardiner couldn't do this alone and the Council wouldn't back him. Lord Paget led the lords in revolt, Mary was furious and nothing was sorted out by the time the wedding took place.

## Getting Parliament on side

Mary used her common sense and didn't take Cardinal Pole's advice to ignore Parliament. The pope's man had been out of England for years and had lost touch with what was going on.

So Mary's first Parliament repealed all the acts brought in under Edward (see Chapter 8 for details of Edward's reformation):

- ✔ The 1552 *Book of Common Prayer* was withdrawn.

- ✔ The Sarum Use (the old Latin mass) was brought back officially.

- ✔ The pope would now appoint bishops, not the monarch.

- ✔ Priests couldn't marry.

Various visitations were carried out and many bishops were sacked. If they wouldn't give up their 'concubines', bishops lost their jobs. The human cost was huge – families broken up, women suddenly left destitute.

The Catholic Church was very old, and Edward's reforms had only been around for a few years. So most people probably accepted Mary's changes. The English Bible stayed and for the moment the Royal Supremacy stayed. Things were more or less back to the state of play that King Henry had left.

## *Furthering the faith*

If Mary had left it at her first reforms, fine, but neither she nor Lord Chancellor Gardiner were prepared to do that. And with Philip now on the scene (see Chapter 9 for details of Mary's marriage), they could open the Catholic door still wider because Philip was the son of the Holy Roman Emperor Charles V, and he ruled a country – Spain – where the Inquisition was all-powerful (see the sidebar, 'The Holy Inquisition').

---

## The Holy Inquisition

The Catholic Church set up the Holy Inquisition in 1248 to stamp out heresy. With the rise of various Protestant sects in the 16th century, things got pretty heavy and the Inquisition began to use torture against its opponents. The nastiest Grand Inquisitor was probably Torquemada (1483–98) but they were all prepared to use barbarous methods to keep people loyal to the faith. All it needed was for one informer to point the finger at somebody, and arrests and torture would follow.

The Inquisition dealt with all sorts of sins – infidelity, seduction, sorcery, witchcraft, blasphemy, heresy and even being a Jew. Punishments carried out after secret trials included burning alive, loss of property, banishment and a life sentence in the galleys (oared warships).

Charles V was easily the most powerful ruler in Europe and his son Philip was very close behind him. Now that Philip could claim to be king of England by virtue of being Mary's husband, he could bring all the authority of the Catholic church to England, backed if necessary by serious money and lots of soldiers, and of course the full terror of the Inquisition.

Pope Julius III wanted to get England back under his control – that would be a huge feather in the papal mitre. So the pope was persuaded to lift Church sanctions against people who'd bought ex-monastic lands (including, of course, the queen herself).

Meanwhile, Charles V let Cardinal Pole return to England (even though he held him up for a while to let Philip get the credit for the big Catholic comeback). In England Pole was a bit of a problem because he was actually a traitor for his part in the Pilgrimage of Grace in 1536 (see Chapter 6). So Parliament rushed through a bill to clear him of his treason and Pole talked to both Houses, telling them that all they had to do was to beg the pope's forgiveness and all would be well. So they did.

But that was the easy bit! Now the Council had to work towards legal documents, scrapping the Act of Supremacy and getting the pope to put something on paper in case he changed his mind.

Parliament overturned the Royal Supremacy on 16 January 1555, but Mary had left a loophole. The repeal of the Act of Supremacy could also be repealed (in other words, back to Henry VIII's final Church). This wasn't likely to happen while Mary was alive, but who knew what the upshot would be after that?

Mary agreed that Parliament had the right to decide what the religion of the country was going to be, but she couldn't give up her control of the Church completely, even with the Act of Supremacy gone. So she tried to have her cake and eat it:

- ✔ She didn't call herself Supreme Head (because she wasn't!).

- ✔ She didn't carry out royal visitations.

- ✔ She did set up commissions to censor heretical writings and sermons (not her job).

- ✔ She did encourage persecution of heretics and the final decision on whether to burn people or not came from her (see the following section 'Beginning the burning').

## Polarising Pole and Paul

Sod's Law of History is that events that ought to run smoothly somehow don't. So it was with Mary and the pope. The new man in Rome in 1555 was Paul IV, so terrifying that it was said that sparks flew from his feet as he strode through the Vatican. He was the most hated pope of the century and people held street parties in Rome when he died. Pope Paul IV hated Cardinal Reginald Pole and any kind of Catholic comeback while these two were involved was going to be difficult.

Pole was concerned about churchmen's education. Half a generation of laymen had already grown up reading their English Bibles and were in some cases better read than their priests. Universities, Oxford and Cambridge, turned out competent clerics, but below that (and these universities were tiny) only a sort of apprenticeship scheme that wasn't very good existed. So Pole saw an urgent need to upgrade the education of curates.

But before Pole could achieve much he lost his status as the pope's ambassador (*Legate a Latere*). Why was this? Well, when Philip II attacked the papal states (see 'Squabbling with the pope', later in this chapter), Paul IV pulled

his people out of Philip's territory – hence he recalled Pole from England.

Twenty years earlier, when Martin Luther was making waves against the Catholic Church (see Chapter 6), Pole had been one of those who was looking for some sort of compromise with the man. But Paul IV was a hard-liner – if you so much as glanced at a Protestant without a lighted match in your hand, you must be a heretic.

Paul demanded that Pole come to Rome to explain why he hadn't acted harshly enough, but Mary had already given the Cardinal Cranmer's job as archbishop of Canterbury and didn't let him go. The result was Anglo–papal relations going into deep freeze.

A furious Mary refused to accept Paul's new appointment as ambassador, the friar William Peto. So what, we have to ask, was the point of it all? England's return to the Church of Rome caused huge emotional upheaval, but the return hadn't quite happened.

When Mary died in November 1558 the pope was delighted, but even more so by the news that Cardinal Pole followed her 12 hours later.

## Beginning the burning

Mary believed that the punishment of heretics was a duty. God had put her on the throne, and so any attack on her faith was a personal attack on her (treason) and an attack on God (heresy). Either way, the punishment was death. Her view of Wyatt's Rebellion (see Chapter 9) was that it was a Protestant revolt, and so heretics and traitors went hand in hand.

### Measuring Protestantism

Simon Renard, Charles V's ambassador, believed that the Protestants were still a strong political force and must be watched. The country couldn't easily forget all that had happened during Edward VI's reign – the events of that time weren't just a flash in the religious pan.

Mary's view was that:

- ✓ Ordinary people were simple folk who'd been deluded and misled.

- ✓ Protestant leaders were wicked people whose religious views were wrong and they were clearly in it for money or power.

- ✓ The Protestants most likely figurehead might be sister Elizabeth, but she was in prison after Wyatt's Rebellion and had been told to keep the Catholic faith.

Lord Chancellor Gardiner's view was that:

- ✓ Ordinary people were idiots. They'd do as they were told.

- ✓ Protestant leaders were hoping things would go their way. Put a few of them on trial, threaten them with the stake and watch them grovel and recant.

### *Making martyrs*

Gardiner gave the Protestant preachers in prison in London a straight choice: recant or die. They all turned him down. John Hooper, John Rogers and John Cardmaker were earmarked for the flames on 29 January; Cardmaker cracked and recanted. Rogers was one of those whose charred remains were found at Smithfield (see the nearby sidebar 'Fanning the flames'); Hooper died in front of his own cathedral in Gloucester. Worse was to come.

By the summer of 1555, high profile Protestants Rowland Taylor, John Bradford, Laurence Sanders, Robert Farrer and Edward Crome were all charged with heresy. Crome recanted; the others died. John Cardmaker, wracked with guilt, withdrew his recantation and was burned on 30 May.

---

## Fanning the flames

In 1849 excavations at Smithfield near St Bartholomew's Hospital in London uncovered charred oak posts, an iron staple and ring and burnt human remains. This was all that was left of 43 people burned alive on the orders of Mary. Burning was specifically the punishment for heretics (including, everywhere except England, witches). It was widely used by the pope's Holy Inquisition throughout Europe. In Spain the public burnings were called Auto da Fe and the first thing Philip did when he left England for the first time was to watch 14 people killed in this way. In the heat of Spain, especially when the 'spear of mercy' was thrust into the mouth first, death was relatively quick. In a damp, foggy London, it could take two hours.

Something was going wrong in Gardiner's and Pole's plans. Protestants weren't recanting; they were becoming martyrs – the last thing Mary's Government wanted.

Gardiner's death (from natural causes!) in November did nothing to stop the persecution.

When bishops Nicholas Ridley and Hugh Latimer were burned in Oxford in October 1555, an enterprising London waterman took a day trip of ghouls up the Thames to watch the spectacle. They got good value for their money – Ridley was fully conscious for 45 minutes and he roasted in agony from the feet up.

### Taking responsibility

The Church was, by law, not able to shed blood, so even though Cardinal Pole's fixed show trials found men guilty they had to be handed over to the secular authorities for the actual punishment.

Mary, of course, was comfortable with the burnings: she was doing God's work and her duty as queen. The Council, however, could have stopped her – they weren't afraid to take her on over other matters – but they didn't. Philip wasn't happy with the persecutions, simply because he could see the whole thing was counter-productive. He knew the English would blame him and he kept a low profile throughout.

---

# Cremating Cranmer

Thomas Cranmer crops up in plenty of previous chapters. He was vital to the creation of Henry VIII's Church (see Chapter 6) and a powerhouse when it came to the Edwardian Reformation, prayer books and all (see Chapter 8). Mary hated him because in religious terms he was a traitor. She had Cranmer put on trial in September 1555 and his dilemma was obvious. As long as Mary was supreme head of the Church, he backed her, but he wouldn't say the mass or follow the pope.

It's not much to his credit that Cranmer recanted, but Mary wasn't buying it. She believed Cranmer had been behind her father kicking her mother out (see Chapters 5 and 6) and was responsible for every bad thing that had happened since 1533!

On the stake in March 1556, Cranmer had no more to lose. He withdrew his recantation and died a martyr after all, thrusting his right hand into the fiercest of the flames – 'This hath offended,' he shouted above the fire's roar, 'Oh, this unworthy hand.'

## An inconsistent approach

The Marian burnings followed a peculiar pattern. On the one hand, Pole went so far as to have dead heretics' remains dug up and burned in public. On the other, some people weren't only allowed to leave the country, but were given plenty of time to do it. For example, the duchess of Suffolk, taking the kitchen sink with her, took five days to reach Gravesend from London (less than one hour by car today).

## *Punishing the people*

By 1557, with most high profile targets dead or in exile, the government set its sights on the rank and file. Brief rigged trials of several people at once took place to save time, and pardons were usually turned down. Public burning was abandoned and victims were put to death early in the morning to avoid the crowds. Ordinary people went to the stake as bravely as the preachers and bishops.

Between 50 and 60 of the total 300 burned were women. In one particularly ghastly incident in Guernsey, Perotine Massey gave birth at the stake and her baby was delivered and burned too. In another instance, the stake wasn't used and 'loose women' were running around screaming and on fire.

Public reaction to the burnings was mixed. Protestants weren't always popular with Catholic neighbours, who felt a sense of justice about what was happening. On the other hand, a lot of people couldn't get worked up about heresy as a crime and thought burning was over the top. The more ordinary the victims were, the more support they got – hence the move to early morning burnings.

Most of what we know about Mary's burnings comes from biased Protestant accounts like Foxe's *Book of Martyrs*. Some of those who died were fanatics who'd probably have been burned by the Protestants had Edward VI lived. Some of the 'spontaneous' demonstrations were actually carefully staged Protestant propaganda.

## *Looking on the good side*

Mary only became 'Bloody Mary' in the 19th century, when attitudes had changed completely. Some good things *were* going on in her reign:

> ✔ Books of spiritual guidance were published.
>
> ✔ Pole spent a lot of time improving the education of the clergy.
>
> ✔ Pole promised a new Bible translation in 1556.
>
> ✔ Bishop Bonner of London wrote homilies like Cranmer's (see Chapter 8).

The bottom line, however, was that everybody saw the burnings as the work of the pope, the Inquisition and Philip. So the huge natural reconversion to the old faith that Mary had planned never happened.

## Planting Rebellion in Ireland

The burnings that took place in England just didn't happen in Ireland. That was largely because Ireland had so few Protestants that when Mary became queen they either gave up and went back to Rome or got out of the country.

The unpopular and not very competent Anthony St Leger was governor between 1553 and 1556 and he had no new ideas.

When St Leger was recalled from Ireland in disgrace at the end of May 1556, he was replaced by Thomas Radcliffe, Lord Fitzwalter, who was about to become the earl of Sussex.

The key feature of Sussex's deputyship on Mary's behalf was the setting up of plantations run by Englishmen with farming experience who usually happened to be ex-soldiers. At a stroke, these men could form their own military garrisons (saving the government money) and would hopefully make the country more stable.

---

### What's your poison, Ormond?

Back in December 1546 Governor St Leger had held a dinner party at his home in Limehouse in London. James Butler, the earl of Ormond and Ossary, was in the capital to settle a dispute between him and St Leger over Irish affairs, which was to be arbitrated by the Privy Council.

It was generous of St Leger to invite his rival round for a bite, but it all turned sour (literally)

when everyone became ill and 17 of them (including Ormond) died. Poisoning everybody was a very neat solution to St Leger's immediate problems, but it seems a rather high-risk strategy. Maybe it was just the dodgy fish from Billingsgate . . .

---

The targeted counties were Leix and Offaly, renamed King's and Queen's counties. In some cases, the Englishmen removed the landlords only from the estates, setting up the system that would cause bitter resentment three centuries later – Irish tenants paying rent to English landlords who didn't even live in Ireland.

# Securing Succession

Philip and Mary were two minds with one thought – they both wanted a son. The boy would be king of a Catholic England and a foreign territory – Spain and the Spanish Netherlands (Low Countries) – would be thrown in.

But their union wasn't plain sailing:

- Philip couldn't take Mary out of England (even for a honeymoon), because the law at the time said that, by doing so, Mary might lose her claim to the English throne. Unlike today, when foreign visits by heads of state are an important part of what they do, leaving the country in the 16th century usually involved leading an army in the field.

- Philip had to abide by English law.

- England wouldn't take part in the ongoing war between the Holy Roman Empire and France.

- The marriage was unpopular with Philip (because his father had done the deal).

- Some people resented a foreigner on the English throne.

## Settling into the role of king

In public, Philip was very attentive to Mary and she, increasingly plain and frumpy, was besotted. She was an old fashioned romantic in some ways and had a plain gold wedding ring because 'that was how maidens were wedded in olden times'. She kept out of sight at Court after the wedding (as was the custom) while Philip went sight-seeing and tried to find himself a separate palace.

Philip had a real problem learning English (see the sidebar 'Tudor-speak') but his pre-nup had said he had to have English servants. So he came out with a compromise: English servants in public; Spanish in private. This, of course, was the worst of both worlds: Englishmen complained they had no access to the king; Spaniards felt dishonoured in the eyes of the world.

## Tudor-speak

Philip couldn't speak English. Mary could understand Spanish up to a point, but probably couldn't speak it. Mary spoke good French; Philip didn't. So we can't be sure how the couple communicated. Maybe Mary spoke French to Philip and he answered in Spanish? Maybe they canoodled in Latin (after all, thousands of Romans did for centuries!)? Even so, misunderstandings must have been common. What's Latin for 'I've got a headache'?

As far as dealing with the Council goes, Gardiner and a few others spoke fluent Latin. Some of the nobility outside the Council, however, only spoke and wrote English and some were illiterate. Interpreters must have been on hand, and it may be that some gentlemen of the king's Privy Chamber did that job from time to time.

Some of Philip's Spanish and Italian courtiers had nothing to do after the wedding and found themselves at daggers (literally) with their English counterparts. To avoid further embarrassment, Philip packed them off to the Low Countries.

From then on, Philip's life was oddly semi-detached.

- ✔ He played war games for the benefit of the nobility, went to the state opening of Parliament (the equivalent Cortes in Spain had nothing like the power of the Lords and Commons) and went to mass in St Paul's Cathedral.

- ✔ Much of his time he spent closeted away with his Spanish advisers, chatting about European politics. He probably shared few of his political ideas with Mary.

Only on the issue of the new Rome/England understanding (see the earlier section 'Furthering the Faith') was Philip truly open.

## *Expecting great things*

Mary was sexually very naive. When she overheard the lord chamberlain call a lady-in-waiting a whore, she thought that was a compliment and started using it herself until the lady in question explained that the lord chamberlain was a foul old *&^%$£, which presumably Mary didn't understand either.

Luckily, Philip knew which end of the bed was which, so it came as no surprise to anybody when Mary thought she was pregnant. Some of the Spanish courtiers thought 'it would take God himself to drink of this cup', but events seemed to be about to prove them wrong.

The early weeks of 1555 were Mary's high water mark. She was pregnant, the old faith was back (so was Cardinal Pole), hubby was attentive and nasty noises came from Scotland or France. Then everything went pear-shaped.

# *Waiting for nothing*

Early in April Mary retired from Court (which was usual for a pregnant queen). She tired easily and her abdomen was swollen. A nursery was decorated at Hampton Court (the same room where Edward VI was born), a cradle set up and an army of nurses and midwives were on hand. They even brought a set of triplets, newly born to a little woman as old as Mary, to encourage the queen.

But nothing happened. Her doctors wondered whether their dates were wrong, but rumours in and out of Court were (as always) far wilder:

- ✔ The queen was bewitched/ill/dead.

- ✔ A substitute child had been smuggled into the palace (writer John Foxe recorded that a woman who'd just given birth was asked to give the boy up by Court agents, no questions asked – but then the arch-Protestant John Foxe would say that, wouldn't he?).

- ✔ Mary's child was born on 30 April. This was so widely believed that people in London began to celebrate.

People prayed for the queen's safe delivery, but in late July everything was scaled down. Mary hadn't been pregnant after all. The royal nursery was dismantled and Mary, emotionally shattered, went back to her normal duties.

By now, Mary was flat-chested and thin with a deep, rasping voice and a bad complexion. She'd always had problems with her periods and it was irregular periods that had led her to believe she was pregnant. Her weight loss led her doctors to believe that the baby's head (there was, of course, no doubt that it was a boy) had engaged inside the pelvis. Two years later, Mary would go through this deeply traumatic faux pregnancy experience a second time (see Chapter 11). Today, the symptoms sound like an ovarian cystic tumour or possible cervical cancer.

Whatever the cause of Mary's illness, nothing could be done, and to all who knew her it was obvious that Mary wasn't well. Not only could the queen not conceive, but she didn't have long to live. For the Protestants, the lack of an heir for Mary and Philip was good news. The old faith might die (again) with the queen.

Charles V now realised that empire-building with the Tudors (at least this one!) wasn't going to happen. At least he'd got Philip into the Low Countries with English backing (see the following section), and if the queen was barren, that was good reason enough for the pope to grant a divorce.

# Drifting and Shifting: Philip Flexes His Muscles

Philip sailed for the Low Countries on 26 August 1555. Mary and the Court went with him as far as Greenwich, east of London. People were glad to see Mary back in public and equally glad to see Philip go, though the king had left an inner group in the Council to keep him in the picture during his absence and he promised to be back by October. Everybody noticed a chill in the atmosphere between the royal couple.

## Eyeing the crown

Philip didn't come back for Parliament's opening in October. In fact, he pulled his Household out of England a few weeks later. What was going on?

- ✔ To Philip, the whole venture was falling apart. Without a son he could make no headway.
- ✔ The queen wasn't well. If she died, would Elizabeth succeed?

The whole thing boiled down to Philip versus Elizabeth – a foreign Catholic ruler versus a home-grown and (probably) Protestant one.

Philip had been talking to his lawyers, and he now pushed for a separate coronation as king of England. In England the act of coronation was vital, far more so than in Europe, and perhaps Philip wanted to push the claim in his own right. After all, if Mary died, he'd be sitting on the throne of England – and possession was nine tenths of the law.

Mary now had a dilemma. If she let Philip be crowned, it would look like power sharing and this had never happened before in English history. She knew that nobody in England would accept power-sharing monarchs. Philip argued that the decision about a coronation wasn't Parliament's, but Mary's. On the other hand, Mary was writing long, pleading letters to Philip to come back; she missed him and England needed his 'firm hand'. She even wrote to cousin Charles to use his influence on his son, but Charles was now living in retirement at the monastery of San Jeronimo in Spain and was pretty tired of the hurly-burly of European power politics.

According to one story, Mary kicked Philip's portrait around the Privy Chamber in frustration, but she wouldn't give in to his request.

When news of Philip and Mary's disagreement got out (leaks were nothing new, of course) people trotted out predictable arguments:

- Philip planned to grab England when Mary died (probably true), and then England would be subjected to Spanish tyranny (yes – and that included the Inquisition).

- Elizabeth would be out (undoubtedly).

- Philip was leaping into bed with all and sundry behind Mary's back (quite possibly).

## Double dealing with Dudley

No – not *that* Dudley; he'd been executed in August 1553 (see Chapter 9) but his cousin, Henry, who'd set himself up as a go-between for the exiled Protestants and potential rebels in the West Country (what is it about the West Country? – see Chapters 7 and 8 for other rebellions).

Dudley's plan, hatched before Christmas 1555 and involving some MPs, was that a French-backed invasion of exiles would oust Mary and Philip and put Elizabeth on the throne. The whole thing fell apart when Henri II signed a treaty with Philip and pulled out of the hare-brained scheme, leaving the plotters without cash.

Undeterred, the rebels planned to steal £50,000 in silver and whisk it across the Channel. This part of the plot was betrayed and the ring-leaders, including Richard Uvedale, captain of the Isle of Wight, were arrested and interrogated. Several of the plotters were executed in the summer of 1556. Slippery Dudley was already out of reach in France.

At this point, Philip realised that his coronation ambitions weren't going to come off and he dropped the whole idea. But he realised that getting on-side with Elizabeth may be a good idea, just in case . . .

---

## Managing from afar

Philip kept in touch with events at the top via his select Council. He commented, but rarely intervened, leaving Mary to govern which was, after all, her job. When Gardiner the Lord Chancellor died in 1555, Philip was consulted over his replacement. His military hatchet-man in the Low Countries, the duke of Alba, strongly advised him to appoint 'king's men' not 'queen's men', but the appointment seems to have been a compromise.

Nicholas Heath was archbishop of York (the Church's second top job), a good administrator and an honest man. But he couldn't hold a candle to Gardiner with all his experience. He was probably neither Philip's nor Mary's first choice, but he got the job anyway.

---

## The fabric of frustration

The all-important cloth trade took a down-turn during Mary's reign, and Philip didn't help matters:

✔ Charles had asked Mary to restore the privileges of the European Hanseatic League (big business), which Edward VI had removed. This meant that Antwerp-based merchants were now back in English ports, which annoyed the merchant adventurers, the most powerful economic group in London. And whenever Antwerp and English merchants got into disputes, Philip always backed Antwerp.

✔ Philip kept English traders out of the Spanish–American market. True, he was also keeping Naples and Flanders out of this, but that didn't reduce English annoyance.

✔ English merchants tried to pinch some of the Portuguese trade in Guinea, West Africa. Because Philip's mother was Portuguese, he stopped this too.

The one thing Philip didn't block was the setting up of the Muscovy Company in 1555 to trade with the newly expanding Russia, because he had no interests there!

---

## Taking a turn for the worse

England was depressed in 1556. The previous summer had been unusually wet, three successive harvests had failed and food prices were three times greater than those of 50 years earlier. One eyewitness wrote: 'What diseases and sicknesses everywhere prevail, the like whereof has never been known before. Hot burning fevers and other strange diseases.'

Many people felt that the depression was all Philip's fault (see the nearby sidebar 'The fabric of frustration'), and so were the burnings (a Spanish idea) *and* thanks to him, England was bound to be dragged into war with France again sooner or later (see the following section).

## Squabbling with the pope

Philip became king of Spain in January 1556 and he was already lord of the Low Countries. This meant he'd got involved in the half-hearted war with France that had been going on since 1552. But when he became king he cut his losses and made peace with Henri II at Vaucelles in January 1556.

The pope, Paul IV, hated all things Spanish (he even refused to make the long dead Spanish hero El Cid a saint because of this) and he began to take land off Spain's allies and even imprison the Holy Roman Emperor's spokesmen.

Philip dithered before attacking the papacy. After all, an attack put him in a difficult position as far as God was concerned; two champions of Christendom having a go at each other wasn't good for publicity. But on 1 September he sent his viceroy as king of Spain, the duke of Alba, to Naples to hit the papal states.

The pope was all mouth and no vestments. He couldn't fight Alba, one of the best soldiers of his generation, so he called in the French for help. The duke of Guise crossed the Alps in January 1557 – and here we go again!

# Trying to drag England into a war

Philip naturally wanted England in on this fight. That way, he could hit France on two fronts – the great dream, in fact, of Henry VII all those years ago (see Chapter 2).

Mary was keen but the Privy Council and even Cardinal Pole were against going to war. Pole couldn't allow war against his boss, the pope, even if Paul IV couldn't stand him, and the Council reminded Mary that her pre-nup with Philip expressly said 'no war with France'. Anyway, the Council couldn't afford war – times were hard and the national debt stood at a staggering £180,000.

Philip came back to England to plead his case– this was a new war, he said, not the old one. France was at the gates of Naples and Philip and Mary both knew that war was the decision of the monarch; the Council could only advise.

What was the state of play?

  - ✔ The Council was divided. Most of them opposed war but Paget and the earl of Pembroke muttered things about honour, and backed Philip.

  - ✔ Nobody cared what Parliament thought – it was nothing to do with them.

  - ✔ The powerful London merchants opposed war because they were scared of losing valuable ships and cargo to the French (and almost certainly Scottish) pirates.

  - ✔ Some of the nobility and gentry longed for a good scrap under a king. There had been few opportunities recently and Philip was a fighter who'd lead them to battle.

  - ✔ Some nobles saw their chance to get back into Mary's good books by backing Philip.

  - ✔ Most ordinary people were against fighting – war always meant more taxes.

With the situation still unresolved, Philip left England in June 1557, and he did so for the last time. He'd never see the country – or Mary – again. And the next time he tried (see Chapter 15) he'd send the most terrifying fleet the world had seen – the Armada.

# Chapter 11

# Ending the Dream: The Last of Mary

*T*he last year of Mary I's reign was grim, both for her and the country. The queen had her second phantom pregnancy, after which Philip never came back; the last English stronghold in France fell; and, above all, Elizabeth and the spectre of Protestantism waited in the wings.

## Going to War with France

In Chapter 10 we explain that Philip was gung-ho for a war against the French. But the king hadn't expected that it would be so difficult to get England in on his war with Henri II. He said as much to the bishop of Arras, his chief minister on the Low Countries.

Then, help came from an unexpected source.

### Revolting with Stafford

Some noble families just won't lie down. The dukes of Buckingham had been right there at the top of the power tree since Richard III's reign (see Chapter 2) and they were still pushing their luck now.

Thomas Stafford was the grandson of the last duke of Buckingham and related to Reginald Pole: cardinal, archbishop of Canterbury and papal head man (Chapter 10 has more on Pole). Stafford had been involved in Wyatt's Rebellion (flip to Chapter 9) and had high-tailed it to France where he spent most of his time annoying people. He believed he had a claim to the English throne, and early in 1557 he decided to try his luck.

Henri II offered help at first, then thought better of it. Even so, Stafford hired two ships, got a ragbag force together and landed at Scarborough on the Yorkshire coast (it's a tourist resort today – check it out). Amazingly, Stafford took the feebly defended castle and issued a proclamation that said:

- ✔ Mary wasn't the rightful monarch because she'd given the crown away to a foreigner (Philip).
- ✔ Stafford was the 'protector of the realm' – a vague phrase, but one degree down from claiming the throne and it had echoes of Somerset who'd ruled on behalf of the young Edward VI (see Chapter 7).

Stafford was soon rounded up by the troops of the earl of Westmoreland and the rebellion was over. The 'protector of the realm' was executed.

What's all this got to do with Philip's war? Well, the Privy Council blew the rebellion up out of all proportion and claimed heavy French involvement. So Mary declared war on France on 7 June 1557. Taxpayers, relax – Philip's paying!

## *Fighting the French – again!*

Philip needed to get moving on his attack before winter set in.

Before real modern warfare the campaigning season was May to September. There weren't many good roads in Europe and they quickly turned to bogs when it rained. Cannon were heavy and the largest of them could only fire a few times a day because they over-heated and the barrels clogged with powder that some poor soldier had to scrape out. Fighting in the winter was nobody's idea of a good time.

Philip got to Calais on 5 July with 7,000 men under the earl of Pembroke. His commanders were good men – Robert, Ambrose and Henry Dudley (the three sons of the late duke of Northumberland [Warwick] – see Chapters 7 and 9), Peter Carew, Nicholas Throgmorton and William Courtenay. Do these names sound familiar? They did to the Venetian ambassador, who realised that all Mary's troublemakers were at the front. Her loyal supporters stayed at home.

Philip attacked and took the border town of St Quentin (see Chapter 15 for a map of the Low Countries), but Pembroke's English troops had to make sure that Calais was safe from attack first; so they got there late. Philip was less than pleased and sent them home rather than pay for their winter quartering. As it was, the campaign had so far cost him £48,000, an enormous sum for one small town.

## Warring in winter: the fall of Calais

By the end of November Philip's army was in winter quarters at Hainault in the southern Netherlands and the English Government was saving money by cutting back troops defending Calais (will they never learn?).

Psychologically, Calais was important. At one time half of France had belonged to England, but most of that had been lost by the end of the Hundred Years War in 1453 (you can find out about this era in *British History For Dummies* by Sean Lang, published by Wiley). Check out Mary's coat of arms – it has the fleur-de-lys of France on it. So does Elizabeth's – and she didn't own any of France at all.

The duke of Guise (the most powerful man in France after the king) had been thrashed in battle by Philip's man Alba (see Chapter 10 for more on him) and he was looking for a quick, morale-boosting comeback.

Calais' defences weren't what they should have been and Guise's spies told him now was the time to strike. Philip's spies were telling him the same thing but the Calais governor, Lord Wentworth, and the Council in London weren't listening – until it was too late.

On 1 January 1558 Guise and the French struck, literally skating over the frozen marshes that in warmer weather saved Calais from attack. Guise grabbed the fort of Ruysbank, which protected the harbour, so the English fleet, sent out at the last minute under command of the earl of Rutland, couldn't get in. On 7 January the French guns smashed through the castle walls and the town fell. English civilians ran and Wentworth surrendered with 2,000 of his men.

Shocked and surprised, the Council now ordered Rutland to save the very last English stronghold, Guisnes, but that surrendered on 21 January and the English fleet was badly damaged by storms in the North Sea. The Council decided to cut their losses and call the whole thing off.

## Following the fall

Mary was devastated by the fall of Calais. 'When I am dead and opened,' she wrote, 'they shall find Calais engraved in my heart.'

Recriminations flew thick and fast:

- ✔ It was Wentworth's fault because he was a secret heretic and was part of the Protestant plot.
- ✔ It was the Government's fault; Calais hadn't been properly defended for years.
- ✔ It was Philip's fault, because his half-hearted 'rescue' of Calais with only 200 *harquebusiers* (musketeers) was too little, too late.

## Simmering in Scotland

War with France usually meant war with Scotland because of the Auld Alliance (see Chapters 4 and 7). This time it didn't happen. Philip was careful not to declare war on Scotland as well as France and the Scots/French nobles weren't too keen to invade England. The regent in Scotland, Mary of Guise (her daughter, Mary Queen of Scots, was still only 15) was all for war, but nobody else wanted to know.

In a slightly bizarre situation, the continuing peace was announced at Carlisle and Dumfries on 18 July. Scotland simmered with discontent (when didn't it?) over the arrogance and wealth of England and the Council tried to persuade Philip to declare war. The truth was that Scotland was useful to Philip for his Flemish merchants, so he wasn't prepared to risk a war. The expected attack across the border from Scotland never happened.

In fact, the Council hadn't spent enough money on fortifications and Wentworth's garrison was seriously under-manned. That said, Guise had caught the English napping and the English had paid the price. Philip was all for launching a counter-attack the following summer, but the Council wasn't keen, claiming lack of cash.

Philip's spring offensive would have cost £170,000 over five months. Add to this the £150,000 needed to keep existing garrisons, plus £200,000 necessary for a sea defence, and the total price tag was a staggering £520,000. This would mean new taxes; new taxes would mean revolt.

Mary and Philip were furious that the Council wouldn't back them in another attack. All the queen could do was appoint Lord Clinton as lord admiral (the top naval man) in February, but the amphibious operation he tried to launch in Brittany in the summer fizzled out.

## *Feeling the fallout*

The fall of Calais was a psychological blow that Mary's Government never recovered from.

Parliament met on 20 January 1558 just before Guisnes fell and the Council asked members to vote for an increase in direct taxation – a traditional subsidy to be collected over two years. The money was needed:

- ✔ To build up the fleet (ships were expensive and had to be refitted regularly because of wear and tear)
- ✔ To pay for a garrison at Berwick on the Scots' border (check out the Elizabethan fortifications next time you're there)
- ✔ To raise an army in case of a Scots' invasion

Direct taxation was slow to boost the coffers, so by the end of June the Council pushed through two defence bills that:

- ✔ Streamlined the method of recruiting men to stop corruption
- ✔ Told Households to provide armour and weapons to equip a militia

Increasingly, the gentry, as opposed to the nobility, took over control of local troops.

## Getting the jitters

The Council thought that, come the good weather in the spring, France would invade.

When the French had last tried to invade, only 13 years earlier, fierce fighting had followed on the Isle of Wight and the *Mary Rose*, the pride of Henry VIII's fleet, had sunk (refer to Chapter 3).

Lords lieutenant of counties paraded their militias and got them busy with battlefield drill and musket practice (although a lot of the soldiers were still relying on bows and arrows).

The marquis of Winchester was empowered to use martial law against 'rebels, traitors and other offenders'. These powers already existed but were only used occasionally against deserters from the navy. Suddenly, Big Brother had come to England and panic reigned in Whitehall.

# Catching a Cold: The Flu Epidemic

The harvests of 1555 and 1556 had been dreadful, with food shortages and starvation. Twice as many people died from disease in 1558 than the year before. Nobody knew what the 'strange diseases' were and so no cure existed.

In some places (but not everywhere) the poor were hit harder than the rich. No age group was safe but the elderly suffered very badly. County militias had to be disbanded, and some workshops were closed down. If the flu didn't kill you, it left you weak and vulnerable, and the last thing you could handle was dragging a plough across the furrow or cutting down timber on the lord's estate. The economy was hit hard through lost work days.

The outbreak kept Philip away, even when he heard that Mary was seriously ill – he probably thought she had the flu and couldn't take the chance of catching it himself. Nobody was immune – Cardinal Pole died from it in November 1558.

# Defending the Faith

Throughout history when disasters or epidemics happened, simple (and not so simple) people thought it was the work of the devil or the wrath of God. The poor harvests, the economic depression (see Chapter 10), the lost war and the flu epidemic of the last two years just reinforced these ideas in people's minds.

The Church's leaders and university types didn't argue have much to say, but others did:

✔ Some, like the hosier (tights-maker) Miles Huggarde, thought the flu was the result of plots against the queen and people moaning about her godly work.

✔ The Protestants, of course, believed that Mary's return to the old faith had led to God's anger. Exiles Edmund Grindal and John Foxe, who were writing their martyrology, kept up a steady barrage of criticism against the queen, Philip and the Council, all of whom were tarred with the same (papist) brush.

Few people criticised the queen directly but Philip was fair game. Never popular, by the summer of 1558 he might as well have been the devil himself.

Trying to make Catholicism acceptable wasn't easy in the face of a foreign king, a failed war and flu. Here's an outline of the Church at this time:

✔ The Church stressed the importance of the mass and Thomas Watson, bishop of Lincoln, wrote books to guide ordinary people through the complicated rituals of the mass (which had fallen into disuse under Edward VI – see Chapter 7).

✔ The English Bible (see Chapter 6) wasn't recalled, even though it had been written by heretics, because Mary – and even Cardinal Pole – quite liked it. Rabid Catholics like Bishop James Turberville of Exeter grabbed copies and burned them. Presumably, this was less traumatic than burning people!

✔ The pastoral care that the Catholic Church offered was old-fashioned by Protestant standards, fussing about sacraments and ceremonies; ceremonies were good for discipline.

✔ The Church wasn't generally too keen on sermons, because in the wrong hands they gave people wrong ideas.

✔ The Church didn't restore the shrines.

✔ Nobody made a pilgrimage in Mary's reign. Though you expect have expected Mary to go, what with the old Virgin's shrine at Walsingham in Norfolk and a lot to pray for, she didn't.

✔ No real return to the monasteries occured. The only great abbey set up was at Westminster and very few *novices* (trainee monks) were recruited.

# Encountering Elizabeth

Henry VIII's will named three heirs to his kingdom. If Edward VI died childless, the throne should pass to Mary; if Mary died childless, it should go to Elizabeth. It was a sort of Doomsday scenario and nobody at the time of Henry's death thought Elizabeth would be queen, but by 1558 there seemed no other alternative.

Mary was opposed to Elizabeth because:

- ✔ She couldn't forget that Elizabeth was the hated Anne Boleyn's daughter and she believed (wrongly) that Anne was a heretic (her sixth finger and spooky witchcraft rumours didn't help – see Chapter 4).

- ✔ She thought that Elizabeth was only *pretending* to have gone back to the old faith – she was obviously a Protestant.

- ✔ The law said Elizabeth was a bastard and Mary didn't even like to think of them as half-sisters. In her more snide moments, she commented loudly on how much Elizabeth looked like Mark Smeaton, the music teacher who'd been executed for having an affair with Anne Boleyn (see Chapter 5).

Mary had a love–hate relationship with Elizabeth, seeing her as a sort of daughter on the one hand and a deadly rival on the other. The only film with Mary in anything like an important role is Cathy Burke's portrayal in *Elizabeth*. Check out the scene when she tries to persuade Elizabeth (Cate Blanchett) to go over to Rome; her mood swings say it all.

## Locking up a rival

In Chapter 9 we explain that following a rebellion in England led by Thomas Wyatt, Mary had her sister sent to the Tower. As Charles V's man in England, looking out for Philip's interests, the ambassador Simon Renard was delighted when it looked for a while as though Elizabeth was involved in Wyatt's Rebellion. Renard did his best to have the princess executed and was livid when the 'evidence' against her wouldn't stand up.

The story goes that Elizabeth refused to enter the Tower by water because that meant passing under the archway called Traitor's Gate (check it out when you're there next) and she was no traitor.

The cringing letter Elizabeth wrote to Mary from the Tower has survived. She denied any involvement with Wyatt and said there'd never been a more devoted sister. The frequent scribbling out, however, reveals a scared woman desperately searching for the right phrase.

Despite urgings from various members of the Council like Paget, Mary refused to have her sister killed. Instead, she released her from the Tower in 1554 and put her under house arrest at Woodstock in Oxfordshire.

Mary and Elizabeth met face to face at some point in 1554 and Elizabeth sobbed and swore loyalty to Mary, but the queen wouldn't let her go. Mary's attitude to her half-sister bordered on the schizophrenic – she hated and loved her at the same time.

Lord Chancellor Gardiner's idea was to have Elizabeth barred from ever being queen by scrapping Henry VIII's last Succession Act. Because this would mean bastardising Mary too, the whole thing was quietly dropped.

## Searching for a suitable suitor

The laws of England – and most of Europe – were that when a woman married, her property became her husband's. The generally held view – going all the way back to Adam and Eve – was that women were inferior to men and wives were expected to do as they were told.

So the solution, in the case of Elizabeth, was simple – find her a good man and the Elizabeth problem would go away. Philip took on the job of matchmaker himself. He decided that the lucky groom would need to be:

✔ Be a good Catholic

✔ Be a crony of Philip's or at least loyal to his family

✔ Have the time and energy to keep Elizabeth in check (for her famous temper, see Chapter 12).

The obvious choice was Emmanuel Philibert, the duke of Savoy (see Map of Europe in Chapter 9).

Philibert had actually lost his land to the French and he'd been brought up at Charles V's Court. He was a competent soldier and was prepared to move to England to live with Elizabeth (although Philip probably had ideas of shipping her overseas at the earliest opportunity).

Philip's problem was that he had to convince two women:

✔ Elizabeth was clever and shrewd. She knew exactly what was going on, and in fact for the rest of her life she never lost her own power to a man (despite huge pressure).

✔ Mary was surprisingly snobby. She had no qualms about marrying Elizabeth off, but the girl was the bastard (as far as Mary was concerned) of Anne Boleyn and Mark Smeaton, so a duke was far too high ranked for her.

When Philip came back to England in the spring of 1557 he brought with him the duchesses of Parma and Lorraine, two pretty feisty ladies from his Spanish Court. They worked on Elizabeth – and probably Mary too – but got nowhere.

We know that Philip issued instructions after the Dudley conspiracy (see Chapter 10 for details) that Elizabeth was to be left alone, so maybe Mary's paranoia was particularly bad then and Elizabeth needed protection. Philip could have whisked Elizabeth back to the Low Countries or Spain, but the Council had said no and Philip needed the Council's backing for the French war.

So Elizabeth stayed put, biding her time and keeping everybody guessing. Philip tried to push the Savoy marriage again in 1558, but it was still no go.

By now, Mary had suffered her second phantom pregnancy (see Chapter 10 for details of the babies that never were), and so in October 1558 she added a new clause to her will. If she produced no 'heirs of her body' the crown would pass 'by the laws of England'. She still couldn't bring herself to name Elizabeth.

## *Naming Elizabeth as successor*

Mary was paranoid in the last months of her life. Two phantom pregnancies, a half-hearted comeback of Catholicism, the smell of burning flesh over Smithfield (Chapter 10 gives the grisly details of the burnings) – it wasn't much of a legacy to leave.

Elizabeth was a born plotter. Much later in her life (see Chapter 16) she gave her increasingly frustrated Parliaments 'answers answerless'. She was highly intelligent, secretive and enigmatic; nobody quite knew how to play her. Even with Wyatt's Rebellion (see Chapter 9) it wasn't clear what her involvement was and no jury was prepared to convict her.

By the summer of 1558 it was clear that Mary was seriously ill and Philip sent a close adviser, the count of Feria, to talk to Elizabeth at Hatfield House, north of London (check the place out next time you're in Hertfordshire). No records of what went on exist, but it's likely the pair talked of what would happen when Mary died.

Now Philip faced a dilemma. He knew by October that Mary was probably dying and many in England thought he should do the decent thing and be with her. He had two problems though:

- ✔ If Mary had flu, he might catch it.

- ✔ If he was in England when Mary died, he'd have to claim succession, which he wasn't ready for and which would turn pretty nasty.

So Philip sent the long-suffering Feria instead. The count saw Mary early in November. She recognised him, but couldn't read the letters he'd brought from Philip.

Everybody seemed to be holding their breath, wondering what would happen. Heretics due to be burned were held in prison. But by the time of Elizabeth's next meeting with Feria, everything had changed. Elizabeth was more confident, less reliant on Philip. When Mary was gone, she knew the Council and the people would back her. As for the Church . . . well, that remained to be seen.

It was probably now that Mary named Elizabeth as her successor. She asked that her debts be paid and the Church she loved so dearly should be kept intact. Her request received no reply.

## Preparing for power

Count Feria is very useful for the history of these weeks because he wrote a thumbnail sketch of Elizabeth:

- She was vain and clever, taught by her father to get her own way.
- Her ladies-in-waiting were all Protestant, so Feria assumed (rightly) that she'd choose male advisers of the same persuasion when she became queen.
- She had a huge backing in the country at large. To quote the count: 'There is not a heretic or a traitor in the kingdom who would not rise up from the grave to support her.'
- She was seriously annoyed about the way Mary had treated her, whisking her from one prison to another.

Feria let Elizabeth know that Philip had told his pension-holders to back her. This was supposed to make Elizabeth grateful, but it didn't work – Elizabeth wasn't sure anybody should be receiving cash hand-outs from a foreign king (thanks, sister-in-law).

So the smooth count and the soon-to-be-queen talked money, marriage and foreign affairs:

- Elizabeth wanted to know whether Mary had been funding Philip. Feria told her no; it was the other way round.
- Elizabeth reminded Feria that Parliament had a right to know what Philip's money was being spent on.

✔ Elizabeth showed her dry sense of humour by telling Feria about the advances of the duke of Savoy and that being married to a foreigner had caused Mary a lot of grief. Now that the marriage was linked to the royal succession, it was altogether a more serious – and sensitive – subject.

✔ Feria told Elizabeth that Philip would fight on against the French until they gave Calais back. Elizabeth told him she'd behead anyone who thought otherwise.

✔ Elizabeth (who may only have been half joking) said she worried about the English hatred of foreigners. Becase Feria was about to marry Elizabeth's friend, Mary's lady-in-waiting Jane Dormer the following month, he already regarded himself as an honorary Englishman. In fact, he found English habits barbarous and their politics appalling.

# Claiming the Crown

Mary died on the morning of 17 November at St James's Palace in London, possibly of cancer. She'd been drifting in and out of consciousness for days and wasn't in pain. She told her ladies in the last hours that she'd had dreams of little children playing with angels.

The story goes that Elizabeth was walking in the knot gardens of Hatfield when she was brought the news of Mary's death. She took a deep breath and thanked God for a happy conclusion. The lord chancellor, Nicholas Heath, proclaimed Elizabeth as queen and Parliament was dissolved.

## The other Mary

Practically speaking, the only rival who could have rained on Elizabeth's parade was Mary, Queen of Scots, her cousin once removed. Elizabeth was the country's rightful queen under the will of Henry VIII, but Mary of Scots, now 16, did have a claim. She was the granddaughter of Margaret Tudor, Henry VIII's elder sister, but because her father was the Scots king James V, she was an 'alien'. That's why Henry hadn't included her in his will.

When Mary Tudor died, Mary of Scots was in France, about to marry the dauphin and eventually become queen of France as well as Scotland. It was this French connection that made Mary unacceptable to Philip. The last thing he wanted was a Guise empire stretching from the Pyrenees to Scotland.

But although she wasn't to be queen of England, for the next 20 years Mary of Scotland was to be a thorn in Elizabeth's side.

It was the smoothest handover of power in 50 years. Elizabeth's backers had got men together, ready to face opposition from Catholics, Philip, *anybody*, but no one argued and the Elizabeth's men quietly put their weapons away.

What was the state of play in 1558?

- ✔ Pope Paul was hopeful. He'd lost faith in Mary because the Catholic comeback had stalled. He couldn't stand Cardinal Pole and the pair's deaths on the same day delighted him. Maybe Elizabeth would see sense and continue Mary's work. Oh dear – Part IV illustrates how naive his hope was!

- ✔ Philip needed England in his war against France, but Elizabeth was as devious as he was. Only time would tell how it would all work out (see Chapter 12).

- ✔ The bishops were uneasy. They received Elizabeth loyally (although some refused to go to her coronation) and they urged her not to make sudden, rash decisions but to check with the pope first.

- ✔ The Protestants hoped their time had come. Rumours of the new queen's religious leanings were too many not to be true. They expected a field day.

At Mary's funeral on 14 December 1558, Bishop John White of Winchester warned the congregation about the threat to religion. 'The wolves,' he said, 'be coming out of Geneva and other places . . . and have sent their books before them, full of pestilent doctrines, blasphemy and heresy to infect the people.'

He must have hoped, as many Catholics did, that the queen would marry a champion of the old faith who'd channel her in the right direction.

But nobody was ready for Elizabeth, as you can see in Chapters 12 to 18.

# Part IV
# Ending with Elizabeth

## The 5th Wave
### By Rich Tennant

"Hail, Elizabeth, By the Grace of God, Queen of England, France, and Ireland, Defender of the Faith, and Bachelorette Number One..."

# In this part . . .

After Henry VIII, Elizabeth is the other Tudor everybody knows about; red hair, white face, big ruff, hell of a temper. She was her father's daughter all right, and more of a man than many of her courtiers. She brought Protestantism and a bit of sanity back to religion, played house with at least two of her noblemen, had her cousin executed and went to war with Spain, the superpower of her age.

She was Gloriana, Orianna, Good Queen Bess. She only had the feeble body of a woman, but she wore the trousers in 16th-century England before trousers were even invented. A lot of people loved her (Leicester, Essex, Ralegh, Cecil, Walsingham) and a lot of people hated her too (Mary of Scots, Philip of Spain, most of Europe).

If Henry VIII was big, Elizabeth was bigger still, if only because she was a woman in a man's world. Her death in 1603 marked the end of a family whose like England shall never see again.

# Chapter 12

# Dancing with Elizabeth

· · · · · · · · · · · · · · · · · · · · · · · · · · · · · · · · · · · · · · · · · · · · · · · · · · · · ·

▶ Making over the Council and Chamber

▶ Playing the marriage game

▶ Entertaining Elizabeth

▶ Playing pirates

▶ Annoying the king of Spain

· · · · · · · · · · · · · · · · · · · · · · · · · · · · · · · · · · · · · · · · · · · · · · · · · · · · ·

*E*lizabeth took over the reins of government smoothly. Like a breath of
fresh air, she cleared out her Court, negotiated with foreign powers,
organised the navy and backed overseas voyages. Over it all, she kept everybody guessing about her marriage – would she? Wouldn't she? Who to?
When? Everybody asked and nobody got an answer.

But the first ten years of Elizabeth's reign were nervy ones: the new queen
lived on the edge as enemies closed around her.

## Clearing Out the Court

The queen was crowned at Westminster Abbey on 15 January 1559. Paintings
of the occasion show the 25-year-old with long golden hair flowing down her
back, her dress and stomacher of gold cloth, holding the orb and sceptre in
her hands. On her head is a glittering golden crown, set with rubies and emeralds. None of this stuff has survived today – the Crown Jewels in the Tower of
London only date from Charles II (1660) – but check them out even so.

This was a different style of coronation to Mary's or Henry VIII's or Henry
VII's. Elizabeth's service was performed by the bishop of Carlisle because the
archbishop of York refused to go; and the ceremony was in English as well as
in Latin. Protestant pageantry was everywhere you looked – a sign of things
to come (see Chapter 13).

Elizabeth's first job was to sort out her closest advisers.

# Purging the Privy Chamber

The Privy Chamber was meant to comprise the queen's most trusted confidantes (see Chapter 1), so all 23 of Mary's closest circle got the elbow and were replaced with Elizabeth's relatives, especially the Seymours, Dudleys and Greys.

Because the monarch was female, ladies-in-waiting were now closest to the queen. They dressed her, bathed her and put her to bed. She can't have been able to keep many secrets from them. Katherine Ashley was her closest confidante, a sort of mother figure who'd been with Elizabeth since she was a child. Two new girls on the block were Lady Knollys (pronounced Noles) and Lady Carey. Others were the wives and daughters of new ministers (see below).

Some of the men of the Chamber stayed put, like Katherine's husband John, the grooms and ushers (who looked after horses and opened doors).

Out of a total of 50 Chamber members under Mary, Elizabeth changed nearly 40. If that didn't send a message as to how the new queen was going to operate, nothing would.

# Choosing the Council

When it came to the Council , Elizabeth was more cautious (see Chapter 1 for the Council's responsibilities). Courtiers could come and go but statesmen were important, and she chose men who hopefully would stay loyal for life. Here's how the new queen shook up the Council:

- **Kicked out:** Principal Secretary John Boxall was fired – the man was an ardent Catholic. The dodgy Lord Paget (see Chapter 11 for his views on Elizabeth) was also shown the door, as was Nicholas Heath as lord chancellor.

- **New blood:** Elizabeth recruited two of the cleverest men of their generation. William Cecil (later Lord Burghley) became the queen's secretary of state and right-hand man, and Nicholas Bacon became lord keeper of the great seal. Elizabeth tasked these two men with sorting out her Church (see Chapter 13).

- **Retained:** The old marquis of Winchester stayed as lord treasurer and Lord Clinton kept his job as lord admiral (even though he was a crony of Philip's). Elizabeth also kept the earls of Arundel, Shrewsbury and Pembroke. They were Catholics, but not rabid, and were intensely loyal to the queen.

About a dozen of Mary's advisers stayed on.

It was all about balance. When Elizabeth came to the throne she had a country that was broke, divided, unhappy and disease ridden. She had to mend fences as well as jump over them. So the old faces in the Council represented continuity and experience, and the new ones, like the earl of Bedford and Lord Cobham, stood for change. Elizabeth's Council was 20 strong, half the size of Mary's.

This Council was the first one without a single churchman in it. The councillors were mostly elderly (the marquis of Winchester was 85) and were either university men or lawyers from the London Inns of Court, but not one of them had a religious background. Even when Matthew Parker was appointed archbishop of Canterbury in 1559 he couldn't join Elizabeth's exclusive club.

# Marrying the Job

From Sarah Bernhardt to Cate Blanchett, actresses have longed to play Elizabeth because her reign has it all – vicious politics, terrible tortures, naval battles on the high seas and discoveries of the New World. And the story of Elizabeth's personal life is just as colourful – child molestations, sexual abnormality, did she/didn't she, and if so, with whom . . .

## Getting a picture of Elizabeth's sexuality

So what do we know about Elizabeth's sex life?

- ✔ She was examined by doctors at the age of 13 and we don't know a) why and b) what their findings were. Today we still wonder whether Elizabeth had some sort of physical abnormality that made sex difficult or impossible.

- ✔ She was seduced at 14 by Lord Thomas Seymour in 1548. He liked to chase her through the garden and slap her backside. In a bizarre scene, Catherine Parr once held the girl down while Seymour cut Elizabeth's dress to gawp at her undies and presumably the body underneath. Weird or what?

- ✔ Descriptions of the princess/young queen tell us she was attractive, with golden hair, a high forehead (considered a sign of intelligence) and very beautiful hands with long fingers that she fluttered while she talked. She liked wearing particularly low cut dresses, not always on the most appropriate occasions.

- ✔ She was a notorious flirt, fluttering her eyelashes at ambassadors like Count Feria (see Chapter 11), courtiers like Robert Dudley (see the later section 'Dallying with Dudley') and even the odd servant.

## Looking for Mr Right

It was expected – and Elizabeth's first Parliament suggested – that the queen would marry. So it wasn't a matter of whether but whom, and Elizabeth had a number of options:

- ✔ **The duke of Savoy:** Been there, done that. In Chapter 11 you see that this was Philip's idea to shut up his sister-in-law and remove her as a threat to Mary.

- ✔ **The earl of Arundel:** A nice old boy, but at 46 he could've been Elizabeth's father.

- ✔ **Sir William Pickering:** A handsome soldier but he made no effort.

- ✔ **Philip of Spain:** He put himself forward (largely as a matter of duty) as early as 10 January 1559, before the coronation. Elizabeth turned him down (politely) on the grounds of the Leviticus warning about marrying your dead wife's sister that had caused Henry VIII so much grief (see Chapter 6).

Parliament wasn't best pleased when they asked Elizabeth about marriage and her answer was, 'And in the end, this shall for me be sufficient, that a marble stone shall declare that a queen, having reigned such a time, lived and died a virgin.' Well, okay; Parliament had other problems just then, but they weren't going to let the matter drop.

## Wanting it all

Elizabeth didn't want 'a man about the kingdom', as Mary had with Philip, but marriage and child bearing was still at the heart of the Tudor problem. She was the last child of Henry VIII and beyond her the line got very murky indeed.

Even if Elizabeth had no physical problems in conceiving, the idea of marriage can hardly have appealed. She'd seen Mary's unhappiness first-hand and her life had been dominated by her father's string of marital mess-ups (see Chapter 5).

The Enabling Act of 1554 had *ungendered* the crown – the queen was a man as far as the Constitution went. Even so, Mary's marriage to Philip (see Chapter 11) had shown everybody the risks. A foreign husband would have his own agenda, and as king he'd be able to use England in any future alliance or war. A home-grown husband would be more acceptable to the foreigner-hating English, but he'd stir up the old family squabbles that had made the Wars of the Roses possible (see Chapter 2).

With hindsight, we can see that all Elizabeth's flirtations with proposals (see the following section) were a bluff, but it wasn't like that at the time. Each proposal seemed genuine and Elizabeth had weigh each up carefully.

---

# The political and the personal

Tudor marriages weren't to do with love; they were all about politics. This is what was happening in the politics of 16th-century Europe:

✔ Spain was becoming *the* superpower, thanks to silver from the New World. Spain's power led to clashes with Barbary (North African) pirates, the Ottoman (Turkish) Empire in the east and the Dutch (see Chapter 15).

✔ France was falling apart. The accidental jousting death of Henri II in 1559 led to a power struggle and years of warfare called the Wars of Religion, which let in the English, the Spaniards and the Germans.

✔ The Counter-Reformation was a comeback by the Catholic Church that brought all kinds of problems involving Spain, England and of course the papacy. Elizabeth changed marital direction depending on who was top dog in Europe. By the 1560s the Roman Empire was on its way down, but Spain was on its way up. As Spain got pushier in the 1570s, however, Elizabeth went right off the idea of a Habsburg connection.

---

# *Toying with the talent*

European princes were lining up as soon as Elizabeth was crowned.

✔ **Eric XIV of Sweden:** He'd already tried it on before Mary died but the Council turned him down because he was a Lutheran. Elizabeth rejected Eric, partly because his little brother, John, duke of Finland, was sent over to woo her. She may have known Eric was as mad as a March hare, paranoid and suspicious to the point of having several courtiers murdered. He was dethroned in 1569 and spent his last years writing psalms before somebody poisoned him with arsenic. Good call, Elizabeth!

✔ **Charles of Austria:** He was Philip's cousin and the son of the new Roman emperor, Ferdinand. He was Catholic but 'flexible' and not in line for the throne so he was free to pop over for a life of bliss with Elizabeth. Charles wasn't very keen but Elizabeth pretended to be (at first) and William Cecil liked the idea. After two years of Elizabeth putting religious and financial obstacles in the pre-nup, Charles gave up.

✔ **Henri of Valois, duke of Anjou:** He was the younger brother of King Charles IX of France and son of the terrifying Catherine de Medici. Elizabeth only considered him as a possible rebuff to the ever more threatening attitude of Philip II of Spain. Henri was only 18 at the time and a rabid Catholic. Negotiations dragged on between 1569 and 1572 when it all went to hell in a handcart when Elizabeth discovered that Catherine de Medici and Henri were up to their necks in the slaughter of 40,000 Protestants in Paris on St Bartholomew's Day, 24 August. Another narrow escape!

✔ **François, duke of Alençon:** Catherine de Medici (see the previous bullet) had other sons and wasn't going to give up a crack at England that easily. As pushy mothers go, de Medici takes some beating. François was her youngest boy and Secretary of State Lord Burghley was getting desperate. The queen was 39 – only three years younger than Mary when she died – and her biological clock may well have stopped already. Elizabeth was old enough to be Alençon's mother, but by 1578 she seemed keen to start on him again. Spain was on the rampage (see 'Sailing in New Directions', later in this chapter) and the duke of Anjou (as Alençon was by now) seemed a likely prospect to keep Philip at arm's length.

The protestant John Stubbs wrote *The Gaping Gulf* as an attack on the Anjou marriage. The poet Spenser had a go at it too in *Mother Hubbard's Tale* but he got away with it, probably because he was usually buttering Elizabeth up with stories about the Faerie Queen. Stubbs had his right hand cut off (it was an Elizabethan belief that whatever body part had offended should be removed) but still had the guts to sweep off his hat with his left hand and shout 'God save the queen!' before fainting. Cool, or what?

Marriage negotiations with Anjou went on until 1581 (by which time Elizabeth was 48), and when he arrived in England Elizabeth went all schoolgirl over him, giving him a ring and telling everybody they were in love. This was either a rush of blood to the head or a scam of some kind all along, because days later Elizabeth told Anjou marriage was impossible. 'Goodbye' was all she wrote.

In this whirlwind ride through marriage proposals from foreigners, we've travelled over 24 years. As each one passed, the queen's likelihood of pregnancy diminished and the succession faded. The quest for a groom was all about politics – Elizabeth's heart, though not her head, lay elsewhere.

## Dallying with Dudley

Did they? Didn't they? The one man who undoubtedly held a special place in Elizabeth's heart was Robert Dudley, whom she made master of the horse and earl of Leicester. This book contains so many Dudleys (check them out in Chapters 7, 8 and 9) that for clarity's sake we'll call this one Leicester, although he wasn't given the title until 1564.

### Childhood sweethearts?

Leicester was the fourth son of the duke of Northumberland and was almost exactly the same age as Elizabeth. They knew each other well and may have had joint lessons with the same tutor. At the age of 17 Leicester married Amy Robsart, the daughter of Sir John Robsart, a Norfolk gentleman.

Three years later Leicester was imprisoned in the Tower for his part in his father's attempt to keep Mary off the throne (see Chapter 9) and he found himself a cell or two away from Elizabeth. The story goes that he lent her cash when they were released, although she was richer than he was. William Cecil, who watched over Elizabeth like a mother hen (he'd run her estates even before she became queen), found Leicester pushy and didn't like him.

## Favouring the favourite

When the queen made Leicester her master of the horse, ears at Court began to prick up.

The first master of the horse was Thomas Brandon, brother of William, who'd saved Henry VII's life at Bosworth (see Chapter 2). Then, under Henry VIII at the Field of the Cloth of Gold (see Chapter 3), the master of the horse was Henry Guildford. Leicester held the job for 14 years. The job was a government appointment until 1924, changing with each ministry; since then it's been permanent. Next time you watch the Trooping of the Colour on TV, check out the master of the horse – he's the guy with a scarlet tunic and cocked hat riding the white horse. You can't miss him.

Because the position involved running the royal stables as well as advising on cavalry horses for the army, it gave Leicester unlimited access to Elizabeth who, like her father, was very keen on riding and hunting. Elizabeth had Leicester's apartments moved nearer hers and she popped in to see him at all hours. Her ladies, who'd usually be present as chaperones with any male visitor to the queen, were told to make themselves scarce.

So were they actually lovers? Here's the evidence:

- ✔ The Spanish ambassador, de Quadra, saw the couple canoodling on a barge in 1561.

- ✔ When Elizabeth made him earl of Leicester, people noticed her tickling his neck as she put the collar on.

- ✔ In August 1565 Leicester rode under the queen's window on his way back from a hunt. She appeared at the casement 'undressed' (relax, guys, that really means in her nightie, but in Tudor times nighties were naughty).

- ✔ The French ambassador told the Spanish ambassador in 1566 that Leicester had slept with the queen on New Year's night.

- ✔ There were rumours that Elizabeth had given birth to a son – Arthur Dudley – who was spirited out of Hampton Court and brought up by somebody else.

When Elizabeth was ill with smallpox in October 1562 and thought she was dying she said that she loved Lord Robert dearly, as God was her witness, and that nothing improper had ever passed between them.

In the various films on Elizabeth, Leicester hardly gets a mention until Cate Blanchett's version. Joseph Fiennes is a swaggering, petulant Leicester (and a hell of a dancer), childishly upset because the queen has to spend time with various suitors, but 21st-century audiences have to have it spelled out, so Leicester and the queen go to bed.

Did they really? Didn't they really? We'll never know. The important thing is this – whatever their relationship, Elizabeth kept Leicester in his place, once shouting at him, 'God's death [Elizabeth swore like a trooper] my lord, I will have here but one mistress and no master.' The earl of Leicester kept a slightly lower profile after that!

The man most alarmed by the Leicester fling was William Cecil. Leicester was married and the scandal, if the affair was exposed, might well lose Elizabeth the throne (her first years were pretty insecure, with two serious illnesses and a Church to sort out; see Chapter 13.) Cecil knew that Leicester wasn't very bright and was a poor judge of character. At the very least, any marriage would upset the Council's apple cart and Cecil had set his sights on Archduke Charles of Spain.

### Clearing the path for marriage: by foul means?

By 1560 the queen seemed to be in love. De Quadra, who'd taken over from de Feria as Philip's watchdog, spread the rumour that Elizabeth and Leicester were planning to poison Amy Dudley so they could marry. He called Leicester 'the king that is to be'.

On Sunday 8 September Amy told all her servants at the family home at Cumnor, Oxfordshire to go to a local fair at Abingdon. Only three ladies stayed with her and they 'played at tables' (probably chess or backgammon). At some point, Amy got up, left the room, tripped on her way out and fell downstairs. Her neck was broken. What are the options?

- **Accident:** You try walking in a heavy Elizabethan farthingale dress (on the other hand, Amy was used to it).

- **Suicide:** Had she heard the rumours about hubby and the queen and decided to end it all? On the other hand, throwing yourself down the stairs isn't a certain way to kill yourself.

- **Murder:** If so, who? Leicester, obviously, but he wasn't there at the time. Somebody suggested one of his cronies, Anthony Forster.

Whatever actually happened to Lady Dudley, the inquest jury returned an accidental death verdict. But the murder rumours wouldn't go away. Leicester didn't help himself by not going either to the inquest or the funeral, but nevertheless, as was customary, he had to stay away from Court. There were rumours of jury tampering and counter-claims that Amy Dudley had breast cancer that had caused depression.

SEEN ON SCREEN

## Faking it as a pale redhead

Remember that scene at the end of *Elizabeth* when Cate Blanchett decides to dump her live-in lover Robert Dudley and become a professional virgin, complete with ghastly white make-up and curly red wig? Well, it never happened. The make-up and wig belong to a much later period in her life and were supposed to make her look more attractive, not less, and Dudley hung around until his death in 1588. Elizabeth only pushed the virgin queen bit when it was obvious she was past child-bearing age.

REMEMBER

If it *was* murder and Leicester was behind it, the whole thing backfired because the scandal made Elizabeth see sense and the idea of marrying went out of the window.

Even so, on paper Leicester prospered. He got his earldom in the September of 1564 and was made a member of the Privy Council. This meant that Cecil could keep an eye on him but it didn't stop the reckless Leicester from getting involved in a coup against Cecil in 1569. It failed; he apologised to the queen; they kissed (maybe!) and made up.

### Blowing hot and cold

After 1569 the relationship between Elizabeth and Leicester changed with the seasons. In 1578 he secretly married the countess of Essex, Lettice Knollys – so she became Lettice Leicester! Elizabeth was very touchy about her ladies, expecting to be told their every move and whim. After the hush-hush wedding, the Leicesters were barred from Court for a while.

Later, in 1585, Elizabeth cooled down and made Leicester her agent in the Low Countries (today's Netherlands). He was soon feathering his nest with the local Government, the Estates General. Elizabeth recalled him in disgrace.

When Leicester died in 1588, the queen was genuinely heartbroken. She always kept his last letter, a reminder of the nearest thing to a love affair she'd ever known.

# Riding a Cock Horse

One way in which Elizabeth kept in touch with her country in the days before television and the queen's speech at Christmas was to go on *progresses,* riding with half her Court through the south of England. She never went too far from London, probably because of the risk of a coup if she did.

The old nursery rhyme goes:

> Ride a cock horse to Banbury Cross,
>
> To see a fine lady upon a white horse.
>
> Rings on her fingers and bells on her toes,
>
> She shall have music wherever she goes.

And if the fine lady isn't Elizabeth, who is it?

The company travelled less than 10 miles a day and put up at other people's country houses, where they expected to be fed, wined and entertained – at ridiculous expense.

On 4 September 1566 the queen went to Oxford. What for?

- ✔ She listened to sermons and disputations by the university's scholars. She understood their Latin perfectly and this impressed the scholars – their queen was intellectual, just like them.

- ✔ She watched a play, *Palomon and Arcite*, performed in Christ Church College, proving how much she loved the theatre and could identify with classical drama.

- ✔ She honoured Robert Dudley whom she'd appointed as chancellor of the University in September of 1564.

- ✔ Most importantly of all, she made sure that the town and the university accepted her as supreme governor of the English Church and let them know what she thought of heretics.

Just like her father, Elizabeth enjoyed glittering social occasions. In Coventry in 1565 she 'won the hearts of all her loving subjects', according to the town's mayor, but the high points of her progresses came in the mid-1570s.

The queen was in Warwick in 1572 and Bristol in 1574, and in 1575 she pulled out all the travelling stops by visiting Worcester, Lichfield, Reading, Woodstock and Windsor. In Warwick the entire town turned out to see their monarch and the recorder of the town read out a five-page (count them!) history of the place. At the end Elizabeth sent for the man: 'Come hither, little recorder.' He knelt and kissed her hand. She said, 'It was told me that you would be afraid to look upon me or to speak boldly, but you were not so afraid of me as I was of you.'

Next time you're in Warwickshire, check out Kenilworth Castle. It's a ruin today and if you stand in the low ground to the south of the curtain wall and shout, you'll hear your voice come back to you – that's because you're in Echo Fields. The area was deliberately flooded in 1575 by Lord Leicester who lived there, and when the queen arrived there was boating on the lake and the whole place was lit up by fireworks. The knot garden where they walked is still there. Okay, so Leicester had the hots for the queen and wanted to marry her, but the three-week stay must have seriously damaged his bank balance. Leicester put on poetry by George Gascoigne, top poet of the day, bear baiting, hunting, music, dancing and incredible banquets. Somebody painted Elizabeth and Leicester dancing the Volta; the cheeky nobleman is throwing the queen in the air to wild clapping and music – and she's loving every minute of it!

But the progresses weren't just remembered for their lively parties. It was very unfortunate that the queen's progress to Norwich in 1579 went horribly wrong. Norwich was delighted with the usual speeches, music, hunting and frivolities. But it was a bit like hosting the Olympic Games today – huge prestige but at a price. Thousands of townsfolk caught bubonic plague – the Black Death – from somebody in the entourage and thousands died before the disease burnt itself out.

For about six years before the Armada (1588; see Chapter 15) the progresses stopped. But they started again in the 1590s when the queen was old and perhaps wanted to recapture her youth – because she was worth it. She often ordered her coachman to drive her into the thickest of the crowds to talk to the ordinary people and she stood up on the carriage steps and thanked them.

On one of her later progresses Elizabeth took the opportunity to kiss and make up with an old acquaintance. She'd once put Edward Seymour, earl of Hertford, in prison for daring to marry Catherine, the sister of Jane Grey. When she arrived at his home in Odiham in Hampshire in September 1591, all seemed forgiven. After three days of fireworks, feasts and fun, a choir sang 'Come Again, Fair Nature's Treasure' as the queen left.

Elizabeth made her last progress, through Middlesex and Buckinghamshire, in the last year of her life.

# Sailing in New Directions

Ever since Christopher Columbus had gone West in 1492, Europe had been poised on the brink of a brave new world. Henry VII had famously backed the wrong ship (Cabot rather than Columbus – see Chapter 2), and government investment in overseas trade and exploration was slow to take off under Edward VI. Under Mary, the investment had ground to a halt because she had no interest in the trade and exploration and had clashed with the largely Protestant merchants of the City of London on religious grounds.

The livery companies of the City were like stockbrokers today. They made huge profits buying and selling and often lent money to the Crown. Leaders of the mercers', goldsmiths' and fishmongers' companies were also courtiers, so close government links existed. Thomas Gresham continued as the crown agent in the Low Countries so business picked up again under Elizabeth (see Chapter 9).

## *Slaving with Hawkins*

John Hawkins was the son of a Plymouth merchant who moved to London in 1554 to work closely with the Navy Board and the City, both of which invested in overseas voyages. He was determined to cash in on one of the biggest money spinners in history – the slave trade (see the nearby sidebar).

One problem was that Spain and Portugal had got the jump on the English and had already grabbed several markets. That would all change in 1562 when Hawkins hijacked a slave ship.

---

### The queen is in her counting house

Elizabeth seems to have inherited her grandfather Henry VII's careful ways with money (see Chapter 2). Her prudence was quite handy in the Protestant days of Edward because she could wear the dull clothes that were the fashion of the time and these were cheap. Under Mary she was genuinely strapped and got used to checking her figures herself. She saved £1,500 in 1552 largely because she only gave away 7 pounds 15 shillings and 8 pence to charity.

In the year of the Armada (1588 – see Chapter 15) Elizabeth actually sold bullets to her own soldiers, and when the earl of Essex (see Chapter 16) came back from his expedition to Cadiz she wanted an account of every penny spent. She worked out that in 1599 the king of France owed her 401,734 pounds 16 shillings and 5½ pence! She told her Parliament in 1566, 'I thank God that I am imbued with such qualities that if I were turned out of my realm in my petticoat, I were able to live in any place in Christendom.'

Elizabeth borrowed more and more from the City of London and less from Antwerp, but she always had ongoing cash flow problems.

# The slave trade

Slavery was widespread in the ancient world of Greece and Rome, which Renaissance men looked back on with a mixture of awe and fondness. In Tudor England men like Hawkins were muscling in on an institution that was already making serious money in the Middle East, Africa and the Americas – the movement of black Africans, in chains, to wherever they were needed for back-breaking manual labour. Between 1450 and 1870 an estimated 11.5 million slaves were taken to the Americas, mostly from West Africa (then called, for obvious reasons, the Slave Coast).

Arabs and Europeans benefited from the slave trade and African development was held up. Nobody, even devout Christians, seems to have had a moral problem with buying, selling and owning somebody else in the Tudor period.

## *Voyage #1 (1561)*

Hawkins got hold of slave cargoes on two ships and sailed them to Tenerife in the Canary Islands (a gorgeous holiday destination now – check the islands out!). He sold all his slaves to Spanish colonists in exchange for hides, sugar, ginger and pearls. The sales were illegal because Hawkins wasn't a Spaniard (see Chapter 11 for Philip II's ruling on this) and his goods were confiscated in Seville. The Spaniards called him a pirate (which is fair enough), but Hawkins still made a huge profit.

## *Voyage #2 (1564)*

Nothing succeeds like success and suddenly everybody wanted in on Hawkins' second trip. Several councillors, like Cecil and the earl of Pembroke, invested and the queen, ever with an eye to the main chance, gave Hawkins a fully armed ship stuffed with provisions – 'God bless all who sail in her'.

This voyage took royal involvement to a new level. Monarchs had leased ships to merchants occasionally in the past, always going to European ports, but Elizabeth now showed a new commitment to sea power.

Once again the Spaniards and the Portuguese objected, and once again Hawkins bullied people into buying from him. At various places in the Caribbean, Hawkins claimed to be trading on behalf of the queen (not true) and his chat placed Elizabeth and England in troubled waters. But because most people were making loads of money out of the voyages, they thought it was worth the hassle.

# The not-so-common market

Nearer to home Elizabeth faced commercial problems. After the slump in the 1550s English cloth exports had picked up a bit but not enough. Why?

✔ Dutch Protestants were complaining about Philip's high-handed government of the Spanish Netherlands and England sympathised with them. This in turn niggled with the merchants of Antwerp, who put petty restrictions on cloth being shipped through the port.

✔ Margaret of Parma, the regent of the Low Countries, put an embargo on English cloth in 1564, so trade now switched to Emden in Germany. Cecil thought the move would widen the market; the merchant adventurers disagreed. The embargo ended in 1566 but others had now grabbed the markets, and when Margaret was replaced by Philip's hardliner, the duke of Alba (see Chapters 10 and 11), the English had to leave again.

### Giving Lovell a go

Anglo–Spanish relations were at a low in 1566 and the Spanish ambassador demanded that the queen stop Hawkins from his slave-trading raids by not letting him sail. A voyage by the inexperienced John Lovell was entirely backed by private enterprise and came back in September 1567 with a small profit. At least Lovell's trip didn't worsen the diplomatic situation.

### Voyage #3 (1567)

Elizabeth changed her mind (she was good at that) and backed another Hawkins trip in October 1567. He sailed from Plymouth (one of the major ports in the West Country – check out the town's links with Francis Drake and see his statue on the Hoe) with four of his own ships and two provided by the Crown. Again, he claimed to be sailing under the queen's commission and again, it wasn't true.

Things got tough for Hawkins in Guinea late in 1567. The Portuguese authorities there had had a tip-off and he lost men in a fire fight before getting involved in black tribal warfare in today's Sierra Leone. He still got his slaves, though, and sold them at Cartagena in Columbia before heading home.

### Harassing Hawkins

On the way back to England from his third voyage, Hawkins' luck ran out. One of the ships in his fleet, the *Jesus of Lubeck*, belonged to the queen. It was leaking badly and Hawkins put in to San Juan d'Ulloa, the port of Mexico City. Unfortunately, a Spanish fleet arrived at the same time, bringing the new viceroy of the Indies, Don Martin Enriquez.

All hell broke loose and Hawkins had to cut and run, leaving the *Jesus* and her crewmen behind. At sea, Hawkins' remaining ships became separated,

Francis Drake's *Judith* making so much headway that Hawkins accused him of desertion (hot tempered lot, these sea dogs!). Hawkins limped into Vigo and got back to England in January 1569 with only a handful of his original crew.

Hawkins had a go at Drake and the Spanish authorities in Mexico, demanding huge compensation via the Admiralty Court. He hadn't got a leg to stand on of course, because he shouldn't have been in San Juan d'Ulloa in the first place.

Elizabeth had shot herself in the foot and relations with Philip went further down the tubes.

## *Menacing from Spain*

Hawkins and Drake's 'Boys' Own Adventures' (see the nearby sidebar 'El Draco') didn't impress the Spaniards. Philip demanded compensation for the looting of the Spanish colonies and this renewed aggression may have been why Elizabeth started smarming around France and the duke of Anjou again (see the earlier section 'Toying with the talent').

Elizabeth continued the complicated dance of diplomacy and marriage negotiations. She knew that her navy was fast becoming (thanks to John Hawkins – see Chapter 15) the best in the world and that Philip was probably behind various plots on her life (see Chapter14).

---

## Turning a blind eye to the privateers

Since the 14th century ships had sometimes acted on behalf of the crown with *letters of marque*, the official green light to attack foreign ships and steal their goodies. A slice of the action went to these pirates, who called themselves *privateers*, and to the rest to the Crown. If challenged, as Elizabeth frequently was by Spain, she'd deny all knowledge and tut tut about her unruly subjects. The Hawkinses of Plymouth were at the cutting edge of this privateering and Elizabeth's attitude was typical of her fence-sitting for England.

Philip II had said that England couldn't take part in the American trade, which was exactly what Hawkins did. Francis Drake, Walter Ralegh, John Hawkins and Martin Frobisher were among the famous names (mostly from the stroppy West Country) who attacked Spanish and Flemish ships in the Channel and the Western Approaches. (See the map in Chapter 15).

Nearer to home, the captain of the Isle of Wight, Edward Horsey, was taking a cut from French smugglers and pirates operating out of Mead Hole on the island (it's now a tourist spot in the grounds of Queen Victoria's Osborne House – check it out). Elizabeth turned a blind eye to all of this, knowing that much of it would annoy Philip and that later, when the Dutch revolt in the Spanish Netherlands broke out, he'd keep his warships elsewhere.

# El Draco

Francis Drake was making a name for himself by the 1570s. He hit a Spanish silver convoy near Nombre de Dios on the coast of Panama in 1573 with French Huguenots (Protestants), neatly offending Spain, Catholics and the French Government in one swift movement. Both his brothers were killed, but he was now feared by the Spaniards. El Draco was a clever pun on his name – in Spanish it means *The Dragon* or *The Devil*.

In November 1577 Drake set sail from Plymouth to explore the South Pacific. His investors included Leicester, Hawkins, the lord admiral and other members of the Council and Navy Board. The queen gave him one ship, the *Swallow*.

The exploration turned into a mega raid. Drake executed his number two, Thomas Doughty, for

insubordination and hit the Spanish colonies' towns on the West Coast of South America. He got to Southern California, looking for the mythical Straits of Anian, which were said to link the Atlantic with the Pacific. Good seamanship and luck brought him across the Indian Ocean, round the Cape of Good Hope to Sierra Leone by July 1580.

Drake came home a hero, the best known privateer of his day and the first Englishman to sail round the world, and he brought back a lot of loot. The queen was delighted and knighted Drake on the deck of his ship, the *Pelican* (renamed the *Golden Hind*), at Deptford on the Thames in London.

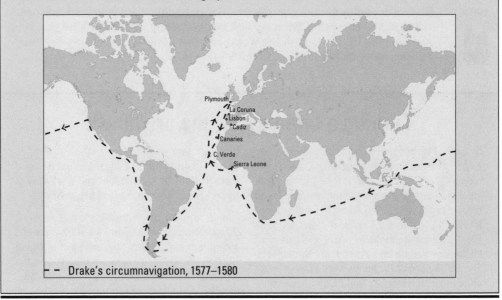

Plymouth
La Coruna
Lisbon
Cadiz
Canaries
C. Verde
Sierra Leone

– – Drake's circumnavigation, 1577–1580

Philip, on the other hand, knew that English pirates had been attacking his treasure ships for years. It could only be a matter of time before outright war broke out.

# Chapter 13

# Choosing the Middle Way between Protestants and Catholics

. . . . . . . . . . . . . . . . . . . . . . . . . . . . . . . . . . . . . . . . . .

## In This Chapter

▶ Setting up a new Church

▶ Underlining the Royal Supremacy

▶ Imposing on Ireland

▶ Saying goodbye to France

▶ Uncovering plots (and Mary Queen of Scots)

▶ Weighing up Elizabeth's first decade

. . . . . . . . . . . . . . . . . . . . . . . . . . . . . . . . . . . . . . . . . .

*W*hen filling in a form today that asks about religion, many people in Britain write *C of E*. This is shorthand for the Church of England, which was essentially the brainchild of Elizabeth I.

When she became queen, Elizabeth was only too aware of the upheavals in religion throughout her life. In some ways, because of who her mother was (Anne Boleyn), she could be said to be part of those upheavals. Now she was determined to build her *via media* (a middle way, or compromise) that would bring Catholics and Protestants together.

## Settling the Faith

What was the religious situation when Elizabeth became queen?

> ✔ Everybody expected the new queen to make changes. Anybody in the know knew that Elizabeth was a Protestant; her vague pretence to be Catholic had been for her sister Mary's benefit only.

> ✔ The Catholic Counter-Reformation in England (see Chapter 8) had stalled badly between 1557 and 1558 because Mary fell out of favour with the pope and Cardinal Pole died.

Elizabeth could easily have carried on without change until she'd found her feet, but that wasn't her way.

## Gauging opinion

The bishops supported Elizabeth as queen (but not the archbishop of York, who was unhappy with her religious settlement; see Chapter 12), but they warned her that if she changed things, God would send his lightning bolts.

In 1559 the same sort of attitudes prevailed as at the start of Mary's reign six years earlier (see Chapter 10):

- ✔ Some people wanted to see a return to the Church 'as King Henry left it' – Six Articles, an English Bible, no monasteries, no pope (see Chapter 6 for details of Henry and the Church). The difference now was that Catholic and Protestant had become more obvious and more opposed. The clergy of 1559 once again looked to the pope as their boss.

- ✔ Some wanted a full Protestant set-up – English services and prayer books and no Catholic 'hocus-pocus'. Men who'd run for their lives when Mary became queen started coming back from exile in Europe.

Most people – the mildly conservative silent majority – decided to wait and see.

A Protestant Church would be a fresh start, a clean break and a chance to promote very clever men (many of them still in exile) to be bishops. It would also put Elizabeth in the driving seat. On the other hand, those who were strongly Catholic were still a large minority and the move would be bound to upset them.

## Pinning down the queen's beliefs

What did the queen actually believe?

- ✔ Her mother, Anne Boleyn, may have supported the religious reformers to an extent but Elizabeth could have few memories of her, so it's not very important.

- ✔ Under Edward she no doubt went Protestant – hence the simple, cheap clothes. She accepted the 42 Articles of the Faith in 1553 (see Chapter 8) and believed in only two sacraments – baptism and communion.

- ✔ Under Mary Elizabeth went through the motions of Catholicism, taking the mass, but even Mary realised her commitment wasn't for real. But Elizabeth did like a bit of Catholic colour – music in church, crosses and candles – and was suspicious of married priests in line with Catholic beliefs.

✔ Elizabeth followed in the footsteps of her father in dismantling the few monasteries that Mary had set up.

✔ She believed in Church government by bishops (the *episcopalian system*) and that they should be appointed by her, not the pope (who was now out forever). She was careful to choose conscientious churchmen, not mere yes men, and she paid them well.

✔ She had no opposition to Church courts, and they went on as before, with no change from Mary's reign.

It may have been Elizabeth's intention to turn the cathedrals into power-houses of reformed teaching, but she met a lot of resistance. Some of the cathedral clergy lost their jobs because they wouldn't take the oath of Royal Supremacy (Henry VIII had men killed for that – see Thomas More in Chapter 4). It would take a generation to make a real difference in the cathedrals.

No doubt Elizabeth was a Christian, but she often consulted her magus, the astrologer Dr John Dee (Chapter 17 has the lowdown on him).

## Clashing over uniformity

Parliament accepted a new Bill of Royal Supremacy in January 1559. Only the bishops in the Lords voted against the bill, and they were a small minority. Elizabeth now called herself supreme governor of the Church of England, and the bishops and an Ecclesiastical Commission handled the day-to-day business.

The House of Commons had no real Catholics in 1559 – so much for Mary's old faith having won the hearts and minds of her subjects.

The Royal Supremacy was one thing, but bringing back the 1552 prayer book (see Chapter 8) was altogether more difficult. The Commons accepted the book but the more conservatively minded Lords said no – they wanted a return to the Church as King Henry VIII had left it, stepping back from the full Protestantism of Edward VI.

Elizabeth suspended Parliament over Easter 1559 to give herself time to think.

Although Elizabeth can't have known it, the Lords blocking the prayer book was a warning for the future power balance between monarch and Parliament (see Chapter 14 for more on this). Seeking backing from Parliament of course meant the risk of not getting backing at all. For Elizabeth merely to suspend or dismiss Parliament until they came up with the answer she wanted wasn't the right thing to do. In 1642, clashing with Parliament led to Civil War and in 1649 Charles I lost his head because of it. Today, the actual powers of the monarch are very limited and Parliament calls the shots. The last time a monarch stopped an act of Parliament was in 1884, when Victoria vetoed a bill on lesbianism.

Elizabeth's strategy was clever. She let the members of Parliament fall out among themselves. Over Easter the old and new bishops agreed on a debate to iron out the situation. The old party blew the rules of procedure during the debate and two of the bishops went to jail for contempt. In this weakened state, when Parliament was recalled the Lords' vote went Elizabeth's way by one vote. Phew!

After building her *via media* (middle way) Elizabeth made no more religious changes. Religious ideas were changing, however – more and more extreme forms of Protestantism were gaining ground. Many reformers wanted a Church run by *synods* (assemblies of clergy and important laymen) not by the bishops and the queen. Elizabeth saw this as an attack on the Royal Supremacy and her own role as governor of the Church. She believed her role was God-given. The methods may be negotiable; the authority itself wasn't.

Elizabeth's Church remained Protestant, emphasising preaching and the use of the English Bible, but the clergy still wore flashy clothes (vestments) and stuck to the set services from the prayer book. By the end of her reign, people unhappy with the Church broke away to form a number of sects on the 'left' of Elizabeth's compromise. The dissenters were every bit as rabid as the Catholics on the 'right', and we have a detailed look at them in Chapter 14.

## *Telling little white lies to Rome*

Pope Paul IV died in August 1559 (hurrah, all of Rome cheered! – see Chapter 10) and the new man was Pius IV. He didn't terrify people like Paul, he had three illegitimate children and he spent most of his time finding jobs in the Vatican for his relatives.

England had no papal ambassador for the rest of Elizabeth's reign, so all news about what was going on in the country reached Rome via the Low Countries (today's Netherlands) or the Spanish ambassador.

No important Catholic was in the mood for a crusade against England. Elizabeth claimed that her Church was essentially Catholic, only a bit different 'in certain particulars' (which was nonsense). Pius chose to believe it (anything for a quiet life) and Philip of Spain still wanted England as an ally.

When Pius invited England to send representatives to the ongoing Council of Trent (see Chapter 8) however, Elizabeth was put on the spot. She ignored the invitation, so blowing her 'Catholic' cover in terms of European diplomacy. Had she really been a supporter of Catholic ideas, she would have sent somebody; no representatives were ever sent.

## *Enforcing her will*

Elizabeth was well aware that getting the prayer book reaccepted by one vote (see 'Clashing over uniformity') wouldn't cut the mustard, so her ministers persuaded her to get heavy (the queen herself was all for toleration).

- ✔ Non-attendance at church cost a fine of 12 pence (1 shilling).

- ✔ The queen's right-hand man William Cecil made sure that a few prominent Catholics still celebrating mass went to jail.

- ✔ Matthew Parker, the new archbishop of Canterbury, got the job of making sure that people everywhere accepted the 39 Articles of Faith (reduced from the 42 of Cranmer's time – see Chapter 8 for details). Parker sent out his 'advertisements' in 1566 demanding that his priests play ball, but Elizabeth wouldn't let him use her name to force the issue.

But if Elizabeth was trying to stand aloof from Protestants and Catholics in the hope religious rows would go away, she was wrong.

## *Conforming clergymen?*

The debate between Catholics and Protestants went on for the rest of Elizabeth's reign. Bishop John Jewel wrote an article defending the new Church; Catholic pamphleteer Thomas Harding wrote one attacking it . . . and so on.

---

### Stoking the fires

Most of Elizabeth's grief over religion came from the universities of Oxford and Cambridge. Under Mary, Cardinal Pole had made sure that all lecturers were Catholic and many of them were rabid. Between 1559 and 1562 many of these men left the country for European universities like Bologna and put their talents to good use on behalf of the Council of Trent and the Counter-Reformation.

In 1568 William Allen set up 'a nest of scorpions', an English college at Douai in France that was a training ground for disaffected Englishmen, whose mission it was to win England back to the old faith by whatever means necessary.

---

In 1559 Elizabeth sent a royal visitation that was supposed to get the backing of the bishops for the Acts of Supremacy and Uniformity, but all but one of them refused and the deans and archdeacons followed suit. Bishops who wouldn't play ball lost their jobs. Some went abroad and others were imprisoned. (Nobody died.) Most of the rank and file clergy took the oath, however, probably to keep their jobs and because if the queen wanted to upset God, that was her business, not theirs.

A lot of clergymen and their flocks went to prayer book services in the morning and had a quiet mass celebration in the evening when they hoped nobody was looking.

# Converting Ireland?

Elizabeth probably realised that re-imposing the prayer book in Ireland wasn't going to work (see Chapter 10 for how far anglicisation had got there).

The Irish Parliament met briefly in 1560, just long enough to re-impose Royal Supremacy, which Thomas Radcliffe, the earl of Sussex, would manage at ground level.

## Tackling the tribes

Sussex's approach was a no-nonsense military occupation. On the grounds that the French might invade at some point (always a useful one to keep up your doublet sleeve) he raided and burned tribal lands, put his cronies into key positions and built up an army of 2,500 men.

---

## The O'Neill

Shane O'Neill was the brother of the earl of Tyrone and he wanted to inherit the title. He was pushy and dynamic and the question everybody was asking was whether he was only after his brother's title or trying to get the English out of Ireland. He had massive backing across Ireland.

A compromise was reached in 1562 when O'Neill came over to Elizabeth's Court and she gave him the title of captain (but not earl) of Tyrone. His powers were very vague and although the queen recognised him as tribal chieftain of the O'Neills, all this did was put him at loggerheads with Sussex. For details of Shane O'Neill's ongoing rebellion, see Chapter 14.

Elizabeth kept Sussex on a tight financial leash (remember, she was Henry VII's grand-daughter) and told him how to do his job in terms of the plantations (see Chapter 10). Not unnaturally, the local nobility and tribal chieftains took exception to Sussex's high-handed approach.

## Setting up the counties

Sussex realised that the only way to stop the endless squabbling between the Irish tribes was to conquer the whole island and bring in a hard-line English overlordship, which in the past the English had only ever tried in the Pale (Chapter 2 explains the geography of Ireland at this time).

Sussex was recalled in 1564 and was replaced by Sir Henry Sidney, who carried out a low key and usually peaceful anglicisation over the next 14 years. The most obvious outward sign of anglicisation was the creation of counties: Clare and Wicklow, 1560; Galway, 1569; Longford, 1571; Mayo, 1576; and Donegal and Coleraine, 1585.

Creating the counties didn't just involve changing names of areas. The counties had their own sheriffs and courts based on the English model, which sat uneasily alongside the Irish tribal set-up that most Irishmen continued to follow. Setting up counties was a bit of a cosmetic exercise but it gave Sidney a pretext to intervene if he wanted to.

## Polarising the faiths

The arrival of the new counties offended the old English, the families who'd held land and power in Ireland for generations. Ireland had technically been made a kingdom in 1541 when Parliament passed an act that said 'The King's highness, his heirs and successors, kings of England, shall be always kings of this land of Ireland.' Since then, a situation that favoured the Irish had been developing:

- ✔ The Anglo-Irish community became *more*, not less Catholic as time went on.

- ✔ After 1570, as you see in Chapter 14, Ireland was the target of Catholic missionaries who realised that Irish hostility to the English was useful in their bid to get England back to the old faith.

- ✔ Getting people to take on Church of Ireland jobs was difficult – they were badly paid and unpopular.

# Claiming Calais

The last English strongholds in France, Calais and Guisnes, had fallen to the French in Mary's reign, but a lot of Englishmen (and Elizabeth was one of them!) looked back with nostalgia to when their great-grandfathers had owned half of France and thought, wouldn't it be nice to get some land back?

England, France and Spain signed the Treaty of Cateau-Cambrésis on 2 April 1559 after months of negotiations that had started under Mary, bringing an end to the long conflict between Spain and France. In the treaty both Henri II of France and Philip II of Spain recognised Elizabeth as queen of England. They agreed that Calais would stay French for eight years, but in 1567 it was to go back to England or the French would have to pay a whacking fee for the land (nobody thought they'd have the money). If this all sounds familiar, it's because Francis I and Henry VIII struck a similar deal (see Chapter 3).

## Feeling uneasy

The new friendship between France and Spain was worrying to Elizabeth and the Council. Henry VIII's and Edward VI's advisers had kept the Valois–Habsburg feud going because it kept France and Spain at each other's throats and England could cash in on that. The prospect of two Catholic powers cosying up led to the myth of a great Catholic conspiracy, which had knock-on effects on various plots against Elizabeth (see Chapter 14).

## Getting involved in a French squabble

The accidental death of Henri II in a tournament in July 1559 (ironically, to celebrate Cateau-Cambrésis) led to chaos in France. The new king (Francis II) was only 15 and his meddling mother was Catherine de Medici, who was so unpopular in France that it gave a green light to other families who believed they had a right to the throne. The gloves were off and three rival families jostled each other for power – the Guises, the Bourbons and the Montmorencys. The struggle was heightened by the fact that the Bourbons were Protestants and the Guises arch-Catholics, determined to stamp out heresy. The complicated ins and outs of years of French in-fighting didn't really concern the queen, but with only 21 miles of sea between France and England, Elizabeth couldn't sit on the sidelines for ever.

The leading light of the Bourbon family was the Prince of Condé and he was looking for Protestant allies to help his cause and that of the Huguenots

(Protestants) in France. In 1562 he got help from Robert Dudley, the queen's favourite you meet in Chapter 12, and the queen sent Henry Sidney (her man in Ireland; he gets around, doesn't he?) to France to negotiate with Condé. Cecil didn't like Elizabeth's decision, but most of the Council did because here was a chance to get Calais back *now*. Condé got £45,000 cash aid plus 4,000 troops under Ambrose Dudley, earl of Warwick, who took over the town of Le Havre in pledge until Calais could be recovered.

In the fighting that followed the Protestants were beaten all over the place and the English garrison at Le Havre found itself cut off. When both French sides came to a peace settlement (with the Guise Catholics getting the better of the deal), everybody seemed to have forgotten about Le Havre. But by May 1562 Catholic and Protestant Frenchmen united against the English garrison, and to cap it all, plague broke out in the town. The earl of Warwick had to surrender Le Havre.

The final upshot – humiliating but inevitable – was that Elizabeth signed the Treaty of Troyes in April 1564, giving up Calais forever and bringing the curtain down on 300 years of history.

# Stirring Things Up with the Stuarts

Mary Stuart Queen of Scots was Elizabeth's nearest relative and her nearest rival for the throne of England. In 1560 she'd face a double blow, losing both her husband, Francis II of France, and her mother, Mary of Guise (regent in Scotland), and would returned home to sit on the throne of Scotland. But the succession was far from straightforward.

## Securing Scotland

Scotland didn't join France (her usual ally) in the war against Spain between 1557 and 1559 because Philip kept the Scots out of the loop and Mary of Guise, regent in Scotland, couldn't get support from the Scots nobility.

A group of Scottish Protestant lords called the Lords of Congregation of Jesus Christ rebelled against Mary of Guise and asked Elizabeth for help. That put the queen in a cleft stick. She was torn between using the request as her excuse to sort Scotland out and the fact that supporting rebels who were against their lawful government was a bad idea – it could be her turn next to face rebellion.

By February 1560 Elizabeth felt she had no choice but to interfere and she sent a fleet to prevent any more French troops landing in Scotland and sent Thomas Howard, the duke of Norfolk, across the border with a small army.

Signing a treaty with the Lords of Congregation was a clever move. Elizabeth claimed to be protector of the liberties of Scotland against the French and this agreement would only come to an end with the deaths of Francis II, Mary or Elizabeth. The queen wouldn't repeat the mistake of Henry VIII's reign (see Chapter 3) of having to fight Scotland as well as France.

After some inconclusive skirmishing in the Scottish Lowlands and an attempt to capture the town of Leith (which didn't work), Mary of Guise died and representatives from both sides signed the Treaty of Edinburgh.

Under the Treaty of Edinburgh:

- ✔ Mary (then queen of France) was recognised as queen of Scotland in her absence.
- ✔ Scotland was now governed by the Lords of Congregation.
- ✔ The English and French agreed to leave Scotland.
- ✔ Francis II and Mary stopped using the arms of England in their heraldry.

Mary never actually agreed to this treaty, but the important point was that Scotland seemed sorted out. The death of Francis, however, meant that Mary came back to Scotland to step up as the Catholic queen of an increasingly Protestant country, and that led to problems.

## Landing right in the thick of trouble

When Mary arrived in Leith near Edinburgh on 19 August 1561 she came with princes, courtiers, musicians and a pretty large chunk of the French crown jewels. Thick fog made her crossing difficult, but it might have saved her life because her malevolent half-brother, James Stuart, earl of Moray, was waiting for her in English ships. Moray was determined to run Scotland his way and if that meant kidnapping Mary, so be it.

The previous year, Scotland had gone through a religious revolution of its own:

- ✔ The Scottish Parliament banned the Latin mass and broke with Rome.
- ✔ The new faith, along the lines of John Calvin in Geneva, was spearheaded by John Knox, who'd been exiled under Mary Tudor but came back to Scotland under Elizabeth to lead the Protestant rebels.

Despite what looked like a clean sweep on paper, the Protestants were in the minority, centred around Ayreshire, Fife and Perth in the Lowlands. In the Highlands, the lawless clans, like the Irish in the Wild Lands, did their own thing – and that meant remaining Catholic. And in Mary, of course, the country still had a Catholic monarch.

The 18-year-old Mary had intelligence, wisdom and charm – and she'd need all that in the years ahead, especially because John Knox was making loud noises about the unfitness of women to rule (today, he'd probably have ended up in an institution of some kind).

In *Mary Queen of Scots*, a far-too-tall Vanessa Redgrave tramps up the beach in the company of half-brother James, played by a Machiavellian Patrick McGoohan, while John Knox, flat-capped and wild-bearded, screams at her from the dunes. In fact, they met indoors in Edinburgh a few days later in rather more civilised surroundings.

Mary's arrival concerned Elizabeth deeply and it kick-started 25 years of intrigue against the queen of England.

## Wearing the crown, and losing the crown

In Scotland Mary kept her nose clean for four years. She saw herself as the eventual rightful queen of England despite the Treaty of Edinburgh (see 'Securing Scotland'), which said she wasn't. The Lords of the Scottish Council (Congregation) asked her opinion on some things but Mary's input was slight.

To hard-bitten Scots politicians, the queen was a lightweight. She'd been brought up with French manners and attitudes, and many politicians probably agreed with Knox that she shouldn't have been on the throne in the first place. Everything would be fine as long as Mary confined her Catholicism to her own Chapel Royal and didn't interfere with the Kirk, the (now Protestant) Church of Scotland.

### Loving a loser

Subjects expect queens to marry; it's one of their duties. What were Mary's options?

- ✔ **Robert Dudley, earl of Leicester:** Elizabeth put Dudley forward (very generous of her, considering they were involved; see Chapter 12) and she may well have given him the Leicester title to make him more acceptable. Elizabeth's thinking is clear – she wanted the king of Scotland to be somebody she knew and could control. But Mary didn't want one of Elizabeth's cast-offs and said no.

- ✔ **Archduke Charles of Austria:** He was the Pope's choice.

- ✔ **Don Carlos, son of Philip II:** He was weak, vicious and cruel. He'd later be sentenced to death for plotting to kill his father's courtiers.

If you think you've heard some of these names before, that's because you have in Chapter 12. Charles and Carlos were in line to hook up with Elizabeth too – there weren't too many eligible European princes knocking about in those days!

In the end, everything went pear-shaped because Mary fell in love with Henry Darnley, son of the earl of Lennox. He had the right credentials, descended as he was from Henry VIII's sister, Mary, but he was vain, handsome, ambitious and empty-headed.

In *Mary Queen of Scots* Darnley is Timothy Dalton (later James Bond) in a very silly blond wig. He came across as petulant, egotistical and bisexual.

The marriage was made in hell. Mary quickly became pregnant but the couple had private and public rows over almost everything and eventually Darnley left her. In a moment of reconciliation, Mary made him the duke of Albany, but when she refused to give him the crown matrimonial he stormed off again and even took part in a coup that saw the queen imprisoned (see the nearby sidebar 'Save me, lady, save me!').

---

## 'Save me, lady, save me!'

In a particularly low period in Mary and Darnley's relationship, Darnley was involved in the murder of Mary's Italian secretary David Rizzio. On 9 March 1566 Mary was having supper with Rizzio in Holyrood Palace in Edinburgh (the headquarters of the Scottish Parliament today – check it out when you're north of the border). The queen was six months pregnant and decidedly alarmed when armed men burst in, led by Darnley himself, and plunged their daggers into the Italian as he clung to her skirts, begging her to save him.

Rizzio, as an Italian and a Catholic, had got too close to Mary for the liking of the Protestant lords, including James Stuart, earl of Moray. His corpse had 60 stab wounds.

Mary was held prisoner after the coup, but in a scene straight out of a Hollywood epic she got Darnley on side again – presumably by using her womanly wiles – promised everybody involved a pardon and was smuggled out of the palace via the crypt with the help of James Hepburn, earl of Bothwell. The pair rode through the night to Dunbar, then Mary sent out a call to arms and the Rizzio plotters ran to England.

### Giving birth to the future king

On 16 June 1566 Mary gave birth to a boy, James, in Edinburgh Castle. There were the by-now familiar rumours of a substitute child replacing the actual baby born to Mary and of 'the coffin in the wall' that was supposed to contain a baby's skeleton wrapped in a shroud with a royal monogram. But check out the later portraits of James and Lord Darnley and you'll be in no doubt that James was the true son.

The importance here, of course, is that baby James was heir to the throne of Scotland, and as long as Elizabeth had no children, England too. When she heard the news of Mary's new baby Elizabeth was furious, saying, 'The queen of Scots is lighter by a son and I am of but barren stock.'

### Getting rid of Darnley

Darnley was a political liability, with enemies in Scotland from coast to coast. In the early hours of 10 February 1567 his house at Kirk o'Fields in Edinburgh was blown up and his and his servant's bodies were found strangled with a rope in the garden. Darnley was still wearing his nightshirt.

Who did it?

- ✔ The earl of Bothwell was chief suspect. He married Mary three months later and some accounts say he raped her and that she lost the twins she was carrying. Love letters were found later, however, which make both the rape and the forced marriage seem unlikely.

- ✔ Mary herself may have been in on the murder – Elizabeth certainly believed this (but then, she would, wouldn't she?).

### Ousting Mary

The Lords of the Council had had enough of their Catholic queen with her renegade politics and they forced her to abdicate, imprisoning her in the grim Lochleven Castle. Reluctantly, Mary passed the crown to little James (just over 1 year old) and agreed that Moray would act as regent for him.

Mary tried to raise an army to get her throne back, but ended up as a refugee in England (her new husband Bothwell high-tailed it to Denmark for his own safety). For the next 19 years Mary of Scotland was the prisoner of Elizabeth of England.

A mutinous Edinburgh mob marched round the streets, chanting, 'Hang the whore!' John Knox, who could have been content with an 'I told you it would all end in tears' went on to compare Mary from his pulpit with those sneaky ladies of the Old Testament, Jezebel and Delilah.

When Mary arrived in England in August 1568 she didn't get the reception she'd hoped for. Elizabeth refused to see her – the meeting between them in *Mary Queen of Scots*, where Glenda Jackson (Elizabeth) meets Vanessa Redgrave (Mary) in a wood and Glenda ends up bashing Vanessa with her riding crop, never happened. Elizabeth rather spitefully sent the refugee queen some tatty old clothes with darns and mends all over them.

### Marrying off Mary

Ignoring the Bothwell marriage, the Council thought it would be a good idea to marry Mary off as soon as possible to someone they could trust and control (the good old Tudor policy). Who was in the running?

- **The Austrians:** Part of the Habsburg power fixation.

- **The Swedes:** Gaining reputation in this period as a European power.

- **Thomas Howard, duke of Norfolk:** Powerful, popular and a former Catholic.

With Mary now in England, the Spanish and French ambassadors were involved and were busy feeding back information to their governments.

Elizabeth was furious once she knew about the proposed Norfolk marriage and she gave the man a dressing down for his arrogance in September 1569. The Spanish ambassador backed off, Howard went to sulk on his Norfolk estates and, as usual, when the queen was in one of her temper tantrums other lords ran for cover. In the event, Mary married nobody.

## Triggering revolt

The far north of England had a reputation for being difficult, ignoring commands from London and doing their own thing. Thomas Percy, the earl of Northumberland, and Charles Neville, the earl of Westmoreland, were known Catholics and owned the lands that ran right up to the Scots Border.

### Uniting against Cecil

By 1569 William Cecil was in the driving seat alongside the queen but he was unpopular for a number of other reasons:

- The old nobility regarded him as an upstart (he wasn't Lord Burghley yet).

- Some didn't like the religious settlement that he, as much as Elizabeth, represented.

- Some blamed Cecil for ordering the attack on the duke of Alba's pay ships at the end of December 1568 (in fact, this had been the queen's idea).

In the Council, Norfolk, Northumberland and Westmoreland were conspiring against Cecil, as was Leicester until he chickened out and confessed all to the queen (see Chapter 12). Their idea was to stage a protest, get the queen to kick Cecil out, go back to the Church 'as king Henry left it' and perhaps even name Mary of Scots as Elizabeth's heir.

The earls of Northumberland and Westmoreland were left exposed by the attack on Cecil. Northumberland had the largest following of any nobleman – over 200 household servants as well as tenants all over the north who'd been loyal to his family for generations.

The earl of Sussex, president of the Council of the North, got wind of the plan and he arranged a meeting with the potential rebels to clear the air. The peace talks failed, and Sussex asked the Council of the North to appear at Court in London, they got their people together ready for a fight.

### Burning themselves out

As they moved south in mid November, the rebel Earls realised how small their support base was and desertions increased daily. As with Kett's Rebellion (flip back to Chapter 8), the rebels weren't happy leaving their own area and by the time they were within 50 miles of Tutbury in Staffordshire, where Mary of Scots was being held, the whole movement began to crumble.

By 25 November the rebels were back in Durham and three weeks later they crossed the border into Scotland. Various noblemen took advantage of Sussex's arrival to welcome his pursuing army and tell him how loyal they were to the queen.

## The plot within the plot

Richard Norton and Robert Tempest were rabid Catholics working for the northern Earls. They wanted to kick Elizabeth out, replace her with Mary of Scots and bring back (yet again!) the old faith. They tried to link up with the pope, the duke of Alba and the Catholic Leaguers of Scotland (who opposed the government of the Lords of Congregation). The rebels had around 10,000 men and they marched on Durham, took the city and publicly tore up the copies of the *Book of Common Prayer* in the cathedral. The earl of Sussex, sent north with an army, proclaimed them all traitors on 13 November.

The only skirmish of the rebellion was fought on 20 February 1570 when Lord Dacre, a disgruntled nobleman who'd just lost his family inheritance, took on Lord Hunsdon and was defeated. Dacre called himself 'Lord of the North', which was building up his part a bit, and Hunsdon was a member of the Privy Council and a cousin of the queen. The Scots clansmen who were supposed to be joining Dacre never materialised and he fled to the Highlands for safety.

### Strengthening the Crown

The collapse of the Northern Rebellion proved two things:

- ✔ Not even the most anti and backward part of the country was willing to go to the wire against the new religious set-up or the queen.

- ✔ Philip II wasn't willing to wade in; neither (directly) was the pope.

The failure of the rebellion was good news for Elizabeth, strengthening her claim to the throne and putting a big tick for success on the first ten years of her reign. It also, however, prompted the pope to get heavy with his attitude towards Elizabeth and indirectly perhaps sparked off other attempts to remove the queen permanently (see Chapter 14).

The North was reorganised, the earldoms of Northumberland and Westmoreland were reduced or abolished and the Dacre inheritance went to the Crown in 1572. Hundreds of executions took place and the writing was on the wall for the duke of Norfolk, who went to the block too.

# Assessing the Decade: Girl Done Good?

A lot of historians like to divide up long reigns to make sense of them, and Elizabeth's first decade as queen does stand alone because in 1570, partly because of Pope Pius's excommunication (see Chapter 14), Elizabeth's England went in a rather different direction. So how did the queen do in her first ten years?

- ✔ She was too slow to get involved in Scotland but what happened there settled Anglo–Scots relations for the next 40 years.

- ✔ She shouldn't have encouraged Robert Dudley in the marriage stakes (see Chapter 12) although in the end this only affected her – and him – personally and didn't cut much ice with anybody else.

- ✔ She behaved badly over her marriage: shilly shallying, dipping out, teasing and ignoring – all of this led to the end of the Tudor line.

- ✔ Backing John Hawkins (see Chapter 12) was a mixed blessing. Yes, she got a large slice of his profits and broke Philip II's stranglehold on Spanish/American trade. But she also cranked up the tension levels, which eventually led to open war with Spain (see Chapter 15).

✔ Until 1572 she was generous enough to welcome refugees from the Low Countries seeking sanctuary in England.

✔ She sat on fences, endlessly delaying on decisions in the hope that problems would go away.

✔ She seemed obsessed by her father, copying his dominance. Her religious settlement was based partly on Henry VIII's and partly on brother Edward's with hardly a glance at the 'new' Reformation ideas coming back with exiles from Europe.

Check out the moment in *Young Bess* when Jean Simmons strikes the Hans Holbein pose of Henry VIII – hands on hips and legs thrust defiantly apart. Three hundred years after the Tudors, the poet Rudyard Kipling wrote 'Bess was Harry's daughter', and he was right.

Historians shouldn't look back with hindsight, but they can't help themselves. No one at the time (least of all Elizabeth herself) knew how where England was headed, but looking back we can see that a lot of her policy made sense:

✔ If she'd married a European prince, England would have been dragged into the swamp of European politics and 'Englishness' would have been lost. And giving birth, particularly later in life, carried dangers in a time of high infant and maternal mortality (see Chapter 1).

✔ Keeping her councillors guessing meant that the queen stayed in control. Parliament was getting more powerful in Elizabeth's reign (see Chapter 14) but was nowhere near governing like in today's democracy.

✔ In religion Elizabeth's middle way Church of England upset Catholics at one extreme and Puritans at the other. The bottom line was that Elizabeth had to go with her own beliefs and the knowledge that the majority of her people were very conservative, illiterate and superstitious, and she had to lead gently. The ravings of John Knox (see 'Landing right in it', earlier in this chapter) wouldn't have gone down well in England.

Most of the criticisms of Elizabeth, whispered in her first decade and muttered more loudly as the years went by, is that she was a woman so was swayed by female emotions. She should have been married and she should have been bringing up children, tied to the kitchen sink (even if the sink was scrubbed by her scullions); leave government to the men. Saying that Elizabeth was a women's libber isn't right; she was more an honorary man.

# Chapter 14

# Gunning for Elizabeth

In This Chapter

▶ Plotting for Mary of Scotland

▶ Lighting the powder keg: Ireland

▶ Posturing with Parliament

▶ Dealing with Puritans

▶ Getting magical with witchcraft

A s Chapter 13 explains, the first ten years of Elizabeth's reign had mixed reviews. Then, she was feeling her way along while carrying all the baggage of the earlier Tudors. But between 1570 and 1590 the queen found her feet and became a legend, even though these were dangerous years – a time of plots and intrigue, international tension and the rise of two new phenomena – pushy parliaments and prickly Puritans.

## Attempting to Remove Elizabeth

Pope Pius V had been a shepherd in his early life and became grand inquisitor under Paul IV (see Chapter 13). He lived on vegetable soup and shellfish and wore a friar's hair shirt under his papal robes. He hated Spain, Jews and heretics and aimed his beady eyes (check out his portrait in the Vatican in Rome) at the highest profile heretic in Europe – the queen of England.

Pius V published *Regnans in Excelsis* on 27 April 1570, which told all good Catholics that they had no need to obey 'the English Jezebel'. The papal bull was virtually a declaration of war.

The Bull caused a conundrum for Catholics, forcing them to choose between their monarch and their faith:

- ✔ If you obeyed the pope (as good Catholics should) you couldn't regard Elizabeth as your lawful queen.

- ✔ If you obeyed your queen (who, after all, had been put there by God) you couldn't be a good Catholic.

Those loyal followers of the pope who opted to obey him had a choice of two ways to get rid of Elizabeth:

- ✔ Mount a Catholic rebellion – not likely after the attempt by the northern earls. Most Englishmen of whatever religious persuasion stayed loyal to her.
- ✔ Send out hit men to kill her.

The first casualty in this religious war was John Felton, who pinned a copy of the pope's Excommunication Bull to the bishop of London's palace gates. Felton was tortured and executed, the first of several martyrs to die in the cause of removing Elizabeth.

In the meantime, Mary of Scots' adventures in Scotland (see Chapter 13) had led to her imprisonment in England from 1568, and a number of plots against Elizabeth were hatched in Mary's name.

In the 16th century the powers that be would usually obtain information about plots through torture. Not only would this be inadmissible in any Western court today, but it means we can't rely on the information being true.

## Bring back the rack

By the early 16th century barbaric torture contraptions had almost disappeared from England, but they made a big comeback under the later Tudors. Only the monarch of the day could allow their use.

Margaret Clitherow, a devout Catholic, was pressed to death in the Tollbooth, York on 25 March 1586. She was tied to posts on the ground and a stone placed under her back. Then her executioners piled stones on top of her so that her ribs broke and pierced the skin. She died in about 15 minutes.

The *rack* was a frame on which you were tied that stretched until your joints were dislocated.

For the Tudors, the rack was the ultimate torture implement. In England it was called the Duke of Exeter's Daughter. Skeffington's Gyves, an iron hoop that constricted the body and crushed the chest, was popular too.

Elizabeth's top torturer was Richard Topcliffe, the member of Parliament for Beverley in Yorkshire. He used the Iron Maiden (a sort of coffin with spikes on the inside) and strappado (hanging people up by their thumbs) as well as thumbscrews in the Marshalsea and Clink prisons in London. It was ironic that Topcliffe was using the same objects used by the hated Inquisition (see Chapter 10), which was banned in England.

## Plotting with Ridolfi, 1572

Mary of Scotland's first serious attempt to oust Elizabeth took place with the backing of Roberto Ridolfi, a Florentine banker living in London. As with all plots before and since Elizabeth's time, it involved very prominent people and was half-baked and high risk.

The Ridolfi Plot involved (in theory) Philip of Spain, the duke of Alba, the pope, the duke of Norfolk, as well, of course, as Mary and Ridolfi himself. The idea was that Alba would land at Harwich on the Essex coast with 6,000 men and march on London. The duke of Norfolk, who'd already been implicated in the Northern Rebellion (see Chapter 13) and was lucky to have kept his head, would grab Elizabeth and a cold war standoff would ensue; the rebels would trade the queen for Mary. Then Mary would marry Norfolk, rule over England *and* Scotland and restore the old faith, knocking the hated Protestant John Knox off his pulpit and probably having Elizabeth executed.

How much of this version of the plot is based on reality is difficult to say. Norfolk had, for all his dodgy dealings in the north, agreed to Elizabeth's new Church, and the pope put a lot of restrictions on his offer of help and claimed to speak for Philip of Spain, which of course he couldn't.

Ridolfi was his own worst enemy. He shot his mouth off, and Mary's spymaster Walsingham (see the nearby sidebar 'Enter a spy') intercepted his letters between Mary, Norfolk and the pope and broke their code.

Luckily for him, Ridolfi was out of the country when his plot was discovered, so he just vanished over the horizon and kept going. The duke of Norfolk was less fortunate: he was held in the Tower until 2 June 1572, when he was beheaded on Tower Green.

Norfolk is a rather sadder character than the scheming villain played by Christopher Ecclestone in *Elizabeth*. All three of his wives had died in childbirth and he may have had some sort of breakdown as a result.

Not only had the plot to remove Queen Elizabeth failed, but from now on her men would watch Mary of Scotland like a hawk.

## Dodging the bullet

There were several one-off attempts to kill Elizabeth after 1570. In one, the half-mad Welsh spy and traitor William Parry got the queen on her own in the gardens at Richmond Palace and was only prevented from killing her by seeing a sudden resemblance to fellow Welshman Henry VII, the queen's grandfather, in his sovereign's face. Perhaps Parry was more than half mad, but he was executed in 1585 nevertheless.

---

## Enter a spy

The plots against Elizabeth failed largely because of the attention to detail of Francis Walsingham, the queen's spymaster. As a 16th-century 'M' (think 007) he employed agents both in England and in Europe who fed back vital information to him. *Projecters* were the rough equivalent of James Bond. They were often multi-lingual, had been recruited from the universities and were licensed to kill on behalf of the queen – men like Christopher Marlowe (see Chapter 17). *Intelligencers* were lesser fry who listened at keyholes and behind curtains, passing all sorts of useful gossip to their masters upstairs. Walsingham's intelligence system was probably better than anything run by any other country at the time.

---

Elizabeth sometimes slept with a drawn sword by her bed – bearing in mind, for example, how the Scots had interrupted their queen's supper parties (see Chapter 13), but she refused to cancel any public appearances. True, she was always surrounded by courtiers (and the men were always armed), but none of them could stop a bullet and in Elizabeth's time firearms were improving. She was once travelling along the Thames in London in the royal barge when somebody fired at her from the shore. One of her oarsmen was hit in the arm (goodbye, career!) but she calmly gave him her handkerchief (hello, very floggable present!) to staunch the blood. 'Be of good cheer,' she said to the oarsman, 'for you will never want. The bullet was meant for me.'

You didn't actually have to physically attack the queen to feel the rope in Elizabeth's day. *Coining* (counterfeiting money) was a hanging offence because it not only debased the value of the currency – something only the Government was allowed to do – but it literally defaced the queen. And in 1583 three Catholics were executed in Bury St Edmunds, Suffolk because they'd daubed graffiti on the royal coat of arms in St Mary's Church. Okay, the graffiti was tasteful – a quote from the Bible – but it equated the queen with the harlot Jezebel, so goodbye, that's all they wrote.

## *Plotting with Throckmorton, 1583*

The next Catholic conspiracy after Ridolfi's involved Francis Throckmorton who worked with the clever and dodgy Spanish ambassador Bernardino de Mendoza.

The idea was pretty old hat really – a rising of English Catholics timed to coincide with a joint Franco–Spanish invasion. It's not clear how much Mary of Scots knew about this plot, but Secretart of State Cecil, Walsingham and the Council were taking no chances. They had Throckmorton watched and his houses seized and ransacked. The searchers found incriminating evidence (surprise!) and under torture Throckmorton confessed everything.

## Rooting out Gregory's Jesuits

Plots and rumours of plots came thick and fast during the 1580s, especially as tensions grew between England and Spain over the Low Countries (today's Netherlands; see Chapter 15).

In October 1584 Cecil and Walsingham drafted a document called the Bond of Association, which asked all loyal subjects (in practice, important men) to pursue plotters to the death and never to back a claim to the throne of anyone who'd made an attempt on the queen's life. This was clearly aimed at Mary of Scots. Four months later Parliament agreed a modified version of the Act, which also got tough with Jesuits (Catholic priests whose mission it was to win England back to the old faith) and seminary priests, who'd been arriving in England since 1580.

By 1580 the Pope was Gregory XIII, an ex-lawyer with a bastard son. He unleashed two Jesuits on England – Edmund Campion and Robert Parsons. A two-man mission might not seem very impressive, but they led a larger team and Campion in particular was brilliant at appearing and disappearing at will, leading the authorities a merry chase.

Campion went north from Dover in Kent through Oxfordshire into the north of England, while Parsons hit the counties of Worcestershire and Gloucestershire. They held the mass in secret in people's houses and one justice of the peace complained, 'This brood [the Jesuit missionaries] will never be rooted out.' People were hiding priests in their homes (see the nearby sidebar 'The priest holes'.

Walsingham's men were pretty thorough, however. Of an estimated 13-strong Jesuit mission eventually sent by Pope Gregory, only one, Parsons, got away. Campion was caught in July 1581 and racked three times before they hanged him. At his trial at Westminster Hall he was too weak to hold up his hand to plead and had to be helped. The Council were impressed by his courage – 'It was a pity he was a Papist'.

---

### The priest holes

Anybody who lives in an Elizabethan house will tell you it once had a priest hole. This is an exaggeration but they certainly existed. Towneley Hall in Burnley, Lancashire once had nine! *Priest holes* were small spaces, often under stairs, below floorboards or in toilet crevices, where nervous householders stashed Jesuits on the run.

In 1592 the Council ordered Richard Brereton, a justice of the peace in Cornwall, to examine 'all rooms, lofts, studies and cellars, keeping an eye open for secret and suspicious places'.

The previous year in Baddesley Clinton in Warwickshire, ten men hid for four hours in a dank dark pit while their pursuers ransacked the floors over their heads.

## Plotting with Babington, 1586

This plot involved the Guise family, who were still in Scotland (see Chapter 13), a Franco–Spanish invasion (every good plot has to have one) and a very silly young gentleman called Anthony Babington.

A Catholic priest, James Ballard, persuaded Babington to send a letter to Mary of Scots, now imprisoned at Chartley Manor in Staffordshire, to back the plot that would put her on Elizabeth's throne. It didn't take long for Walsingham's people to find the incriminating letters smuggled in and out of the house via beer barrels and the inevitable torture and confessions followed.

London rejoiced at Babington's execution on 20 September – it was party time and a specially high gallows was been built on Tower Hill so that the crowd could have a good view.

## Counting the costs of the plots

The cunning plans of the popes, the Jesuits, the disgruntled gentlemen and the just plain madmen all came to nothing. In fact, they backfired. Elizabeth became even more popular each time a plot was uncovered. Mendoza, the Spanish ambassador, was kicked out in January 1584 and wasn't replaced. And Mary of Scots was shown to be up to her neck in murder attempts on Elizabeth and the clamour to kill her grew.

---

## What a way to go!

The official method of execution for treason under the Tudors – and it survived until 1820 – was hanging, drawing and quartering. First, the victim was shown the implements that the executioner was going to be using – murderously sharp knives, saws and axes. Then the victim was hanged with a rope until he passed out, then taken down, revived and his stomach ripped open and his entrails burnt in front of him (this was the drawing bit). Quartering followed – the executioner cut through the joints of the victim's arms and legs and horses pulled him in four directions.

For how much of this ghastly business anybody stayed conscious or alive is difficult to say. The crowd loved the spectacle, but Elizabeth was so horrified by Babington's execution that she ordered that the second day's batch (a further seven conspirators) should be hanged until they were dead before the rest of it began.

---

For as long as she could, Elizabeth tried to pretend that cousin Mary was innocent. Cecil had wanted the woman dead over the Darnley murder (see Chapter 13) and most Englishmen agreed.

By keeping Mary alive, Elizabeth could have damaged relationships with the Scots Government and she'd have become the focus for ongoing plots and rebellions. But the Babington affair left her no choice and so she put Mary on trial for treason.

Mary stage-managed her trial brilliantly at Fotheringhay Castle in Northamptonshire (check it out, but it's only a grassy mound today). She pointed to a chair with the royal coat of arms on it and said, 'I am queen by right of birth and my place should be there.' She'd been a prisoner for 17 years by this point and was wracked with rheumatism. She denied any knowledge of attempts to overthrow Elizabeth, saying, 'I have only two or three years to live and I do not aspire to any public position.'

She was bound to be found guilty, but Elizabeth did some monumental fence-sitting for nearly three months. Her hesitation was partly due to genuine compassion, but Elizabeth also knew that signing a death warrant for a fellow queen was risky. What if someone signed hers one day?

Elizabeth eventually signed (much to the Council's delight) and as soon as the deed was done everybody ran for cover to avoid the queen's explosive wrath. She wailed and screamed for days.

Catholics far and wide were outraged by the planned execution, but did nothing to stop it. Elizabeth was wracked with guilt, but Mary was almost certainly guilty of treason and politically, the execution of Mary Queen of Scots made sense. It meant that any later plotters couldn't use Mary as a figurehead. So on 8 February 1587 Mary went to the block (see the nearby sidebar 'I am resolved to die in this religion' for the gruesome details).

# *Dealing with Irish Rebellion*

Elizabeth followed the advice of most of her ministers who believed that the infighting between the Irish tribes and chieftains could only be stopped by military conquest.

## 'I am resolved to die in this religion'

On the night before her execution Mary lay awake, fully dressed, while her ladies read to her from the Bible. At 6 a.m. she got up, said her prayers and walked to the Great Hall of Fotheringhay, dressed in black with a long transparent veil. Three hundred ladies and gentlemen had crowded in to see her off and the dean of Peterborough tried to bully her into renouncing her faith. 'I have lived in this religion,' she told him, 'and I am resolved to die in this religion.'

There was a gasp as her weeping ladies removed the veil and dress, to reveal the bright red petticoat – red being the colour of martyrdom – underneath. Mary knelt and recited the Lord's Prayer in Latin before being blindfolded and helped down to the block.

Bigger gasps were to follow. The executioner was a blunderer and took three strokes to get the former queen's head off. As her head rolled across the floor, her wig fell off – she was completely bald. And her little lapdog, terrified, ran out from under her skirts, yelping hysterically.

## *Tackling the O'Neills*

Shane O'Neill played right into the queen's hands by going back on the deal he made with her (see Chapter 13) and going on the rampage against the Maguires in Ulster. It took the earl of Sussex's troops four months to bring him to heel.

The Irish complained about the harshness of Sussex's soldiers and opposed the English plantations in Leix and Offaly, and by the spring of 1565 O'Neill was at it again, this time attacking the Macdonnells at Glenshesk. (See Chapter 2 for a map of Ireland in the Tudor period.)

In the following year O'Neill burned the cathedral in Armagh and attacked local villages. Elizabeth proclaimed him a traitor and put a price on his head. To make matters worse, O'Neill tried to make the whole thing an international affair, asking Charles IX of France for help against the English.

In November 1565 Henry Sidney, now lord deputy in Ireland, mounted a big campaign against the rebel would-be earl. Sidney's men lived off the harvest and destroyed anything they couldn't eat or carry, and English ships from Bristol trailed them along the Irish coast. Sidney restored Calvagh O'Donnell to his rightful place in Tyrconnel. And as soon as Sidney had gone, of course, O'Neill attacked Derry.

But what O'Neill hadn't reckoned on was the fickle nature of his Scots allies. On 2 June 1567 O'Neill arrived at their camp at Cushendun in County Antrim.

He didn't know his hosts were in the pay of the English and a fight broke out. O'Neill was hacked to death and his head, carried to Dublin pickled in a barrel, was placed on a spike on the castle wall.

But nobody imagined that was the end of Irish rebellion.

## Stamping out the past

Sidney put down another rising in September 1569 by the Fitzgeralds in Munster with his usual ruthless efficiency. But this endless game couldn't go on, and by December 1571 the new president of Munster, Sir John Perrot, laid down some new rules:

- ✔ Townspeople could no longer wear traditional Gaelic dress – cloaks, Irish coats or great shirts.

- ✔ Men must cut their hair and their beards.

- ✔ Women mustn't wear linen cloth on their heads but must wear hats, caps or French hoods.

- ✔ The bards (poets) were to stop singing about Ireland's past – the songs were un-English and the language barbaric (ironically, six months earlier John Kearney had published the first ever book printed in Ireland – the *Gaelic Alphabet and Catechism*).

The fine for breaking any of these rules was a massive £100.

## Proliferating plantations

In Chapter 10 we explain that the English were muscling in with plantations in Ireland, and another spurt of plantation building went on in Ulster between 1572 and 1573. Around 100 colonists landed at Strangford Lough under the leadership of Thomas Smith, but yet again this was just papering over the cracks and the earl of Essex, now in the driving seat, clashed with a number of chieftains who were furious at the way their land was being parcelled up.

It was a vicious circle. As soon as rebellions occurred, the English seized the rebels' lands and created plantations, adding to the bitterness and the likelihood of further rebellion.

## Attempting to liberate Ireland

By 1579 all hell was ready to break loose. The fighting that eventually followed is called the Nine Years War, Tyrone's Rebellion or the War for Irish Independence, depending on whose side you're on.

Gregory XIII wanted Protestantism out of Ireland as much as the English wanted to control the country, so he backed the Irish by sending a number of adventurers.

- ✔ Thomas Stukeley was a maverick and not the right man for Gregory's job. He set off with 1,000 men and what limited resources the pope could give him, got side-tracked in Morocco (don't ask!) and was killed there.

- ✔ James Fitzmaurice had fewer men than Stukeley, but at least he landed in Ireland in July 1579. A confused revolt broke out in Munster. Six hundred Spanish and Italian troops landing as Fitzmaurice's reinforcements gave the governor, Lord Grey de Wilton, a headache. He cornered the rebels on the Dingle Peninsula, and butchered them. Crops were burnt and animals slaughtered in the kind of killing orgy that burned itself into Irish folk memory for years to come.

- ✔ Viscount Boltinglass, hot from Rome, led a rising in Leinster. He won a skirmish against English troops at Glenmalure in August 1580.

## Imposing the peace?

Since 1575 Henry Sidney had been trying to calm down the Irish situation by replacing protection money, the so-called 'coyne and livery', with a tax called *composition*. He hoped his change would help in two ways:

- ✔ The ordinary people would be happy because the new tax was lower than the coin and livery amount.

- ✔ Landlords would save money because they could now disband their private armies (who'd policed protection) and not have to pay them.

But many, even in the Pale (see Chapter 2 for a breakdown of Irish geography), were suspicious of Sidney's reform, and were reluctant to accept English rule.

During a spectacular piece of fence-sitting, Elizabeth recalled Sidney and her endless vacillating led to his resignation in September 1578. By the end of 1580, Lord Grey, Sidney's successor, was seeing Catholic conspirators behind every bush.

On 10 November, English troops under Nicholas Malby out down the rising by James Fitzgerald with viciousness. Perhaps it was the sight of the pope's banner on the battlefield at Smerwick that annoyed them. A series of trials and executions followed – Ireland had never seen such systematic slaughter. The earl of Kildare was arrested and in Munster the earl of Ormond had his commission taken away from him. William Nugent, the chief justice for the Court of Common Pleas, was executed for treason.

Grey's actions – passing out confiscated lands to his cronies – led to the Council recalling him in July 1582, but the revolts continued.

By November 1583 Gerald Fitzgerald, the earl of Desmond who was the leader of the Munster rebellion against the English, had been murdered by Daniel Kelly in Tralee and the violence died down, at least for a while.

John Perrot, the governor from January 1584, could work with the earl of Ormond and days of peace seemed to lie ahead. But the peace was only as strong as the English garrisons in Ireland, however. Nothing had been resolved and the old resentment – of Irishmen versus Irishmen; of Irishmen versus Englishmen; of 'old' English versus 'new' English – seethed under the surface.

# Handling Parliament

In Tudor times Parliament comprised the House of Commons and the House of Lords, and it met in Westminster Hall in London and represented the top end of society.

The Lords was the senior house and was made up of:

- ✔ Peers of the realm (whose titles had been granted by the monarch)
- ✔ Bishops

The Commons had two types of seat:

- ✔ Borough seats, held by *burgesses* (citizens) of towns big enough to be allowed them
- ✔ County seats, held by knights of the *shire* (county) – usually two per county.

By the start of the Tudor period many knights and gentlemen bought borough seats from the burgesses who were struggling to afford them (the cost of attending Parliament was huge), and so only cities like York, Norwich and London were represented by people who actually lived there.

By 1560:

- ✔ Most MPs had legal training, status and knew what they were talking about. (Even today, no direct training for the job of MP exists. It must be the only job in the country today for which no skills qualifications exist at all, scary, or what?)

- ✔ Parliament made laws (as Nicholas Bacon said) 'for uniting of the people of this realm into a uniform order of religion to the honour and glory of God, the establishment of his Church and the tranquillity of the realm'.

- ✔ Parliament voted for cash to be given to the Government by raising taxation to pay for wars, the upkeep of the navy and so on.

- ✔ The members of the Commons regarded themselves with a new confidence – they believed that they spoke for the whole country. This last was hot air, of course. The Lords only represented themselves and the Commons only represented their own (gentleman) class. The middle class and poor weren't given a look in and the only woman in government was the queen.

One problem for Parliament was that it didn't meet often – only 13 sessions (never more than ten weeks long) in a 44-year reign isn't very much. So members of Parliament had to make their views known when the moment presented itself. And because the queen alone could call Parliament and could also suspend and dismiss it, MPs' hands were tied.

## Sparking religious fervour

The Commons was always more Protestant than Elizabeth and it welcomed her Bill of Uniformity, drafted by the Council, in 1559. The 1559 Parliament had been concerned with the Church Bill and paying for the war against France, but the one in 1563 was all about religion. Several exiles had now returned from Europe (see Chapter 13) and a mood of reform was in the air. An increasing number of MPs were extreme Protestants (they came to be known as *Puritans*) who wanted the Church to be changed still further and were disappointed that Elizabeth didn't share their view. The Parliament of 1571 tried to make sure that the queen's religious settlement was strictly enforced, but Elizabeth torpedoed attempts by William Strickland to bring in a new prayer book because she didn't approve.

In the 1570s and 1580s three campaigns were going on in the Commons:

- ✔ Anti-Catholicism reached its height. Plots against the queen, the arrival of Campion's Jesuit mission (see 'Rooting out Gregory's Jesuits', earlier in this chapter) and the ever-growing threat from Spain (see Chapter 15) meant that everybody was on their guard.

✔ The push for the execution of Mary Queen of Scots was clearly tied in with anti-Catholicism.

✔ A small minority worked for a complete overhaul of Church government.

Parliament got heavy with Catholics:

✔ In 1571 anyone bringing papal bulls into the country was a traitor and could expect to be executed.

✔ In 1581 anyone not attending Church of England services got a crippling fine of £20 a month.

✔ In 1585 anyone joining the Catholic Church as a priest would be hanged and Jesuits in England had 40 days to get out or face the consequences.

✔ In 1593 non-churchgoers (*Recusants*) had their freedoms curtailed. They were spied on and the only way some of them coped was to go to Anglican services and let their wives carry on in the old faith in secret, explaining to the Almighty their husband's predicament.

# Controlling the MPs

Members of Parliament believed their purpose was to discuss the big issues of the day – religion, plots, foreign policy. Elizabeth and the Council saw Parliament as a milk cow for cash and a means to get backing for their policies in law.

The next two monarchs in English history – James I and his son Charles – handled their parliaments so badly that it led to civil war and Charles I's execution. So how did Elizabeth avoid all that?

✔ She turned the full Tudor charm on MPs, sending them home to spend the Christmas of 1584 with their families, returning their thanks to her 'ten thousand thousand fold'. In 1593 (a particularly difficult Commons session) she assured her MPs that nobody could have loved and appreciated them more than she did – except, she added to get the old-stagers on side, her father.

✔ She intervened to hold up various bills and suggested changes to them.

✔ She used the royal veto, chucking out bills she didn't like.

✔ She had troublesome MPs arrested. In 1576 Peter Wentworth, MP for Barnstaple in Devon, complained no freedom of speech existed in the Commons because the queen might object to MPs discussing certain topics. Wentworth was kicked out and cooled his heels in the Tower for a month.

# Grumbling with the Godly

If you let in something like the Reformation, you open the floodgates to all sorts of oddballs. Religion was at the heart of everybody's life in the 16th century and what began in Martin Luther's day (see Chapter 6) as an attack on the abuses of the Catholic Church became a fertile breeding ground for evermore wacky ideas.

The new 'left' in religion were the Puritans – Anabaptists, Calvinists and Presbyterians – who took a leaf out of John Calvin's book in Geneva, Switzerland. They were staunchly against the following:

- ✔ **Blasphemy:** If you took the Lord's name in vain you were punished with an iron spike through the tongue.
- ✔ **Flash clothes:** The sign of the worst sin of all – vanity. Puritans stuck to simple clothing.
- ✔ **Playing cards:** These were the 'Devil's picture books' and were banned.
- ✔ **Plays:** Don't even go there! (See the following section.)

As early as 1565 a hard-line group of Puritans was emerging in the Commons and Cambridge University had a nest of them, especially in St John's College.

The following year the tolerant, even laid-back Matthew Parker, archbishop of Canterbury, had to send out his *advertisements* (see Chapter 13) to remind both 'right' and 'left' in the country what the Church of England actually believed. Puritan priests were refusing to kneel to take communion, make the sign of the cross in baptism or wear surplices, which they called 'the livery of Antichrist'.

## Thrashing the theatres (and everything else enjoyable!)

The Puritan killjoys were soon at work attacking the 'vices' of Elizabeth's England. Philip Stubbes wrote his *Anatomie of Abuses* in 1582, which attacked almost everything from country dancing to the size of gentlemen's ruffs:

- ✔ Football (a 300-year-old street game in Elizabeth's day) was 'a bloody and murdering practice rather than a fellowly sport and pastime'. (Fair enough!)
- ✔ Bowling alleys were wastes of 'time, wit and money'. (Okay.)
- ✔ Maypoles were 'stinking idols' (and they were phallic symbols – penis worship for the sake of fertility – so were doubly naughty).

But Stubbes saved his best lines for the theatres.

Stubbes said that theatres were invitations to debauchery of all kinds:

> *Mark the flocking and running to Theatre and Curtains [two London playhouses in the 1580s] daily and hourly, night and day, time and tide . . . where such kissing and bussing [canoodling] such winking and glancing of wanton eyes . . . is wonderful [not in a good way] to behold.*

And what happened after the show? 'Every mate sorts to his mate . . . and in their secret conclaves they play the sodomites or worse.' Worse? Steady on! Can't you just see the steam coming out of Stubbes's ears?

And he wasn't alone. John Stockwood complained that thousands went to the theatre where barely a hundred went to church. Theatres taught you to lie, cheat, steal, scoff, mock, murder, 'devirginate maids' and to ignore God's laws.

By 1588 various tracts signed by 'Martin Marprelate' – not a real person, and the surname means 'evil bishop' in Latin – appeared on walls all over London attacking the bishops in the Church of England. The Godly were gaining ground.

Remember that brilliant scene in *Shakespeare in Love* where a Puritan preacher is ranting outside two theatres in London – 'A plague on both your houses,' he screams. It's a good phrase and Will Shakespeare (Joseph Fiennes), passing at that moment, overhears the words and pinches them for his forthcoming *Romeo and Juliet*. Genius!

## *Pressing the Presbyterians*

In Chapter 13 we explain that some Puritans wanted a church run by *synods* (assemblies of clergy and important laymen), not bishops. One Puritan sect, which came to control the Scottish church, was the *Presbyterians*. They didn't believe in bishops, but wanted a church run by elders who were responsible to their local community. All Presbyterians were Puritans, but not all Puritans were Presbyterian.

What bothered Puritans most was the cop-out clause that allowed people to go to Anglican services now and again (occasional conformity) while they were actually secret Catholics. They realised they wouldn't get anywhere in Parliament so they did their own thing and set up *prophesying*, group training sessions for Bible study. Elizabeth wasn't happy with prophesying and banned it.

Archbishop Edmund Grindal, who succeeded Matthew Parker as archbishop of Canterbury in 1576, ignored Elizabeth's ban on prophesying and lost his job. His replacement, John Whitgift, was an Anglican hard-liner who blasted both Presbyterians and Catholics from his pulpit.

Anthony Cope tried to push Puritan legislation through the Commons, wanting to abolish Elizabeth's Church and set up a Presbyterian model instead. Most of Parliament was horrified and the queen had the move stopped. Cope's timing was appalling – this was 1587 and a great deal of uncertainty existed in the country over the plans of Philip of Spain (see Chapter 15). It wasn't the right time for change of any kind.

## Silencing the separatists

By the 1590s many Puritans believed that the Church of England was so corrupt that nothing and no one could save it. The only way forward was to break with the Church and set up separate sects. Puritans got a real hold on the country in the next century, and of course the Pilgrim Fathers took their ideas to America, but separatists didn't make much headway at first.

In 1593 Parliament passed the Act against Seditious Sectaries, which killed the separatist group in the Commons and in the country as a whole. That year Parliament was difficult, holding up taxes for war costs (see Chapter 15) until religious issues were put on the agenda. Elizabeth refused to cooperate, and dismissed her MPs. On 29 May a leading Puritan, John Penry, was hanged after a dodgy trial accusing him of printing anti-Church propaganda.

# Wondering about Witchcraft

The year before Henry VII became king (see Chapter 2) two Catholic monks, working on orders from the pope, wrote *Malleus Maleficarum* (*The Hammer of the Witches*). The Catholic Church believed (wrongly) that all over Europe people were worshipping the devil and having sex with demons of the night. *Malleus* was a sort of guidebook for recognising witches and a punishment manual too.

The Middle Ages wasn't crammed full of witches. The actual number of trials for witchcraft was tiny. It wasn't until the upheavals of the Reformation that witchcraft's ideas gained ground, and even then different types of witchcraft existed:

✔ **White witches** were cunning women (and men) who'd been around forever. They lived in villages, helped at births, looked after the sick and laid out the dead. Most of their remedies were harmless, some were (unintentionally) dangerous and some actually worked (the life-saving miracle drug penicillin is, after all, mould on bread). At a time when doctors were few, expensive and not very good, cunning women made sense.

✔ **Black witches** could be hired for *maleficia* (bad doings) like making your neighbour's crops fail or his best cow die. The success of spells was largely in the eye of the beholder (sympathetic magic) – if you believed it was possible, then anything could happen.

Punishment for English and European witchcraft differed. In England the crime was a felony, punishable by hanging. In Europe (and in Scotland) it was heresy, punishable by burning. A lot of the information we have about 16th-century witchcraft is European and the so-called confessions of witches were obtained under the torture of the Inquisition (see Chapter 10).

Flying to the sabbat (mass meeting) on a horse or a broomstick *may* have been the result of taking hallucinogenic drugs like hemlock. And if you had sex with the devil at an orgy, that was either some guy in a goat's head getting lucky or wishful thinking.

## Preying on the poor

Very few examples of witchcraft affecting anybody with money or status exist. James VI of Scotland changed all that when he became king of England in 1603 (see Chapter 16) because he was obsessed with the subject and even wrote a book about it, *Daemonologie*, in 1597. Before that, only the poor seemed afflicted (remember, the six-fingered Anne Boleyn wasn't, in the end, accused of witchcraft at her trial for treason; see Chapter 5).

## Going bump in the night

People were very superstitious in Elizabeth's England. In 1584 de-bunker Reginald Scot wrote *A Discoverie of Witches* in which he rubbished witchcraft in a very 21st-century way. He listed nearly 80 sprites and goblins that country-folk were afraid of, saying they didn't exist. Few people shared his views.

At Bungay, Suffolk on 4 August 1577 during a terrible storm (writers call it pathetic fallacy today) a black dog rushed into the church during morning service and tore the throats out of two people before dashing out again, leaving the shocked parishioners to note the claw-marks on the door and the fact that the church clock had gone haywire. Explanation? You tell us.

## The Chelmsford Trials

The first full trial for witchcraft took place at Chelmsford, Essex, in 1566. Three women were charged with bewitching a child and on the stand one of them, Agnes Waterhouse, told an appalled jury that she had a talking cat called Satan that fed on her blood. Like the Elvis song of 400 years later, the cat was 'the devil in disguise'. Satan promised her all sorts of riches in exchange for doing bad works and Agnes was hanged.

If you look at the case of Agnes Sampson (admittedly in Scotland) in the 1590s, you find out how the evidence for these trials was obtained. She had a bridle put on that pressed four iron prongs into her mouth and she was kept without sleep. After that, Agnes was probably prepared to swear that the moon was made of green cheese (which, for all she knew, it was!).

## *Hanging with the witches*

The witch craze didn't catch on in England until James Stuart became king and he brought a lot of superstitious baggage with him from the North.

The best portrayal of witchcraft from the time is Shakespeare's *Macbeth* in which the three weird sisters can prophesy the future and summon up Hecate, goddess of the underworld. But the play was written in James I's England specifically for the king himself, which is why it's about Scotland and witchcraft – James' two favourite topics. Did Shakespeare believe in it? We don't know.

## *Putting things in perspective*

Witchcraft stories have been exaggerated over the years to include all sorts of sexual deviance, pacts signed in blood with the devil and so on. It whipped up hysteria and was infectious but no statements made by witches themselves were obtained without torture.

The old, the lonely and the eccentric were likely to annoy people in a village and it was all too easy to point an accusing finger at them.

No recorded examples exist of witchcraft being used against the queen or her Government in Elizabeth's England. On the other hand, one knack that witches were supposed to have was the ability to cause storms at sea. As you see in Chapter 15, Elizabeth could have used their services in the summer of 1588, the summer of the Armada.

# Chapter 15

# Facing the Armada

· · · · · · · · · · · · · · · · · · · · · · · · · · · · · · · · · · · · · · · · · ·

## In This Chapter

▶ Getting on the bad side of Philip of Spain

▶ Defending the Dutch

▶ Singeing the king of Spain's beard with Francis Drake

▶ Drumming the Armada up the Channel

· · · · · · · · · · · · · · · · · · · · · · · · · · · · · · · · · · · · · · · · · ·

The world was not enough for Philip II of Spain in the 1580s. He owned huge chunks of the world, his treasure ships prowled the seas and the 16th century was Spain's *siècle d'oro* – golden century. But irritated by Elizabeth's privateers (see Chapter 12), Philip was eventually forced into action when England backed the Dutch revolt against him in the Spanish Netherlands.

Elizabeth's approach was cool and pragmatic, making stirring speeches to her troops and relying on the most brilliant seamen of the age – and bad weather – to destroy Philip's Armada: the biggest invading fleet the world had ever seen.

## Provoking Philip of Spain

The king of Spain was autocratic and pious and had no sense of humour. He was the most powerful man in the world in the 1580s, more than the president of the United States today because no one had elected him. He was king of Spain, the Netherlands and much of the New World because, he believed, God had put him on the throne, and he never let anyone forget it.

For much of his reign Philip was at war with France and the Ottoman Turks whom he regarded as something less than human because they weren't Christian. But he knew Elizabeth personally, had once proposed to her, had been married to her sister (see Chapters 10 and 11) and had a grudging respect for her.

## Walking a fine line

In Chapter 12 we introduce you to two seafarers: John Hawkins and Francis Drake. Hawkins had already annoyed the Spanish authorities in the New World, but he'd now settled down to become treasurer of the navy and to use his huge talents redesigning ships and reorganising the fleet. Drake, on the other hand, was still upsetting Spain's apple cart by helping himself to loot in Spanish America.

The 1570s and 1580s were the decades in which Elizabeth turned a blind eye to the piracy of her seadogs, infuriating Spanish ambassadors sent by Philip to sort out the English privateers' antics.

Elizabeth's promise to Philip was half-hearted at best. In theory

- ✔ All unlicensed voyages must stop.
- ✔ All plundering of friendly ships must stop.
- ✔ All loot taken illegally must be handed over to the Lord Admiral's Court in London.

All this was fine but in practice complications existed. Merchant ships had been armed for several years for their own protection on the seas and captains who were a long way from home and without any communication from land did their own thing, firing on foreign shipping as a matter of course.

## Tightening up?

In July 1561 Elizabeth issued a proclamation giving special protection to the subjects of 'her good brother' of Spain and sent out a few warships to arrest and execute pirates. She gave the Bristol merchants a licence to use armed ships for their own protection (which may actually have increased violence on the high seas). In any case, Elizabeth's instruction was too little, too late. The general trend was for captains to shoot first and sort it out with the lord admiral later.

By 1569 Elizabeth was distinguishing between acts of piracy that went along with foreign policy (attacks on Spanish ships) and acts of piracy that didn't (attacks on anybody else).

The international waters were muddied, however, by what happened in December 1568. The English grabbed five ships out of Biscay laden with wool and 450,000 ducats of Spanish silver at Plymouth and Southampton on the orders of William Cecil, Elizabeth's secretary of state. Technically, the treasure didn't yet belong to Spain because it hadn't got there, but nobody could pretend that this was the work of a rogue Devon seadog acting without orders miles from anywhere.

## *Stacking the deck in England's favour*

By 1580 Philip believed that Elizabeth was challenging his naval and political supremacy. What was his evidence?

- ✔ Hawkins' involvement in the Spanish–American slave trade (see Chapter 12).

- ✔ Drake's attacks on Spanish–American colonies (see Chapter 12).

- ✔ John Dee, the queen's astrologer (check him out in Chapter 17), suggested a huge fleet extension paid for by a tax on fishing. It didn't happen, but the Spaniards knew the *intention* existed.

- ✔ Dee came up with the idea of a British Empire (one of half a dozen guys given this phrase as their own) that would include North America and threaten Philip's claim to the New World.

- ✔ An increasing number of trading companies, like the East India Company, were being set up in the last quarter of the century, from Virginia to the Far East.

- ✔ English nobility were keen to invest in trading voyages. We see this with Hawkins (Chapter 12) and Martin Frobisher's expeditions in the 1570s in search of a north-west passage to China (see Chapter 17 for more on Frobisher).

Spain and Portugal had dominated European and world trade for a century. It looked now as if England was ready to take over.

# *Plotting in the Shadows*

Take a look at Chapter 14 and all those plots against Elizabeth – Ridolfi in 1572; Throckmorton in 1583; Babington in 1586. In all of the plots, Philip and/ or Spain appear somewhere. It's almost as if, turned down by the queen as Philip was for marriage, he was determined to get her some other way; hell hath no fury like a king of Spain scorned.

How much did Philip actually know? Well, he had no interest in Mary Queen of Scots (see Chapters 13 and 14). And although Pope Gregory XIII sometimes spoke on Philip's behalf because it sounded more threatening to Protestants, this doesn't mean that Philip himself was in the know. How much Philip knew about the English depended on how well informed he was kept by his ambassadors in England. Until the 1580s Philip's involvement and/or awareness didn't matter and Elizabeth did her own thing in foreign policy.

Philip knew all about the Throckmorton Plot. He encouraged his ambassador, Bernardino de Mendoza, to complain to Elizabeth about Drake's piracy (which annoyed her) and the man was sending secret, coded messages to Philip filling him in on events. But when Elizabeth's spymaster Walsingham uncovered the Throckmorton Plot, de Mendoza was kicked out, marking the end to Spanish ambassadors in Elizabeth's England.

# Helping the Low Countries

The cold war between England and Spain might have gone on for years with acts of piracy, recriminations and the odd hanging. What happened in the Low Countries in the 1580s, however, turned a cold war into a hot one.

Figure 15-1 shows the area known today as the Netherlands as it was at the time before the rebellion against Spanish control. Note how close England is across the North Sea.

In 1548 Charles V, the Roman emperor (see Chapters 3 and 5), gave the Spanish Netherlands (the Burgundian Circle) to his son Philip, who was determined to introduce a strong Catholic government from Madrid.

## Lording it over the Low Countries

When Philip became king of Spain in 1556 he set up his half-sister, Margaret of Parma, as regent in the Netherlands and sent his right-hand man, Cardinal Granvelle, to hold her hand.

---

## The Burgundian Circle

In the 16th century people called what's Holland or the Netherlands today the Burgundian Circle. It was made up of 17 provinces, each with its own economy, customs and local government called *estates*. The south, which included Flanders, Brabant and Hainault, were French-speaking and rich; the great cloth-trading centres of Antwerp, Bruges and Ghent were among the wealthiest cities in the world. Many people here were Catholics.

In the northern provinces like Holland and Zeeland, farming was the usual occupation, poverty was harsh and most people spoke a kind of low German. Those nearest the coast were fishermen and there were large numbers of Protestants who objected to any kind of central government control. In theory, the Estates General was in overall control of all the provinces, but its powers were vague and nobody took much notice.

---

Granvelle had two priorities: to stamp out heresy (all forms of Protestantism) and to set up a strong, centralised Catholic government. Not unnaturally, the locals complained: Protestants were outraged at these big brother tactics and nobles realised they'd lost their power.

Margaret was caught between a rock and a hard place. She was forced to sack Granvelle, but when she tried to give even more concessions to the Dutch Philip recalled her and sent in the hard-line duke of Alba (plus troops) instead.

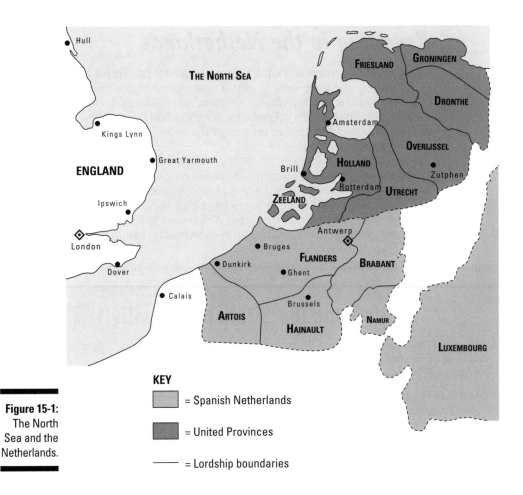

**Figure 15-1:**
The North
Sea and the
Netherlands.

With this iron fist approach, many Dutchmen fled to England and set themselves up as pirates, attacking Spanish and Flemish ships in the Channel. During a thaw in the Anglo–Spanish cold war, Elizabeth kicked them out in 1572 while she negotiated with Philip.

Not to be outdone, the *sea beggars*, as they're known, crossed the sea again and set up operations from Brill, harassing Alba and threatening to link up with France – a two-pronged front that Philip dreaded. The actions of these lawless renegades kick started the Revolt of the Netherlands.

## Revolting in the Netherlands

Clashes went on between Dutch rebels and Alba's troops for four years and by 1580 the battle lines were drawn. Ten southern states (including what's Belgium today) stood with Spain; seven northern states decided to carry on the fight for independence. English volunteers had been fighting for some time on the rebel side, either for pay or the hell of it, and Elizabeth had done nothing to discourage this.

Elizabeth was given a chance in 1581 to become queen of the rebel provinces, but (sensibly) turned it down. It would have meant a head-on clash with Philip. Events hotted up three years later with the assassination of the rebel commander of the United Provinces, William of Orange, known as the Silent (for more on William and his death, see the nearby sidebar 'Silencing the Silent (eventually!).

### Silencing the Silent (eventually!)

Philip and the pope had wanted William the Silent dead for some time and a bounty of 25,000 crowns was on the table for the right man.

Jean Jaureguy had a go, shooting William in the head in Antwerp in March 1582. Remarkably, William survived (although ironically his wife, nursing him, died of a fever). Another attempted hit followed in March of the following year and William moved to Delft for greater safety. Thirteen months later Hans Hanszoom from Vlissingen tried to blow William up, but that didn't work.

Finally, posing as a poor Calvinist refugee, Balthasar Gerard from Burgundy wormed his way in to see William and shot him three times, finally getting the job done. The Spanish authorities saw to it that Gerard's parents got the reward when their son suffered a ghastly and lingering death in front of a huge crowd. Rejoicing Catholics kept the killer's head as a relic and tried to have him declared a saint.

The death of William of Orange forced Elizabeth to face reality. The new military commander on the block was Alexander Farnese, the duke of Parma, who was every bit as hard-line as Alba and probably the best soldier of his generation.

Tempers ran high in the Council as they argued in front of the queen over whether or not England should intervene, and the upshot was the Treaty of Nonsuch in August 1585, which

- ✔ Gave the Dutch rebels an army of 7,000 men led by the earl of Leicester, which would cost England £126,000 per year.
- ✔ Gave Elizabeth two fortresses and the town of Vlissingen (Flushing) as surety that she'd get her money back.

The treaty amounted to a declaration of war, but it was what Drake was up to on the far side of the world that probably tipped the balance.

## *Plundering with El Draco*

Before the Treaty of Nonsuch (see the previous section) Philip had grabbed all English ships in Spanish ports on some flimsy pretext about needing them for some unspecified service. It all sounded a bit dodgy and was – this was actually a pre-emptive strike against England designed to make a point. In 1585 the queen ordered Francis Drake to Vigo in Spain to demand the release of the English ships.

Drake had just refitted a fleet of 20 ships including the 600-ton *Elizabeth Bonaventure* and the Vigo governor wasn't expecting this sudden arrival of force. He handed over ships and crews and Drake probably should've gone home, but being Drake he had other ideas. We don't know what instructions Elizabeth gave him, but the raid that followed was a plain message to Spain: don't mess with the English navy.

Drake burned Spanish settlements in the Canaries and the Cape Verde Islands, and on New Year's Day 1586 he took the town of Santo Domingo on Hispaniola (today's Haiti), hoping to ransom it back to the Spaniards for large amounts of cash. When that didn't happen, Drake burned the place down and moved on to Cartagena and St Augustine in Florida.

In Florida he got an invitation from the newly set up colony at Roanoke and he arrived to find it in trouble. The colonists were running out of food and were surrounded by hostile Native Americans (Drake and his men would probably have called them heathens). The colony was abandoned and Drake took the colonists home, landing in Plymouth on 28 July 1586.

## Leicester in the Low Countries

You'd expect that the leader of the English expeditionary force in the Netherlands would be a nobleman, but the Tudor style of government meant that noblemen with actual battle experience were thin on the ground. Leicester was therefore a bit of a rare bird – a nobleman who did have military experience. At first, the English did quite well, earning the duke of Parma's respect, but their efforts soon went pear-shaped. In September 1586 Philip Sidney, courtier and darling of the literary set, was killed at Zutphen (the silly man wasn't wearing leg armour – will they never learn?). After that, progress went downhill. Leicester lost the vital garrison at Sluys and in February 1586 made himself governor general with Dutch backing. This was clever because it looked to the world as if Elizabeth backed the Dutch all the way; in fact she was furious with Leicester for taking the title on and recalled him.

Drake lost 700 of his 1,700 man expedition, mostly from disease, and his backers only got 75 per cent of their expected return. He did, however, destroy a number of Spanish colonies and humiliate the viceroy of the Indies at very little cost to Elizabeth's government. As an open act of war, Drake's activities would be difficult to better.

Francis Drake has gone down in English history as *the* Elizabethan top seadog, a national hero. No doubt he had guts and was a brilliant sailor, but man-management wasn't his thing and he was no team player. Even in an unruly and violent age, his men were allowed to behave appallingly in their raids on the Spanish colonies.

# *Preparing for Invasion*

What were Philip II's options for a campaign against England?

- ✔ He could invade directly from Spain, hitting the south coast with 150 ships (the fleet he called the *Armada*) carrying 50,000 men.

- ✔ He could take advantage of the ongoing squabbles in Ireland (see Chapter 14) and use the country as a springboard for invasion, hitting England on two fronts from the south and the west.

- ✔ He could link up with Parma's army in the Low Countries and hit England on two fronts from the south and the east.

By the beginning of 1587 Philip had decided on the last idea, but with modifications. The Spanish fleet would now sail up the Channel, collect Parma's troops and invade from the east. But because he no longer had an ambassador in England, Philip had no good idea of the strength of Elizabeth's defences.

Philip had problems:

- ✔ Parma didn't like the plan. He had no deep water port in the Low Countries that could accommodate 150 ships and he told Philip so. Philip ignored him.

- ✔ The marquis of Santa Cruz, Philip's administrator, was useless. He collected troops, gave them no provisions and was astounded when men deserted.

- ✔ Various Spanish towns were supposed to provide ships and guns, but they didn't always, and the guns and ammunition supplied were of such a mixture of sizes and types that it became chaotic.

## *Talking tactics with Elizabeth*

The queen and her Council knew that the Armada was being assembled but they didn't know where and when it would strike. So they tried to cover all bases:

- ✔ John Hawkins was sent to patrol the Western Approaches (see Figure 15-2).

- ✔ Elizabeth ordered new ships to be built, like the *Vanguard*, *Rainbow*, *Seven Stars* and *Popinjay*.

- ✔ Elizabeth licensed more privateers.

- ✔ The queen unleashed Drake (see the following section).

---

## Calculating the cost

The marquis of Santa Cruz was ready to launch Philip's fleet in 1587 but Philip dithered – he wasn't sure it was necessary and it was going to cost an arm and a leg. The original estimates were 4 million ducats (about £1 million) but various changes saw that rocket to 7 million and the actual cost was 12 million – for a plan that would fail.

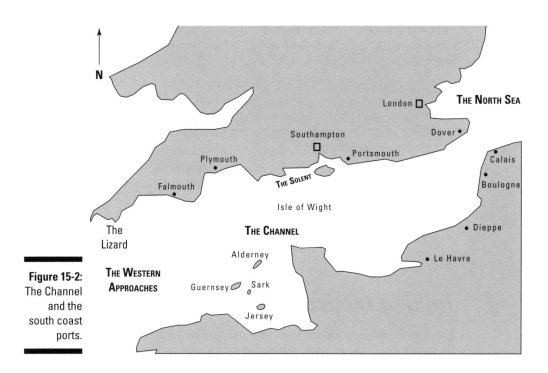

**Figure 15-2:**
The Channel
and the
south coast
ports.

## Firing the fire ships

England sent Drake to raid the Spanish forces, partly paid for by Elizabeth and partly by courtiers and merchants. As a fence-sitter, the queen continued to have doubts about whether she should've sent Drake even after he set sail.

Most of the Armada was being fitted out at Lisbon, but the forts along the Tagus river were too well fortified and Drake hit Cadiz, on Spain's south-west coast, instead. There weren't many ships here, but it was an important supply base for food, weapons, clothing and other necessities for a voyage (see 'A life on the ocean waves', later in this chapter, for life on board a ship).

Drake set fire to *pinnaces* (small boats) and sailed them into the harbour, packed with explosives. He destroyed 30 Spanish ships and the *galleys* (oared warships) sent out against him were no match for the seadog.

Sensibly, Drake didn't try attacking the well-fortified town, commanded by the duke of Medina Sidonia, but sailed off to the Azores in the mid-Atlantic where he captured the huge treasure ship *San Felipe*, which paid for the whole expedition several times over.

## The race-built galleon

If there was one man responsible for saving England from the Armada it was John Hawkins. As treasurer of the navy, he teamed up with a master shipwright, Richard Chapman, and designed the *race-built galleon*, pinched from Spanish blueprints, but modified. Hawkins' ships were lower in the water and more stream-lined than anything in the Spanish navy. Their continuous gun decks meant that they were more deadly while at the same time giving the ships more stability. Hawkins also hit upon the idea of a double sheathing of oak planking below the waterline to lessen the effects of corrosion from barnacles and other sea creatures.

Although no one would know it until put to the test, the English ships could outrun and out-manoeuvre the heavier Spanish galleons and galleasses and would prove invaluable in the Channel fighting.

Drake's comment on Cadiz is the famous, 'I have singed the king of Spain's beard.' Spanish men were very proud of their beards, seeing them as a sign of macho virility. If Drake realised this his comment was psychologically devastating.

The attack on Cadiz put Philip's plans back by a year. The losses were calculated at 172,000 ducats (£60,000) but even worse was the fact that with preparation costs running at 300,000 ducats a month, any delay was disastrous.

## *Losing Santa Cruz, and gaining Medina Sidonia*

The death of Santa Cruz wasn't much of a loss, really. Philip's man was out of his depth with an operation on the scale of the Armada. He died of typhus fever, which had broken out in the Spanish fleet, and was replaced by the duke of Medina Sidonia. Even so, the loss of Santa Cruz brought everything to a standstill until the new appointment.

Because the Armada ultimately failed, people have tended to write off Medina Sidonia as a failure too. In fact, he was a brilliant administrator and worked tirelessly to turn the flagging enterprise around. If Hawkins made the English victory possible with his revolutionary warship designs (see the sidebar 'The race-built galleon'), Medina Sidonia made the Armada launch possible in the first place.

Brilliant and energetic though Medina Sidonia was, he didn't think the Armada would work and wrote to Philip to beg off, claiming (rightly) a lack of naval experience. Philip refused to let him off the hook and Philip's aides intercepted more forthright letters from Medina Sidonia; the king never saw them.

So the admiral set to work. He increased the number of ships from 104 to 130; he nearly doubled the size of his army to 19,000 men; he provided food for the troops; and he improved the powder and shot problem for the guns.

# Smashing the Armada

After leaving, the Spanish fleet sailed in a crescent formation through the Bay of Biscay towards England's south coast, with the slower transports in the centre rear and the faster galleasses on the wings. The problem facing the English was that they couldn't be sure what Medina Sidonia plans were – whether he intended a direct invasion somewhere in the south or whether he intended to link up with Parma in the Netherlands.

## Sighting the Spaniards

The English lord admiral, Lord Howard of Effingham, was based at Plymouth on the Devon coast, because from there he could strike out against the Armada as soon as it was sighted and carry on a running gun battle up the Channel as far as was necessary. Howard also kept a squadron off the coast of Flanders, opposite the duke of Parma's position, to make sure he didn't break out from there.

The Armada sailed down the Tagus on 20 May with 132 ships. They were a motley collection of huge galleons (like Medina Sidonia's flagship, the *San Martin de Portugal*), galleasses, galleys, armed merchantmen and grain ships. Philip called this the *Enterprise of England* and it was underway at last. Its crescent formation when it was first seen off the south coast of England must have been terrifying.

Beacons were lit all over the south coast, linking up to others further inland, so everyone knew the Spaniards were coming.

It's not likely that Francis Drake was playing bowls on Plymouth Hoe and refused to give up his game even though the Spanish fleet had been sighted. That said, he knew the Devon seas like the back of his hand and knew he had plenty of time before engaging the enemy.

But Medina Sidonia had problems. He had no clear instructions on how to link up with Parma (Philip told him God would sort it out – thanks, Your Serene Majesty; nice one!) and an appalling storm off Galicia, northwest Spain, meant that the fleet had to put in to Corunna for repairs.

## Preparing Dad's Army

The Tudors had got rid of nobles' private armies, and apart from a handful of men who'd fought in Scotland or France very little military experience existed in England. Everybody was afraid of Parma because of his warfaring reputation and everybody was relying on the navy to prevent him landing.

By the end of June the county militias had been organised. They were led by the lords lieutenant and were badly armed and equipped. The plan was that

- A third of them would defend the beaches – the best place to stop an invasion.

- A third would form the second wave of defence if the Spaniards got inland.

- A third would fall back on London to defend the queen, who was already gearing up for the speech of her life (see the later section 'Inspiring the troops').

## A life on the ocean waves

You wouldn't have liked working on a Tudor warship. Check out the *Mary Rose* Museum at Portsmouth's Historic Dockyard for an idea of what it was like. For most of the time you were cramped below decks in the dark with rats, fleas and lice as well as the livestock you'd brought on board for food – chickens, geese and sheep. The water had to be rationed – drinking seawater kills your kidneys – and the usual daily food was ship's biscuits infested with slimy little creatures called weevils. Scrubbing the decks was a daily chore and you needed to be quick, strong and agile to climb the rigging to the mast heads 9 metres (30 feet) up in high winds and driving rain.

Tudor warships didn't have hammocks (canvas beds) until the mid 1590s, so men slept on the decks between their guns. Guns came in lots of different sizes and weights with a whole variety of names – culverins, sakers, minions, falcons, port pieces, fowlers and bases. All guns fired round shot (iron cannonballs) designed to smash through the hulls of enemy ships. On firing, the guns jolted backwards with the recoil and so they had to be held fast by ropes. The noise was deafening and some men permanently lost their hearing. Some Spanish eyewitnesses said that the English could fire their cannon as fast as the Spaniards could fire their muskets.

## Keeping the crescent

The appalling weather kept Howard's fleet penned in and then blew him off course far to the south, so he had to put in to Plymouth again to restock with food. Luckily for him, Medina Sidonia's approach was made at the speed of his slowest troop carriers so the English still had time to sail out against the Spanish.

Throughout July Howard's navy bombarded the crescent formation of the Armada, snapping at its heels as it made its way up the Channel. Fearing that the Spaniards would land on and capture the Isle of Wight, Howard divided his command into four. He led one squadron on board the *Ark Royal* and Drake, Hawkins and Martin Frobisher led the others on board the *Triumph*, the biggest ship in either fleet.

The Spanish naval battle system was different from the English. Medina Sidonia's tactic was to fire on an enemy ship (a *broadside*) then get close enough for soldiers to swing across by rope and fight hand-to-hand on the enemy's decks. The English system, by contrast, was to continue firing until a ship sank or surrendered and dart away out of range if the going got tough.

While the others prevented the Armada from sailing into the Solent where the *Mary Rose* had gone down 43 years earlier (see Chapter 3), Drake hit their right wing and drove them further north-east.

But despite the superior English gunnery, the crescent formation was still intact and essentially, the Armada was still on its original course. Gravelines would change all that.

## Battling off Gravelines

When he got to Calais Roads, Medina Sidonia was appalled to see no sign of Parma, who should have been on the coast to meet him as he put in to harbour. The general had been delayed and anyway would not put to sea as long as the English navy was still harassing the Armada. He wasn't to know that Howard's men were desperately short of shot and probably wouldn't have been able to withstand a direct assault by the Armada.

The English admiral sent in his fire ships, which exploded in the crescent formation, sank a few ships and scattered the rest.

Then, off Gravelines in France at the end of July, Howard went in for the kill. Only three or four Spanish ships were sunk but most of the rest were made unseaworthy. The casualty rate on board each ship probably wasn't very high, but the ships themselves scattered, leaderless, and were forced into the North Sea by rough winds.

The Enterprise of England had failed.

## Limping home

Many of the Armada ships never got back to Spain. They sailed all the way round the British coast and many were wrecked on the treacherous rocks of the Western Isles of Scotland (see Figure 15-3 for a map of their route from start to finish). The rocks around Britain are still littered with Spanish wrecks. Some landed on the Irish coast and were greeted as brothers in arms by fellow Catholics who hated the English. In other places, locals cut the Spaniards' throats as they waded ashore.

About 15,000 men had died, mostly by drowning, and the huge cost of the whole project threatened to bankrupt Spain.

## Inspiring the troops

About 20,000 men were ready to defend London if necessary. Even with the fleet scattered, the Council knew that if the Armada could put in to neutral Norwegian ports they might still refit and get Parma across to England.

On 9 August 1588 Elizabeth made speech at Tilbury, east of London. She knew that a renewed attack by the Armada wasn't likely, but the men who heard her speak that day knew no such thing and probably feared the worst. She wore a breastplate and backplate, rode a white horse and waved a sword. The queen told her men:

> *I know I have the body of a weak and feeble woman, but I have the heart and stomach of a king and of a king of England too, and think foul scorn that Parma or Spain or any other Prince of Europe dare invade the borders of my realm . . .*

Elizabeth was deafened by the cheers and applause and her speech has gone down as one of the great moments in history. Check out Cate Blanchett's delivery in *Elizabeth*. She's about 20 years too young for the queen at this point in her life, but catches the combination of bravado and vulnerability beautifully.

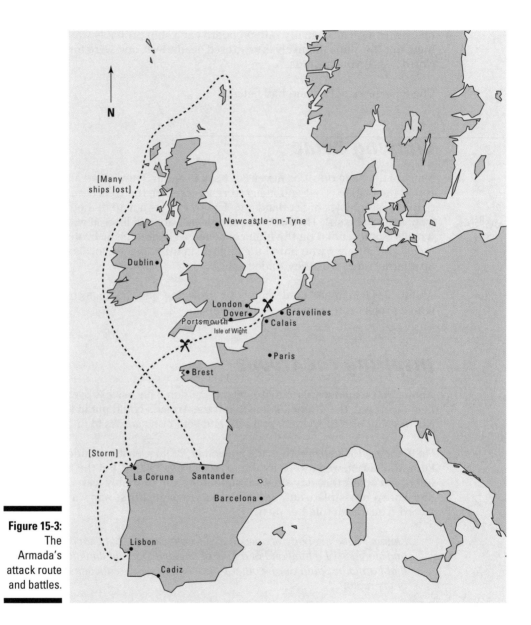

**Figure 15-3:**
The
Armada's
attack route
and battles.

# *Winning the Battle, Not the War*

If this was a Hollywood film, this chapter – indeed this book – would end
here, with triumph and success. History isn't like that. The show must go on.

## Considering another invasion

Could a Spanish invasion have worked in 1588? No, because

- ✔ English seamanship and gunnery made Medina Sidonia's plan to link up with Parma impossible.
- ✔ Bad weather helped the English enormously.
- ✔ Bad Spanish planning meant that there wasn't much of a Plan A, still less a Plan B. No one had any idea how to get Parma's troop transports across the Channel.

Crossing the 21 miles of water to England has always proved a problem. Napoleon couldn't do it in 1804; neither could Hitler in 1940. It only worked in 1688 because the invading army of William of Orange was actually invited over. The last actual enemy who'd managed the crossing was William, duke of Normandy, in 1066.

## Lining up for a rematch?

Philip was, of course, distraught, believing he must have offended God somehow to explain the Armada's loss. But although shaken, he was also stirred and he fought back, entirely rebuilding the fleet by 1593 and improving West Indian and South American defences, so that when Drake attacked the Spanish Caribbean in 1595 he came away empty-handed.

Meanwhile, under threat of yet another invasion, Elizabeth reluctantly spent money updating Carisbrooke Castle on the Isle of Wight to make it a state-of-the art fortress (find out more about the castle in Chapter 19).

---

### The plight of the queen's sailors

More sailors died on board the English ships after the Armada was scattered than during the whole of the action, mostly from plague and typhus. The casualty list was nearly as high as that of the Spaniards. The English sailors stayed on board because Elizabeth refused to pay them, whereas a bitterly disappointed Philip nevertheless welcomed his men home as if they were returning heroes.

Another Armada was launched from Ferrol in Spain in 1597, with 136 ships and 9,000 soldiers. Again, vicious storms destroyed it off the Lizard, the Cornish Peninsula, and no invasion took place.

## Dispensing with Drake

In the autumn of 1588 the English plan was to smash the remnants of Philip's Armada, moored in Santander, Spain. The queen sent Francis Drake to get the job done but he exceeded his authority, as he often did, and he attempted to put the pretender Dom Antonio onto the Portuguese throne, which Philip had held since 1580. The deal was that Antonio was supposed to have a huge following in Portugal (not true) and would give the English all kinds of trade benefits (which never happened).

The campaign's backers lost a lot of cash, the queen herself losing £20,000. Drake's career was effectively over and Elizabeth decided that from now on, war would be conducted solely by warships under direct orders from the Council.

For the queen herself, the last years of her reign lay ahead (see Chapter 16).

# Chapter 16

# Ending an Era: 1590–1603

The end of the 16th century coincided (almost!) with the end of Elizabeth's reign. The queen was 60 in 1594 and couldn't pretend to be a luscious young lovely any more. Children were out of the question – and that meant that crafty English politicians were already looking to Scotland for the next ruling generation in James VI. 'The queen is dead; long live the king.'

But before she went, Elizabeth had unfinished business. Spain was still a threat, Ireland was still grumbling and ambitious men like Robert Devereux, the earl of Essex, and Walter Ralegh, 'that Lucifer', toyed with her affections.

And the men who'd always been there for Elizabeth had gone – William Cecil and Francis Walsingham, who'd guided her policies and watched her back, were dead or dying. A new generation jockeyed for position and got mixed up in intrigue.

One thing was certain – Elizabeth would go out in a blaze of glory that still shines bright today.

## Dashing Devereux: Elizabeth's Last Fling

Robert Devereux was the second earl of Essex and the stepson of Elizabeth's favourite, Robert Dudley, earl of Leicester (we cover their relationship in Chapter 12). He was better looking than Leicester, but just as vain and ambitious, and step-daddy introduced him at Court in 1584 when Essex was 18.

## Did they/didn't they?

Getting a handle on the relationship between Elizabeth and Essex is difficult.

In the film *The Private Lives of Elizabeth and Essex* Bette Davis makes a reasonable Elizabeth, but for all the white make-up, she's 20 years too young for the queen. Essex is Errol Flynn, the greatest swashbuckler of them all and the casting is perfect.

The real Elizabeth and Essex enjoyed each other's company and played cards in her bedroom all night, but probably no more. She was 33 years older than he was but the bottom line is that they each had what the other wanted. Elizabeth was queen of England, the most powerful woman in Europe, and could open all sorts of doors for an ambitious young blade. Essex was young, handsome, funny and outrageous and no doubt he reminded the queen of the now-dead Leicester and the heady days of her youth.

## Climbing the promotion ladder

If one thing stands out about careers in the past, it's not what you know, but who you know. And for every brilliant practitioner, like Thomas Wolsey, Thomas Cromwell, William Cecil and others we meet in this book, you find a lot of idiots. Essex was one of these.

He started out okay:

- ✔ He was made general of the horse (cavalry commander) and went with Leicester to the Low Countries where he fought at Zutphen in 1586 (see Chapter 15).
- ✔ He was knighted on the field (by his step-dad).
- ✔ He was made master of the horse, following again in Leicester's footsteps (see Chapter 12).

So far, so nepotistic, but Essex's arrogance would've been the ending of anybody else's career:

- ✔ He quarrelled with the queen over her treatment of his mother and flounced out of Court. That would've been social death for anyone but Essex.
- ✔ He spent a fortune, both on courtly duties and on a small sailing fleet that was always in the red.
- ✔ He joined the Lisbon expedition (part of the Counter-Armada led by Francis Drake in 1589) when Elizabeth had told him not to and he was recalled. Even so, he wasn't disgraced and his charmed life at Court continued.

## Failing in France

Essex's experience in the Low Countries made him believe he was a brilliant soldier (he wasn't) and he had the cheek to write to the new French king, Henri IV, to ask for a job.

The French Wars of Religion were still going on (see Chapter 13) and Henri (of Navarre, as he was then) was the leader of the Protestants against the Catholic League run by the Guises. In 1591 Henri asked for Elizabeth's support in Normandy and suggested Essex as the man for the job. The queen gave Essex only 4,000 men and kept him (sensibly) on a tight rein. Even so, Essex saw himself as some sort of latter-day Alexander the Great.

The campaign didn't go well, but it wasn't entirely Essex's fault. Elizabeth and Henri disagreed over the strategy (the main objective) of the campaign and Essex wasn't good enough to rise above this. He did, however, knight 24 of his officers on the battlefield, which annoyed the queen considerably.

Elizabeth recalled Essex after six months, but guess what? He wasn't just still a favourite at Court; he got a job on the Privy Council as well.

## Stirring up the Council

By the 1590s Elizabeth's 22-strong Council had dwindled to a hardcore of 13 who met regularly. Of these, only a handful made most key decisions – William Cecil (replaced after his death in 1598 by his son Robert); Lord Howard of Effingham (the lord admiral) and Henry Carey, Baron Hunsdon, (the lord chamberlain). They were a tight-knit bunch and dropping Essex into their little pond was a disaster.

From February 1593, when Essex arrived, people began to flock round him for advancement. Elizabeth was shrewd enough to realise that this was dodgy and didn't promote any of his followers. Essex began to smell a conspiracy.

While Essex was taking part in the capture of Cadiz in 1596 (see 'Looking Beyond England' later in this chapter), Elizabeth promoted Robert Cecil to principal secretary. He'd been doing the job for a while because his dad was too old and ill to cope.

Robert Cecil was deformed, possibly with a spinal condition, and was only about 147 centimetres (4 foot 10 inches) tall. Elizabeth (who of course had known Robert since he was a baby) called him 'my imp', which he hated.

When Essex came back from Cadiz he was furious to find the younger Cecil in the top job and clashed with him constantly.

Essex had his own spy network and was well informed about events in Europe. He dealt directly with leaders in France, Scotland and the United Provinces (the northern Netherlands – see Chapter 15) and his mood swings were affected by how well-informed he was. When his confidence was low, Essex sulked and quarrelled with everybody; when it was high, he was generous and gracious.

In 1597, at a particularly low point, Essex left the Court but came back on the death of William Cecil the following year. Elizabeth made him earl marshal, the senior peer of the realm.

The earl marshal's job today is to organise the great state occasions like Trooping the Colour and the Opening of Parliament. In Elizabeth's day occasions like these (see her progresses in Chapter 12) were the only way in which ordinary people ever saw their monarch, so they were vitally important PR exercises. Even today, nobody does pageantry like the British.

## Tackling Tyrone

Increasingly, after the death of Philip of Spain (see the later section 'Looking Beyond England') and treaties between Spain and France, the mood of the Council was for peace. Essex stood out like a sore thumb over this, looking for military glory anywhere he could find it. He didn't want Ireland, but the death of the governor, Sir Thomas Burgh, in 1597 meant that he got it anyway.

### Understanding Ulster

The most northern of the Irish provinces, Ulster, was divided between Turlough O'Neill and Hugh O'Neill, the earl of Tyrone, who was a Gaelic chieftain and an Anglo-Irish peer (for more on the O'Neills, see Chapters 13 and 14).

Hugh O'Neill had been raised in the English Court, and in spite of his open Catholicism and proud Gaelic heritage he believed he was the man to run Ulster for the English and stop centuries of in-fighting. This became particularly important in 1586–1587 when Philip II had been toying with the idea of mounting a Spanish invasion from Ireland (see Chapter 15).

The Council, however, didn't want to know about Tyrone's offer of stability – neither did the English governor at the time, William Russell. Mightily miffed by this snub, Tyrone became a rebel against the English instead.

The earl of Tyrone isn't the usual hero of any film and the one portrait of him isn't likely to be accurate, so we don't know what he looked like. But check out Alan Hale's performance in *The Private Lives of Elizabeth and Essex*. How could any self-respecting Irishman fail to follow him?

### Reviving hope

Tyrone raised a huge army of 5,000 infantry and 1,000 cavalry. Unlike most rebel armies, which were small and badly equipped, Tyrone's men were trained and had the latest state-of-the-art muskets and pikes. By June 1595 Tyrone had taken Sligo and most of Connaught.

Slightly panicky, the Council sent over reinforcements. Russell now had 600 cavalry and 4,000 infantry.

### Playing for time

In October Tyrone asked for a pardon and got a truce that lasted until the following May. He was hoping that Philip II, still harbouring ever wilder dreams of mounting another Armada (see Chapter 15), would use his services against the English. Tyrone's chance was lost along with several ships that Philip sent out in October 1597.

### Upping the ante

The scale of Tyrone's actions against the English had now amounted to a civil war. Russell was recalled by the Council and replaced by an excellent soldier-administrator, Thomas Burgh. He was outnumbered by Tyrone, however, and died of typhus before he could make any real headway against him.

No hard evidence exists to tell us where Tyrone's cash was coming from. Okay, he had Ulster under his control, which brought in about £80,000 a year in rent, but the war was costing him £500 a day. Perhaps some Spanish loot was coming his way.

### Fighting at the Ford

On 14 August 1598 Tyrone, backed by rebel leaders Hugh O'Donnell and Hugh Maquire, smashed an English army under Henry Bagenal at the Battle of Yellow Ford over the Blackwater River. Bagenal himself was killed and this was a major blow to English hopes of controlling the provinces. More than 3,000 settlers fled from the plantations in Munster, mostly to Cork and Waterford.

Tyrone's rebellion was something new in Irish history. It was organised, disciplined and backed with cash. Using the Catholic religion and Gaelic heritage, Tyrone helped to create a national identity in Ireland that, centuries later, would drive the English out of all provinces except, ironically, his own in Ulster.

It was against this background that Essex took up his Irish appointment in March 1599. His failure in Ireland was more obvious than in France. He had a massive army of 17,000 men but spent weeks marching all over southern Ireland, where no opposition existed, and decided he couldn't meet Tyrone head on.

Forced north on the orders of a furious Elizabeth, Essex inexplicably only had 4,000 men with him when he met the rebels near Louth. He agreed a feeble truce with Tyrone and Elizabeth recalled him.

## *Rebelling with Essex*

This time the queen's darling had gone too far and as soon as he arrived in England Essex was arrested and spent a year in prison. Elizabeth would hear no more excuses – the man was in his 30s by now, an experienced soldier and politician, and he'd made a complete dog's breakfast of Ireland.

Released in August 1600, Essex was a broken man. His finances were non-existent and he was forbidden to attend Court, the one place where he might have smarmed round the queen again. He sulked at Essex House in London throughout October, brooding over the enemies who'd conspired against him – Robert Cecil, of course, Lord Cobham on the Council and one of the most dazzling men of Elizabeth's age, Walter Ralegh (you can find out about him in the nearby sidebar 'That Great Lucifer: Walter Ralegh').

---

### 'That Great Lucifer': Walter Ralegh

Ralegh (he never spelled the name with an 'i') was another Devon seadog like Drake and Hawkins (see Chapters 12 and 15). He loved nothing better than a fight and had abandoned his Oxford University place to fight for the French Huguenots (Protestants) at Jarnac and Moncontour. He raided Spanish colonies with his half-brother Humphrey Gilbert and put down a rising in Ulster in 1580.

Elizabeth was dazzled by Ralegh – his West Country brogue, his dark, brooding good looks – and she heaped honours on him. Ralegh was seriously rich after she gave him total control of wine imports and cloth subsidies. In the 1580s he was exploring North America and setting up the English colony at Roanoke, bringing tobacco and potatoes to England (see Chapter 18 for more on this).

Essex replaced Ralegh as the queen's favourite, and he never had an earldom or a place on the Council. In 1592 the queen found out about Ralegh's affair with one of her ladies, Bess Throckmorton (check her out in Chapter 17), and put Ralegh in prison for four years (over the top, or what?), only letting him out to negotiate with Devon pirates for her cut of the loot from a Spanish treasure ship, the *Madre de Dios,* which was the biggest prize of the entire reign.

Ralegh was supposed to be an atheist and a member of the pseudo-scientific School of Night (see Chapter 17 for more on this group). He lived on after Elizabeth in increasing disfavour under James I and was executed at Whitehall in 1616.

Essex had no intention of harming Elizabeth, but by the end of 1600 he decided it was payback time. He got together like-minded people who had an axe to grind against the *Cecilocracy* (the government of the Cecils) and made plans to overthrow the Court, sack the Privy Council and form a new Parliament.

On 7 February 1601 the Council called upon Essex to explain himself. Robert Cecil (who'd taken over as spymaster) probably knew exactly what was going on – after all, he certainly did in the infamous Gunpowder Plot four years later, which was designed to kill James I.

Essex refused to attend the Council, so they went to him. When the lord keeper, Thomas Egerton, turned up at Essex House, Essex kidnapped him and let 300 swordsmen loose in the streets of London. But nobody backed Essex and when the authorities moved in most of the 300 melted away. Essex surrendered the same evening, despite having vowed to fight to the death.

Essex's guilt wasn't in question. He'd appeared, armed, against the queen's peace and that was treason. At his trial, at the Court of the High Steward, on 19 February Cecil let him have it:

> *For wit, I give you pre-eminence. For nobility I also give you place. I am no swordsman; there you also have the odds. But I have innocence, conscience, truth and honesty to defend me . . . and your Lordship is a delinquent.*

Essex was beheaded privately in the grounds of the Tower on 25 February.

# *Looking Beyond England*

Events of the Tudor era didn't come to an end neatly at the end of a reign, and in 1603, when Elizabeth died, unfinished business remained.

## *Spain*

The war with the world's only superpower dragged on into the next century. As long as Philip II was still building – and actually sending out – Armadas, Elizabeth had to respond.

On 1 June 1596 a huge combined fleet of Anglo-Dutch warships (100 in all) sailed for Cadiz under the command of Howard of Effingham. Essex, at that point still in favour at Court, led the soldiers. The raid was a brilliant success. The English captured the city, and most of the Spanish fleet moored there was set on fired by their own crews, who did a bit of plundering first, and sunk. By the time the Spanish commander Medina Sidonia arrived, it was all over.

No looting (along the lines of Drake) took place, and a vast amount of cash (about £7 million) should have reached Elizabeth, but didn't. The money probably popped into the pockets of the commanders. The taking of Cadiz should have been the high water mark of English success against Spain, but instead people remember the more dramatic if less successful Armada of 1588 (see Chapter 15).

After Cadiz the fire went out of Spanish foreign policy as far as England was concerned.

✔ Increasingly, the country was bankrupt, ruined by expensive war and the hyper-inflation caused by flooding the economy with silver.

✔ Philip II died in 1598 and his son, Philip III, had other problems and other ambitions.

✔ After Elizabeth neither the new king, James I, nor his principal secretary, Robert Cecil, were warmongers.

Spain and England signed a peace treaty in a new spirit of 'friendship and amity' in 1604, and Spain was to begin its long, slow decline into being one of the poorest countries in Europe.

### Ireland

The earl of Tyrone's success in the 1590s (see the earlier section 'Tackling Tyrone') led to an actual tie-up with Spain in 1601, but the timing was bad.

Charles Blount, Lord Mountjoy, took over as governor after Essex's recall and forced Tyrone back on the defensive. By the time the Spaniards arrived, Munster was peaceful. The Spaniards, under Don Juan del Aguila, were outnumbered by Mountjoy and defeated at Kinsale on 2 January. Elizabeth allowed Mountjoy to agree to terms with Tyrone, who gave up the Spanish connection and his authority as head of the O'Neills. By 1603 the Wild Lands (see Chapter 2) had gone and Ireland was divided into counties just like England and Wales.

Ireland was only partly sorted. Further rebellions and vicious retaliation followed in the centuries to come, and as late as 1869 British Prime Minister William Gladstone was saying that his 'mission is to pacify Ireland'. The sad story of that country is that peace still isn't secure.

### France

England's old enemy continued to be tied up in their internal religious and political problems. Elizabeth had backed Henri IV when he asked her for help against the Catholic League, but his sudden conversion to Catholicism in 1593 changed the goal posts and English involvement there ended with the capture of El Leon near the naval port of Brest in 1594.

In 1598 Philip of Spain signed the Treaty of Vervains with Henri, burying the hatchet after years of warfare.

The 17th and 18th centuries are the years of French greatness – as Spain fell, France rose. England, as always, watched from the sidelines and considered carefully whether or not to get involved. Increasingly, many Englishmen believed 'abroad was a bloody place' and wanted little to do with it.

### The Netherlands

English backing of the Dutch proved successful in the short term. When the brilliant duke of Parma died in 1593, no one of his calibre existed to replace him and the Dutch had found their own excellent general in Maurice of Nassau, son of William the Silent.

The Dutch finally became independent in 1609 and remained on friendly terms with James I, Elizabeth's successor.

In the longer term the English and Dutch fought each other over fishing rights in the 1660s, but in 1688 a Dutchman, William of Orange, became king of England. The Tudors would have collectively turned in their graves.

# Saying Farewell to Gloriana

As the century turned it was obvious that the queen wouldn't last much longer. Friends were dying all around her, and increasingly her letters were about old friends she missed and places she'd never visit again. When William Cecil was dying in August 1598 she sat by his bedside and fed him soup.

In her last speech to Parliament in November 1601, when they were complaining about the monopolies they accused her of passing out to favourites, she told them, 'Though you have had and may have many mightier and wiser princes, yet you never had nor never shall have any that love you better.'

The queen remained tetchy and quick-tempered to the last – a man who talked about the succession risked death. And even in her last days when Robert Cecil told her she must go to bed, she said, 'The word must is not to be used to princes . . . little man, little man, you know that I must die and that makes you so presumptuous.'

With the exception of two serious illnesses earlier in her reign (see Chapter 12), which were smallpox and probably malaria, Elizabeth was extremely healthy. She danced, rode and hunted well into her 60s. On the other hand, her teeth were black and rotten and she probably suffered from toothache.

---

## Leaving an image of strength

Image was as important to Elizabeth as it was to Henry VIII (see Chapter 3) – perhaps more so because she was a woman competing in a man's world. So everything was carefully stage-managed and the truth has got lost in the fiction.

She was careful not to let unofficial portraits see the light of day – they were banned in 1563, but the official portraits say it all. The 18th-century gossip Horace Walpole got it right – 'A pale Roman nose, a head of hair loaded with crowns and powdered with diamonds, a vast ruff, a vaster farthingale and a bushel of pearls.'

It screams wealth, it screams power and you cross it at your peril.

Okay, so Elizabeth doesn't, in the portraits, stand like Henry VIII – that would be silly. But everything else you see is a mixture of macho and desirability. In the Armada portrait you see her brilliant warships in the window behind her and her right hand rests lightly on the globe that had been rounded by Francis Drake. It's almost as if she's pointing to the future – her country would one day own vast chunks of that globe and be the greatest imperial power in history.

---

Elizabeth spent Christmas 1602 at her lodge in Whitechapel and caught a severe cold in January, developing a boil on her face. By the end of a wet and gloomy month she was having difficulty swallowing, and on 20 March she collapsed on her way into chapel. She wouldn't go to bed, despite Cecil's attempts, and sat propped on cushions with her finger in her mouth, refusing to eat. She lost the power of speech and died in the early hours of 24 March 1603, almost certainly of pneumonia.

The queen left instructions that she wasn't to be embalmed, but she was, and her heart was enclosed in the same casket as her sister Mary's in Westminster Abbey (check out their tombs there today).

'Some,' wrote the poet Thomas Dekker, 'call her Pandora, some Gloriana, some Cynthia, some Belphoebe, some Astraea . . . I am one of her country and we adore her by the name of Eliza.'

# Gangin' Doon wi' Wee Jamie, or Going Down with King James VI

As Elizabeth had grown older, the issue of who'd take over from her became more urgent. She refused to talk about succession, but the practical men of the Council had a job to do.

Back in 1543, the Succession Act of that year said

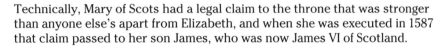

> ✔ Edward would succeed Henry VIII as Edward VI.
>
> ✔ If Edward died childless the crown would pass to Mary I.
>
> ✔ If Mary died childless the crown would pass to Elizabeth I.

Mary and Elizabeth were included despite the fact that both of them had been declared bastards. Mary Queen of Scots was ignored because she was 'alien born' (in other words, although she was descended from the Tudors, her father was James V of Scotland, one of the Stuart family).

Technically, Mary of Scots had a legal claim to the throne that was stronger than anyone else's apart from Elizabeth, and when she was executed in 1587 that claim passed to her son James, who was now James VI of Scotland.

Elizabeth wasn't likely to repeal Henry VIII's Act of Succession because some would say that gave Mary of Scots as good a claim to the throne as Elizabeth, and Elizabeth didn't want Mary and her line to have the throne because Mary was a Catholic (see Chapter 13 for more on Elizabeth's attitude towards Mary). James Stuart, however, was brought up in the Protestant faith, so the problem went away.

The only other claimant possible for the throne in 1603 was Arabella Stuart, a granddaughter of Margaret Clifford and a niece of James's dad, Lord Darnley. But Margaret was never really a front runner and the earl of Essex had been in secret communication with James VI for some time. Essex's fall (see 'Rebelling with Essex', earlier in the chapter) caused a slight hitch, but the queen's crafty adviser Robert Cecil sent emissaries to James and assured him of his support after the queen had gone.

---

## The wisest fool in Christendom

This book is all about the Tudors, not the Stuarts, but it won't hurt to have a look at the man who was to take over in 1603. James had been king of Scotland for 35 years by the time he took over the England job and was now 37 years old. He was married in 1589 to the 15-year-old Anne of Denmark and the couple would eventually have seven children.

James's first appearance in London horrified many courtiers. The man's head was too big for his body, his tongue lolled and he dribbled. His skinny little legs were in marked contrast to his big thighs and body. James wasn't fat – his clothes were double padded to safeguard from knife attacks and because he was terrified of the naked steel of armour. He spoke with a broad Scots accent (which took time for his courtiers to understand), hated tobacco, which he called the 'noxious weed', and was afraid of witches, whose work he'd seen up close and personal.

Time would show James to be bisexual, intolerant and an appalling handler of parliaments, even though he was scholarly and cultured. It was Henri IV of France who called him 'the wisest fool in Christendom'. But James's full story belongs to another book.

When Elizabeth passed away on 24 March, after a gruelling ride of 60 hours, with frequent changes of horse, courtier Robert Carey reached Edinburgh to break the news to James. When asked who should follow her, Elizabeth, in her last coherent moments, had said, 'Who but our cousin of Scotland?'

Looking back, Cecil missed Elizabeth and life working for James was no bed of roses. 'I wish,' he wrote, 'I waited now in her Presence Chamber with ease at my foot and rest in my bed.'

And the legends began to grow about the Tudors and the last of them, Good Queen Bess.

# Part V
# The Part of Tens

## In this part . . .

Like all For Dummies books, this one ends with some fast and fun information. Sample the delights of Hampton Court, find out why bad boy Kit Marlowe died, and dabble in magic with Dr Dee. We have something here for everyone – snippets from a vanished and fascinating age.

# Chapter 17

# Ten Top Tudor People

*W*e could write a whole book about people of interest from the 118-year Tudor period – some of them you've heard a lot about; others, little; and some you haven't heard of at all. But we only have a chapter for this topic, so here we cover ten of the best – people who made their mark not just on Tudor society, but in the world at large and in history generally.

## Anne Askew (1521–1546)

You meet some feisty women in this book, but none more so than Anne Askew. She was born to a wealthy landowning family in Lincolnshire, and with the shadow of the warnings of the Book of Leviticus (see Chapter 5) hanging over her, she was forced to marry her dead sister's husband, Thomas Kyme.

Anne was a rarity – an intelligent woman whose family taught her to read and write. She hated Kyme, and although she had two kids by him she refused to take his surname and began to appal hubby (and lots of other people) by learning huge chunks of the Bible and preaching in public throughout the county.

When Kyme tried to put a stop to his wife's preaching she left him and went to London, where her radical Protestant ideas were more widely accepted than in a rural backwater like Lincolnshire. It's possible that Anne met queen Catherine (Parr) at this time, because when she was first arrested for holding illegal Protestant prayer meetings Catherine sent food and warm clothing to the Tower where Anne was being held and then got her released.

The deal agreed for Anne's release was she had to give up preaching and go back to Kyme. Instead, she demanded a divorce on the Biblical grounds that she wasn't bound to stay married to an 'unbeliever' (a Catholic). Anne's was a clever argument, but the Court wasn't having any of it. Because Anne didn't have the wherewithal to set up a new Church to push her divorce through (which was what Henry VIII had done – see Chapter 6), she meekly obeyed.

Perhaps *meekly* isn't the right word, because Anne left Kyme twice more, came back to London, preached and was arrested all over again. This time, the powers that be used torture on Anne, so vicious that the constable of the Tower, Anthony Kingston, left in disgust. The lord chancellor, Thomas Wriothesley, and Richard Rich, the ex-crony of Henry's adviser Thomas Cromwell, interrogated Anne themselves. Then Kingston came back and put a stop to it – Anne was a gentle-woman and as such shouldn't be subjected to being stretched on the rack . Kingston appealed to the king and Henry agreed to back off as long as Anne recanted. She refused.

Anne was brought to Smithfield just outside London's city wall on 16 July 1546. A huge baying crowd watched as she once again turned down Henry's offer of mercy. Her legs were so badly twisted by the rack that she couldn't stand and she had to be tied to the stake on a chair. While the Catholic priest read out his words for the soon-to-be-dead in Latin, Anne argued with him in English. Then the executioners sprinkled gunpowder over Anne's body and set fire to her.

Wriothesley and Rich had been hoping to get Anne Askew to implicate the queen as a closet Protestant, but she named no one during their interrogations. She richly deserved her place in John Foxe's *Book of Martyrs* (for more on Foxe, scan down to the later section devoted to him).

# Bess of Hardwick (1527–1608)

It isn't often that you hear about women in the Tudor period who weren't queens. And it's interesting that Elizabeth Hardwick is better known for her house than herself!

Bess was the daughter of a well-to-do family who sent her (as was usual) into the service of a great household – the Zouche family of Derbyshire. At their town house in London she met and fell in love with Robert Barlow. She was 13 and her husband wasn't much older, but he died of 'chronic distemper' (which could be anything!) and so she married again.

Bess's second husband was William Cavendish, who was one of the commissioners of Thomas Cromwell (a top adviser to Henry VIII), and he was busy getting rid of the monasteries in the 1530s (see Chapter 6 for more) and making a small fortune buying up Church land cheap. The pair married at 2 a.m. (don't ask!) on 20 August 1547. William was 22 years older than his wife but the marriage was happy and produced eight children.

As a landowner at the time of the Enclosure Riots (see Chapter 7), Bess was a hardliner, depopulating villages on behalf of her husband. Cavendish died in October 1557 and Bess married William St Loe, a wealthy widower with children of his own. She was now a lady-in-waiting to Elizabeth I, owned the impressive Chatsworth House in Derbyshire and was a very good catch. St Loe became captain of the queen's bodyguard.

Bess's good fortune nearly came unstuck, however, when she got involved with Catherine Grey, sister of Jane, the Nine Days Queen (see Chapter 9). Bess knew of Catherine's secret marriage to the earl of Hertford and didn't tell the queen. Because Elizabeth hated being kept out of the loop as far as her ladies were concerned, it was off to the Tower for Bess for six months.

St Loe died in 1565 and Bess married George Talbot, the earl of Shrewsbury. Talbot was probably the richest nobleman in the country and got the job of guarding Mary Queen of Scots between 1569 and 1584. She and Bess became very friendly. Her links with Mary were bound to end in tears, and sure enough, Bess fell foul of Elizabeth again when she was found out for spreading malicious gossip about the queen. Her husband disowned her.

Bess bought Hardwick Hall in 1583 for £9,500 and rebuilt it for her adopted daughter, Arabella Stuart, whom she hoped would be the next queen of England. Bess plotted to get Arabella on the throne when Elizabeth died (see Chapter 16), but she failed.

The woman was hard-headed, calculating, a serial marrier and quite capable of bending the truth when it suited her. In that sense, although she had no links to the royal family, Bess Hardwick was a Tudor through and through.

# Christopher Marlowe (1564–1593)

Like Shakespeare (see the later section on Will), Marlowe was a playwright and poet. The pair were only two months apart in age and both wrote for the London stage. They must have known each other and the relationship portrayed in the film *Shakespeare in Love* is probably right – the Stratford man was in awe of Marlowe because Marlowe hit theatrical London first and wowed everybody with his 'mighty line', the thumping beat called *iambic pentameter* that Shakespeare (and everybody else) pinched later.

In *Shakespeare in Love*, Marlowe is played by Rupert Everett in such a mysterious way that he isn't even listed in the film's credits.

And mystery was what Marlowe was all about. He was born in Canterbury, the son of a shoemaker, but was a bright boy and went to the King's School in the city (it's still there, with a Marlowe plaque on the wall). He went up to Corpus Christi College, Cambridge, getting his first degree in 1583 and his Masters in 1587. Marlowe was probably recruited as an agent by Elizabeth's spymaster Francis Walsingham between those dates. He was 'on the queen's business' in the Low Countries (today's Netherlands) then, though we don't know exactly what he was up to.

Most scholars from Cambridge went into the Church but Marlowe went to London, lodged with fellow playwright Thomas Kyd in Norton Folgate and got his brilliant plays staged. *The Jew of Malta*, *Edward II*, *Tamburlaine* and the *Tragicall Historie of Dr Faustus* were all runaway successes.

Much of Marlowe's short life (he was dead at 29) is lost in the murky underworld of Elizabethan England. As a projectioner (the Tudor version of James Bond; see Chapter 14) he worked in a clandestine way, spying for Walsingham. He had a short temper and fought two duels in broad daylight for which he was bound over to keep the peace (basically, given a good behaviour bond). He was probably homosexual, although much of the evidence for this rests on his play *Edward II*. He was definitely an atheist, denying the existence of God. Some of the articles he wrote – saying that Jesus and John the Baptist were lovers – still shock today.

Marlowe may have been a member of the School of Night, an exclusive club to which Walter Ralegh belonged. The members of this club were actually wannabe scientists, but in those days science and the black arts of devil worship went hand in hand (see the later section on John Dee).

Marlowe was killed in a pub brawl in Deptford, London on 30 May 1593 – or was he? Some people say he didn't die at all, but, on the run from the authorities for his atheism (then a burning offence) he got to Europe and went on to write the plays of Shakespeare! The actual details of Marlowe's death are peculiar. He wasn't in a pub but in an eating house belonging to Eleanor Bull, a cousin of William Cecil (see Part IV). And the men with Marlowe were spies too. Marlowe may have been murdered by the state, on orders from the Council.

After 400 years Marlowe finally has a memorial in Poets' Corner in Westminster Abbey and a society of his own.

# Cecily Bodenham (?–1543?)

The women in Tudor England were expected to know their places and do as they were told. But a surprising number of them were well educated, strong and resourceful. It's a sign of women's status generally, however, that we don't have a clue when Cecily Bodenham was born or precisely when she died.

Cecily was born in Rotherwas, Herefordshire on the Welsh border, the daughter of Roger Bodenham and Joane Bromwich. At some point she decided to become a nun, which wasn't unusual for girls of genteel but impoverished families – being a nun saved a bit of money.

Cecily became a nun at the Convent of Kingston St Michael in Wiltshire and was obviously a bright cookie, rising to be prioress. Check out Geoffrey Chaucer's *Canterbury Tales*, written in 1386. One of the Chaucer's characters who goes on a fictional pilgrimage to Canterbury is a prioress. She wears gold jewellery and spends a fortune on her lapdogs, feeding them fresh meat and bread dipped in milk. Maybe Cecily was a bit like that, not the married-to-Christ virgin she was supposed to be, because in 1511 she was kidnapped by a local curate who also robbed the priory. After various negotiations, she got her old job back.

By 1534 the job of abbess at the huge Wilton Abbey came up. Wilton was an important saint's shrine and very rich, and Cecily, who was known at Court, paid Henry VIII's adviser Thomas Cromwell £100 to get the job (who said money doesn't talk?). With the job came a number of estates nearby, so Cecily was able to make quite a bit of cash.

In Chapter 6 we detail the story of Henry VIII's dissolution of the monasteries. Cecily was one of those who didn't die in a ditch over principles. Complaining that she was all alone – 'without father, brother or assured friend' – she let Cromwell's commissioners close Wilton down on 25 March 1539.

One of Cecily's nuns had got her number, though, and wrote in her diary, 'Methinks the Abbess hath a faint heart and doth yield up our possessions to the spoiler with a not unwilling haste.' Leaving aside the fact that nuns weren't supposed to have possessions at all, the smart sister had got it absolutely right. As Henry VIII sold off the monastic lands, Cecily got a very nice house in nearby Fovant with an orchard, gardens, three acres of meadow and unlimited firewood. She also got £100 a year.

Maybe it was Cecily's conscience that led her to take in ten of the nuns and build the south aisle of St George's Church in the village. Maybe she was buying her place in heaven.

# Elizabeth Throckmorton (1565–c.1647)

Elizabeth was always known as Bess and was one of the ladies-in-waiting to Elizabeth I (who was only ever known as Bess by a very select few). These ladies were titled, clever and often pretty with a lot of social accomplishments, but woe betide anybody who tried to outshine the queen.

Bess was the daughter of a diplomat, Nicholas Throckmorton, and Anne Carew, so she was brought up in Court circles. She was intelligent and feisty, but because of her scheming dad's behaviour, she had to tread warily. In 1569 Nicholas was sent to the Tower for pushing a scheme to marry Mary Queen of Scots to the duke of Norfolk (read all about Mary's adventures in Chapters 13 and 14).

When Bess met the dashing seadog Walter Ralegh (see Chapter 16) she fell for him and he seduced her (up against a tree, according to one account). She came out with all sorts of excuses to explain her thickening waistline but also insisted on marriage, to which Ralegh happily agreed.

The problem came when Elizabeth found out. Ralegh had been her favourite (some even said lover) for 12 years and although Bess's boy Damerei had died in the October of 1591 and Lady Ralegh was back at Court, the rumours finally reached the queen by May 1592. She was furious and jailed them both in separate apartments in the Tower for a time.

Elizabeth expected grovelling from the couple, but didn't get it. Ralegh was out of favour for good, although he attempted suicide in the Tower and was allowed out to carry on the queen's enterprising privateer business (see Chapter 12), raiding Spanish territory in the West Indies.

Bess produced a second son, Walter, in 1593 and another, Carew, later. The pair remained devoted, despite Ralegh's chequered career. After his long imprisonment and execution in 1618, Bess worked hard to clear her lover's name and re-establish his reputation.

The story goes that Bess kept her husband's embalmed head. On the block, the headsman dithered and an astonishingly gutsy Ralegh told him to strike home. The man had to swing the axe twice. Family stories claim that Carew Ralegh had the head buried with him when he died.

Bess Throckmorton has appeared many times on screen. Joan Collins played her in *The Virgin Queen* when Bette Davis was Elizabeth; Abbi Cornish took on the role in Cate Blanchett's *Elizabeth: The Golden Age*; but the greatest portrayal has to be Marge Simpson in *Four Great Women and a Manicure*. You have to be *somebody* to get on the Simpsons!

# Dr John Dee (1527–1608)

We spend a long time in this book looking at the religious beliefs of the Tudors, but despite their religion, they all had astrologers like John Dee at Court to give them advice on what was happening in the heavens.

However much science you know and however much you understand the world, you can't quite shake astrology off even today. Check out the horoscopes in any daily newspaper.

Dee had links to the royals from day one. His dad was a gentleman usher at Henry VIII's Court and he himself claimed to be descended from Rhodri Mawr (Roderick the Great), the 9th-century Welsh king, so working for the Welsh Tudors made a kind of sense. Dee got his degree at St John's College, Cambridge in 1544, and two years later he became one of the first fellows (tutors) at Trinity College (find out about the brilliant building in Chapter 19).

In the late 1540s, while England was becoming Protestant under Edward VI (see Chapter 8), Dee was lecturing in various European universities like Louvain and the Sorbonne in Paris.

Back in England in 1551, England was far behind the Spaniards and Portuguese when it came to navigation, so Dee used his considerable mathematical and astronomical skills to teach English sailors. One of his pupils was Martin Frobisher (see the later section on him).

Dee's life took a downturn in 1553 when he was arrested on charges of conspiracy to kill Queen Mary with sorcery. He'd provided a horoscope for Princess Elizabeth, predicting when Mary would die – that sort of thing wasn't just wishful thinking in the 16th century, it was treason. Even so, Mary pardoned him in 1556.

Under Elizabeth Dee did well, even deciding the best time for her coronation. He was often consulted by the queen and even the Council on all sorts of matters – out of this came his idea for the extension of the English fleet, paid for by a fishing tax (see Chapter 15).

But Dee is best remembered today for his occult dabbling. Like many scholars of his time, he was trying to find the Philosophers' Stone, which would turn scrap iron into gold. He was also looking for the Elixir of Life, which would create immortality. His neighbours in Mortlake, west of London, were so sure he was a black magician that they burnt down his house and laboratory in 1583.

Unfortunately, Dee hooked up with con-men like Edward Kelly and the pair tried for years to bring people back from the dead. Kelly was a convicted charlatan – he even had the clipped ears to prove it. (A common Elizabethan form of punishment was to clip the ears of a conman. To this day, people use the phrase 'I'll give him a clip on the ear', meaning 'to give a punishment'.) He spent most of his time convincing Dee that the spirits wanted him to share Dee's lovely young wife, which eventually happened.

After numerous adventures, mostly in Poland, Kelly was killed jumping out of a window in Prague and Dee came home to carry on his fortune-telling at the newly rebuilt house in Mortlake. In 1604 James I had to bail him out when he was once again accused of sorcery. Dee died four years later in poverty.

# John Foxe (1516–1587)

We come across this man several times in this book, and there's nobody better to record the cruelty of the Tudor age.

John Foxe was born into a middle class family in Boston, Lincolnshire and went to Brasenose College, Oxford at 16 (which was the usual age then). He was a bright spark, and could read Latin, Greek and Hebrew fluently. Foxe got his Masters degree in 1543 and became a lecturer in logic at the university. He was already a priest, as indeed were all lecturers, but two years later he got religion in a more serious way and resigned from the university because he wasn't happy with the idea of *celibacy* (no sex) for priests. Broke and jobless, he went to work as a tutor for the children of the Lucy family at Charlecote near Stratford-upon-Avon. While there, Foxe married Agnes Randall and they had six children.

In London in 1547 Foxe got himself a patron (essential in those days) and found himself teaching the children of the Howard family (the dukes of Norfolk), one of whom, Charles, would later command the English fleet against the Spanish Armada in 1588 (see Chapter 15). Foxe was now mixing with the top flight Protestant reformers of the day, many of whom would be burned in the years ahead.

Under Mary I from 1553 Foxe was walking a religious tightrope. The queen was bringing back the Catholic faith (see Chapter 10) and so Foxe got out of England quickly, the authorities on his tail. He travelled all over Protestant Germany, writing articles as he went and preaching at the English church in Frankfurt, where a lot of exiles had gone. There he got bogged down in a silly argument about which kind of Protestantism to follow. One type was led by Richard Cox; the other by John Knox (see Chapter 13), so it was Coxians versus Knoxians. Foxe was with Knox. (We know, it all sounds like a Dr Seuss book!)

After Mary's death in 1558, Foxe was in no hurry to come back to England. For a start, he couldn't afford the journey and anyway, he wanted to see which way the religious wind would blow under Elizabeth. Finally, back in London in 1559, his friend Edmund Grindal, bishop of London, ordained Foxe. But Elizabeth's Church wanted priests to wear *surplices* (white robes) and Foxe wouldn't. So that was the end of his promotional prospects.

But what we most remember Foxe for is his *Book of Martyrs* (actually called *Acts and Monuments*), which began life in 1554. The book was originally about the 15th-century Lollards, an anti-Catholic sect. While in exile, Foxe heard about the burnings of heretics under Mary and decided to expand the book to his present day. The first edition appeared in Basle, Switzerland in 1559 and a much larger (1,800 page) version in English four years later.

The book was a runaway best-seller, but royalties for writers didn't exist in those days and Foxe stayed as poor as ever. Catholics, of course, didn't like the book – Thomas Harding called it 'that huge dunghill of your stinking martyrs, full of a thousand lies'. The 1570 edition had 2,300 pages and the version of 1583 was four times longer than the Bible. It's a biased book and not much of a rattling good read today (the full title alone fills half a page), but as a diary of events of a ghastly time, it's invaluable.

Foxe died in April 1587 and was buried in St Giles, Cripplegate (London) where the explorer Martin Frobisher would be laid to rest seven years later.

# *Martin Frobisher (c. 1535–1594)*

Most of Elizabeth's seadogs came from Devon, but Martin Frobisher was a Yorkshireman from Altofts, near Wakefield. His father was a squire with quite a few estates and as a 13-year-old Martin was sent to London to get involved in business. This was quite unusual for the son of a man who had landed estates and the boy had no real head for business. We're not even certain whether he learned to read properly, but his involvement in the get-rich-quick schemes of the City of London gave Frobisher a passion for the sea and exploration.

In the 1550s Frobisher was trading with the Africans in Guinea on the West African coast and fighting off the Portuguese who already had the area sewn up (see Chapter 12). At one point he was taken prisoner and spent months in the grim jail of Mina, emerging with the tough resilience he exhibited all his life.

Unlike Francis Drake (whom Frobisher hated) and John Hawkins (see these men in Chapters 12 and 15), we don't know a great deal about Frobisher's life. He was in the West Indies in the 1560s and had something to do with the spread of English plantations in Ireland, but his activities are shrouded in mystery and he may have been acting as an agent for Elizabeth's spymaster Walsingham.

In 1576 Frobisher got the job of searching for a north-west passage to Cathay (China). Ever since the 1480s the overland caravan route to the East had been closed by the Ottoman Turks, so the rich spice trade was badly damaged. This is why explorers like Columbus, da Gama and Magellan travelled all over the world, trying to find a new way east. If, as clever men were beginning to believe, the world was round, then by going west, you could end up east.

Frobisher was backed by a London merchant, Michael Lok, and various members of the Council. Setting off with 35 men and two ships, the *Gabriel* and the *Michael*, he was the first Englishman to reach Labrador and the land he called *Meta Incognita* (Frobisher Bay). Here he found icebergs taller than any building he'd ever seen and was probably the first white man (except maybe the Vikings) to see the local native, the Inuit.

In two later voyages (1577 and 1578) he brought an Inuit back with him – the man could be seen rowing his kayak in Bristol harbour – and some ore that everybody from the queen down hoped was gold. After much testing, the 'black earth' turned out to be pyrites (fool's gold) and Frobisher fell from favour.

Frobisher was raiding with Drake in the Caribbean in 1585 (see Chapter 12), and when the Armada reached England from Spain three years later he was given command of a squadron and was knighted as a result of his bravery.

Six years later Frobisher was shot in the thigh fighting the Spaniards at Crozon near the French naval base at Brest. The wound became infected and he died on the way home. You can see a memorial to Frobisher in Blackwall, London, from where he sailed on his voyages, and a piece of his ore in a wall in Dartford, Kent. But the explorer never did find the North-west Passage.

# *Polydore Vergil (c 1470–1555)*

Okay, so perhaps this guy shouldn't qualify as a Tudor, because he was Italian, but he spent so long in England and worked as Henry VII's official historian so we figure he was in the loop.

Italy was the cradle of the Renaissance, the centre of the rediscovery of classical Greece and Rome that led to new ideas, discoveries and technology; and Polydore Vergil was part of all that.

The Vergils were a pretty cultured lot. Polydore's great-grandfather, Anthony, was a doctor and astrologer. One of his brothers taught philosophy at the University of Paris and another at Pavia in Italy. A third brother (obviously the non-academic black sheep) was a merchant in London.

Polydore was educated at Bologna and worked for various Italian noblemen before coming to England in 1501 as collector of Peter's Pence (one of the taxes that went to Rome – see Chapter 6). As Pope Alexander VI's man in England he got the job of receiver to the bishop of Bath and Wells three years later.

Henry VII knew a clever guy when he met one and got Vergil working on a huge 26 volume *Historiae Anglicae* (*History of the English*) in 1505. He was either a slow researcher or busy on other things, because the book wasn't finished until 1533 and was published the next year.

Vergil fell foul of Henry VIII long before the publication of his book. The king's top man was Thomas Wolsey (see Chapters 4, 5 and 6), who wanted to be a cardinal and probably pope. Vergil didn't back Wolsey and somebody found a letter he'd written that criticised both Wolsey and the king, so Vergil was put in prison. Pope Leo X pressured Henry for his release and Vergil was out after a few months.

In 1525 Vergil published a book on Gildas, the historian-monk from Strathclyde, Scotland in the 6th century. Vergil was a naturalised English citizen from 1510, but after 1538 he went back to Urbino in Italy for prolonged periods and he died there in 1555.

Vergil is important because in some ways he was the first of the real historians. We usually call historians of this period *chroniclers*, and the earlier ones were always churchmen (the only people trained to read and write in the middle ages). Vergil was sceptical and critical, as historians are supposed to be, but he was accused of burning manuscripts to cover his mistakes and stealing books from English libraries to ship them off to Rome.

His Book 27 of the *History of the English* covers the reign of Henry VIII and his hatred of Wolsey comes across very clearly. Even so, no better historian of the Wars of the Roses (1455–1487; see Chapter 2) existed.

# William Shakespeare (1564–1616)

The man from Stratford-upon-Avon, Warwickshire has a huge reputation. He was Man of the Millennium in 2000, the greatest playwright ever and you find more quotes from him than anybody else in a dictionary of quotations. In the

*Dictionary of Biography* Shakespeare gets three times the page space given to his queen, Elizabeth I!

Shakespeare's private life is so ordinary and boring that many people believe he didn't write the famous plays and sonnets at all. His father was a glove maker and wool dealer in Stratford. Young Will probably went to the local school and he married local girl Anne Hathaway (we discuss her house in Chapter 19) when he was 18 and they had three children: Suzanna and the twins Judith and Hamnet. At 25 Shakespeare went to seek his fortune, Dick Whittington style, in London.

In the big smoke Will became an actor-playwright in the trendy new world of the theatre that was opening up in the 1580s, which the Puritans hated (see Chapter 14). He made a reasonable fortune out of theatre profits in the Lord Chamberlain's Company and spent it on a new state-of-the-art house in Stratford, but he seems to have only rented in London.

In his late 40s Shakespeare pulled out of his theatre commitments, went back to Stratford and died there, neatly, on his birthday, 23 April 1616.

Shakespeare (whoever he was) wrote some superb plays that today are divided into comedies, tragedies and histories. Everybody's heard of *Hamlet*, *A Midsummer Night's Dream*, *Macbeth* and so on, and some of the phrases he invented have become part of everyday speech – neither a borrower nor a lender be; more sinned against that sinning; parting is such sweet sorrow; the world's [your] oyster.

Check out the brilliant *Shakespeare in Love* starring Joseph Fiennes as the Bard. Tom Stoppard, who wrote the screenplay, cheats: he has a very 21st-century Will with writer's block going to a psychiatrist and falling in love with a very unlikely heroine who's disguised as a boy. Fiennes has got far too much hair for what we think Shakespeare looked like – but then, what *did* he look like? Accurate it may not be, but the film is great fun from start to finish.

Shakespeare wasn't always popular in his day because he was so successful. Fellow writer Robert Greene called him an 'upstart crow'. Like everybody else in his day, the only reason Shakespeare's plays were put on and his poetry published was that he had a patron, probably the handsome Thomas Wriothesley (pronounced Risley), the third earl of Southampton.

Later generations turned Shakespeare into a literary saint and the word *genius* doesn't begin to describe him. He only ever lived in Stratford and London; he was never an explorer, a soldier or politician. But his plays are rich with experiences. For example, he never went to Italy in his life, yet plays like the *Merchant of Venice* and *Two Gentlemen of Verona* are vivid. Will's real skill, then, was pinching ideas from everybody else, knowing his theatre market very well and having a brilliant turn of phrase.

The Globe Theatre in Southwark, London, has now been rebuilt and is a working playhouse – check it out. Shakespeare's birthplace is a fascinating museum in Stratford, but New Place, the superb house that his success bought him, is just a space surrounded by a wall. You can visit his tomb too in Holy Trinity Church, Stratford.

# Chapter 18

# Ten Things the Tudors Did for Us

*W*hen the Tudors came to power in 1485 England was still a medieval country, run by a king who could barely control his nobles, where violence was a way of life and where the Catholic Church, run from Rome, was a law unto itself. Over the 118 years of Tudor rule, a lot of what people take for granted today was created.

Change happened by degree, not all at once and not always for the better. But by 1603 when Elizabeth I died, England wasn't just that awkward bit out in the sea, a backwater where nothing important happened; it was a sovereign state and a power to be reckoned with, and it had the finest navy in the world.

Later generations would see England become Britain, and Britain become 'the workshop of the world' and the heart of the biggest empire in history. But British development started under the Tudors.

## Civilising the Nobility

The men who ran England in the middle ages were the barons, hard men in a hard age who had castles and private armies. Their castles are all over England today, mostly in ruins – check them out for a feel of this lawless time.

What mattered to the nobility was the length of their pedigree – some families went way back to 1066 and the Norman conquest – and the size of their *retinues* (armed servants).

When the king was weak, as with Henry VI, or unpopular, as with Richard III, the nobles felt it their duty to take over. If several nobles decided on the same thing because of their ancestry, the result was a monumental punch-up like the Wars of the Roses, which lasted on and off for 30 years. (Chapter 2 has all the details of these wars and the pre-Tudor kings.)

Henry VII, the first Tudor, decided to put an end to the strength of the nobility:

- ✔ In 1504 he limited the nobles' followings to household servants (cooks and cleaners, not soldiers).

- ✔ He made the status of the king much higher than it had been – you addressed the king as 'Your Majesty', not 'Your Grace'.

- ✔ He educated his sons in the humanist tradition (see Chapter 2), stressing the importance of honesty, service and competence.

Okay, so it was a slow process, and the odd powerful person in Tudor England tried to be a monarch-maker – Thomas Wolsey under Henry VIII (see Chapter 4); Somerset and Dudley, Edward VI's advisors (Chapter 7); and even, though the attempt was pathetic, the earl of Essex in Elizabeth's last years (Chapter 16).

But by and large, the nobility grew up. Realising that the Tudors brought in new men from humble backgrounds, most of the nobility dropped their personal pursuit of power and worked hard for king and country.

# Encouraging Self-government

One way to cut the power of the nobles (see the section 'Civilising the Nobility') was to give power and responsibility to somebody else. Look at the backgrounds of some of the key men in this book who wielded enormous power: where they started is amazing. Thomas Wolsey's dad was a butcher; Thomas Cromwell's was a blacksmith and brewer. And they're just the tip of the iceberg.

What Henry VII did was to take a system that already existed – local organisations like the Commission of the Peace, Commission of Sewers and so on – and give it teeth. Until that time, *gentlemen* (rich, middle class men with or without an actual coat of arms) were tied to some great lord. But under the Tudors, gentlemen were tied to the king, and so the idea grew up of service to the Crown, not to an individual. And this idea has carried forth to this day: the Government's civil service stays constant whoever is on the throne and whichever political party is in power.

# Building Up Parliament

Parliament began in the 13th century as part of the Great Council of the king. It was made up of peers of the realm at first, then knights of the shire were added and finally *burgesses* (citizens) from towns with royal charters.

Edward I said in the 13th century, *'Quid omnes tangit ab omnibus approbetur'* (That which affects everybody ought to be decided by everybody) – so now you can show off your Latin too! Edward wasn't talking about democracy, though – not at all. Most people – the middle and working classes, the poor and all women – weren't in the loop at all. No elections took place and no political parties existed. Parliament only turned up when the king ordered it and only talked about what he wanted them to talk about.

Henry VIII's break with Rome changed all that (see Chapter 6 and the next section) because he needed all the help he could get. So in the 1530s Henry's top man, Thomas Cromwell, pushed all kinds of acts through Parliament to make them law. The acts were still the king's idea, but it now looked as if everybody in Parliament agreed and the country backed him too.

More and more acts were passed this way and monarchs increasingly had to call Parliament if they wanted money (usually to fight foreign wars). Now the growing role of Parliament was a bit of a double-edged sword. Okay, it gave the monarch support when he or she needed it, but it also made Parliament realise how important they were. As Elizabeth's reign went on, more MPs were demanding changes and getting difficult, and the queen sent one or two to the Tower.

In the next century Parliament and the monarch clashed constantly under the Stuarts. This led to civil war in 1642, the beheading of Charles I in 1649 and 11 years during which no monarch sat on the throne of England.

Today, Parliament calls the shots and the present royal family have no practical powers at all.

# Breaking with Rome

You can read all about Henry VIII's split with Rome in Chapter 6. The break is probably the most important change the Tudors brought about. Certainly, it caused them most bother.

In a nutshell, Henry VIII needed a divorce to get the son he needed to carry on the Tudor line. The pope (head of the Catholic Church) wouldn't grant one, so Henry made himself head of the Church of England instead. Now he could do what he liked.

The Catholic Church had been going for 1,400 years in England and old habits were difficult to break. Most people were illiterate and superstitious, and the Church had been there for them from cradle to grave.

Henry banned all links with Rome – the pope was now called the bishop of Rome – and closed the monasteries because they were places where the pope was regarded as top man.

Under Edward VI truly Protestant ideas took hold (see Chapter 8), but when the king died at 15, his sister Mary, a Catholic, tried to put the clock back and burned heretics who wouldn't follow her orders (Chapter 10). Then Elizabeth I set up a compromise Church in 1559 that was supposed to be half Catholic and half Protestant (Chapter 13), but nobody was fooled – it was a Protestant Church and became even more so as time went on.

Despite attempts by later popes to excommunicate Elizabeth and even have her killed, a number of Catholic plots failed and the Church of England is still alive and kicking today. Now, in a more tolerant age, Catholics and Protestants live side by side peacefully enough.

# Building the Navy

As an island, Britain has always depended on the sea both for trade and defence. The 'wooden walls of England' (the navy) have often kept the country safe from attack – and never more so than in 1588 when Philip II unleashed the Spanish Armada (see Chapter 15).

Before the Tudors England had very few warships and they were used for short periods of time, often being converted from existing trading vessels. Naval warfare was more or less land warfare on water. That's why the front and back of the ships had forecastles and aftcastles; they allowed soldiers to fire arrows and slingshots at each other from the decks.

Henry VIII set to work building a permanent navy with splendid ships like the *Henry Grace a Dieu* and the *Mary Rose*. They patrolled the English coast and took troops to France or wherever they were needed. By 1545 the fleet had nearly 50 ships varying in size from 20 to 1,000 tons. Check out the wreck of the *Mary Rose* in the Historic Dockyard at Portsmouth.

The navy became a government department of its own from 1546 and the lord admiral sat on the Privy Council (see Chapter 2), closely advising the monarch.

By 1580, thanks to the revolutionary designs of John Hawkins (see Chapter 15), English warships like the *Victory*, the *Nonpareil*, the *Dreadnought* and the *Revenge* were faster, more streamlined and more deadly than anything owned by any other European power.

The navy's legacy was picked up in the late 17th century and led to patriotic songs like 'Rule Britannia' in the 19th century. In 1886 the British navy was the largest in the world, the size of any other two countries' navies put together.

# Putting a Woman on the Throne

Some countries, like France with its Salic Law, said it wasn't alright for a woman to be queen in her own right. In theory, a queen could inherit the crown of England, but it had never happened. And people were hesitant. After all, the last queen before the Tudors had been Matilda in the 12th century and she'd spent most of her time fighting her rival Stephen for the crown. Nobody in Tudor England believed a woman could do the job.

The prejudice went back to Adam and Eve really – and medieval people, like the Tudors, believed every word of the Bible. Eve wasn't only made *after* Adam (a sort of reluctant PS), but she let the serpent (the devil) seduce her so that *all* women were naturally weak and more or less immoral.

In England the inheritance of the throne was based on *primogeniture* – the eldest *son* always following on from his dad. That all went a bit pear-shaped during the Wars of the Roses (1455–1487; see Chapter 2) where it was everybody for himself, but the Tudors carried on the primogeniture tradition.

The problem came with the early death of Edward VI (see Chapter 9). The only two real contenders for the throne were Mary and Elizabeth, his half-sisters who were both the daughters of Henry VIII. In fact, Henry had gone to great lengths, breaking with Rome and risking eternal damnation, just to get a son in the first place.

Mary wasn't a great queen – lots of men (like John Knox in Scotland, who hated women) must have said 'I told you so'. But Elizabeth was. She was more of a man than Henry could have hoped for and she told her troops at Tilbury in 1588 (see Chapter 15) that she had the stomach and heart of a king, and a king of England at that.

Although they all had the job in different times and different circumstances, later queens, like Mary II (1689), Victoria (1837) and Elizabeth II (1952), were rather good at it. Oh, except Anne (1702)!

# Messing Up Ireland

However you look at it, Tudor government in Ireland was a complete disaster. Since the 12th century the English had owned the Pale, an area around Dublin, and put castles and garrisons all over the Obedient Lands beyond that. Outside this were the Wild Lands where people spoke Gaelic, poverty was rife and tribe fought tribe as they had for centuries.

Henry VII was happy to let the situation continue, but Henry VIII wanted to sort Ireland out. All his strong arm tactics did was provoke a rebellion from the earl of Kildare and the idea of Irish independence was born. Have a look at the Irish sections in throughout this book and you see a pattern emerging. The map in Chapter 2 makes it clear. Yes, the English imposed the Protestant religion in theory and yes, they carved up Ireland into English style counties, but the rest was about force.

Local heroes like Hugh O'Neill rose in rebellion from time to time and by the 1580s England's fear was that the Irish might link up with Spain to cause real problems. An alliance didn't quite happen, but the establishment of English plantations with Scotsmen under the Stuarts was a festering sore that never healed.

The true start of the troubles between England and Ireland belongs to a later period, but all the warning signs existed already under the Tudors.

# Bringing in Bad Habits

Potatoes got to England by 1586 and people dumped them into stews alongside carrots, peas and beans. But who brought the spud to England? Francis Drake found some in Cartagena that year. They originally came from Peru and were only introduced into North America by the early English colonists in Virginia. On the other hand, Walter Ralegh is also credited with bringing tatties over. So who should be blamed for the chip, crisp, French fry (and they're certainly not French!) and people's ballooning waistlines today? Frank or Walt? You choose!

The natives found by Columbus and the conquistadors were already rolling up tobacco leaves, lighting them and shoving them up their noses by the late 15th century. Spanish and Portuguese explorers brought the leaves back by the 1550s and they got to England, where they really caught on, via raids on the Caribbean Islands in the 1560s. Englishmen smoked tobacco in clay pipes and it made them behave strangely. King James VI of Scotland hated the stuff, writing articles about tobacco and calling it 'the noxious weed'. Since then, tobacco has killed millions of people all over the world.

A discovery that completely passed by the Tudors, meanwhile, was the fork. Traveller Tom Coryat believed he brought the first fork to England in 1611, but that's not likely. People had them in 10th century Constantinople (that's Istanbul today) and it's likely the odd rogue one got to England via Italy and France by the 16th century. Check out the Bayeux Tapestry (made about 1070): everybody's eating with knives and fingers just like they did through most of the Tudor time.

# Widening Horizons

All medieval trade from England was with Europe before the discovery of the New World. Africa and Asia remained closed shops as far as buying and selling went, although the Portuguese in particular were exploring along the west African coast when Henry VII was newly crowned.

The biggest trade was in wool and unfinished cloth and much of it went via the Spanish Netherlands port of Antwerp. Companies like the Staplers and the Merchant Adventurers made huge fortunes out of this trade – the lord chancellor still sits with his feet on a woolsack as a historic symbol in the House of Lords.

The crisis in the wool market in the 1550s (see Chapter 7) led to a search for other markets. Explorers Richard Chancellor and Sir Hugh Willoughby set off in 1553 to find a new route to the East via the frozen Arctic Sea. They failed, but the Muscovy Company of 1555 opened up new trade with Russia, which brought furs and timber to England.

At the same time merchants were operating in Guinea in West Africa and John Hawkins butted in to the Spanish American slave trade. Courtiers and even the queen invested heavily in voyages of discovery (see Martin Frobisher in the previous chapter) and many new companies were set up, such as the Levant, the Eastland, the Virginia and the Hudson's Bay.

Nobody in England cried very much when Antwerp was virtually burned to the ground in 1576.

# Widening the (English) Channel

A long time after the Tudors, Napoleon Bonaparte said, 'The Channel is but a ditch. If I could control it for half an hour, I would have England in the palm of my hand.' And that was the problem. The Channel wasn't just 21 miles of water at its narrowest point, patrolled after the 1540s by English warships; the psychological gap was important.

The English Court had already started using the English language, not French, in the 14th century, and as England lost more and more of France during the 15th century the English felt less and less European as a result.

The last bit of France the English owned was Calais, and when they lost that in 1558 it was a deep shock. The town itself wasn't very important – it was the principle that mattered. Monarchs of England kept the French fleur-de-lys on their coats of arms until 1803. The loss meant, however, that England turned her back on Europe and got on with being first a global trader and then a global power.

Henry VIII's break with Rome added to this 'England first' attitude. The Catholic Church might have ruled Europe (although its grip was seriously weakened as a result of the Reformation) but it didn't rule England, creating a sense of 'them and us'.

The break with Europe wasn't complete, however:

- ✔ The final version of the Church of England was basically Calvinistic. Calvin was a Frenchman operating out of the Swiss city of Geneva.

- ✔ The academic world – lawyers, doctors and scientists – carried on using Latin, which people all over Europe used too.

- ✔ The English eagerly accepted European trends – French hoods, Italian britches, Spanish rapiers. Check out Shakespeare's plays (see Chapters 1 and 17) and notice the many Italian references.

# Chapter 19

# Ten Top Tudor Buildings

*I*f you want to see what's left of the Tudors, go to almost any city in England. And on the way to the cities, stop off at a few country houses, churches and pubs. A hierarchy existed: palaces were for the royals (see the map in Chapter 3); great houses were owned by the nobility; manor houses were the homes of the gentry; merchants lived in town houses. If any other buildings survive, like the homes of the poor, it's always by a sheer miracle.

Be warned, though – subsequent generations have fiddled with many Tudor buildings, and people often live in these period properties today. The Tudors didn't have central heating, hot and cold running water or loos that flushed, and if you see a TV set in a Jacobean (Stuart) cabinet, don't you believe it! And Tudor houses didn't all have priest holes either (see Chapter 14).

Here are ten of the best buildings of the Tudor era that survive in England today.

# Anne Hathaway's Cottage, Shottery, Warwickshire

In case you're wondering, Anne Hathaway is famous for being the wife of William Shakespeare. All the other buildings in this chapter are palaces, great houses or castles. Anne Hathaway's Cottage (which was never actually hers, by the way) is an example of an ordinary country home dating in its oldest parts from the 15th century.

Building in villages like Shottery wouldn't have happened very often and existing cottages would've been updated over time rather than starting from scratch. Major building programmes only occurred in London, often taking over ex-church land vacated by the monasteries in the 1530s (Chapter 6 explains why the monasteries dissolved at this time).

The Hathaway house belonged to a yeoman farmer (Anne's dad) and the oldest part dates to the 1460s. It had a cross passage with a hall to the left and a kitchen to the right. The house was *cruck-built* – imagine a capital letter *A* with the feet as the foundations and the apex forming the ridge of the roof. Joining these uprights were oak beams and the spaces between them were originally filled in with *wattle and daub* (wooden slats and mud). By the early 17th century this infill began to be made of brick. The house had one fireplace, and the very small windows had no glass but wooden shutters to keep out wind and rain.

Later extensions to the house added more rooms on the ground floor with two bedrooms above. The residents of many country cottages had to share their home with their cattle, but because Anne Hathaway's father, Richard, was reasonably well off (on her wedding day to William Shakespeare she received 6 pounds 13 shillings and 4 pence from his will) the animals were kept in outbuildings nearby.

Check out the cottage today – it's part of the Shakespeare circuit based in nearby Stratford and you can see the famous bed that, according to legend, is the 'second best' one that Shakespeare left Anne in his will.

# Burghley House, Stamford

Elizabeth I's principal secretary, William Cecil, inherited Burghley House from his father in 1553 and immediately began to rebuild. In 1563 he bought the manor of Theobalds (pronounced Tibbalds) and started to build there too. But in 1575 Cecil returned to Burghley House, completing the west front in 1577 and the north front ten years later.

Cecil designed his additions in the classical style, much used in France and the Low Countries (today's Netherlands). He'd never been to either country but copied the style from Somerset House in London (www.somersethouse.org.uk), which his former boss, the duke of Somerset (lord protector in Edward VI's reign), built in the late 1540s.

Burghley House is built around a central courtyard. The Great Hall, which is part of this range, originally had many large windows, but the weight of the slate roof began to cause structural problems and so in the 18th century several windows had to be filled in to strengthen the building. The present west range was probably built by Cecil's son Thomas, at the very end of the 16th century when the main entrance was moved from the west side to the north.

Visually, the heart of the house is its great central courtyard, which was designed to impress with glorious classical embellishments of columns, obelisks and carved roundels carrying portraits of Roman emperors – even a king of Troy! Although large parts of the house have been rebuilt and restored, much of it would be readily recognisable to William Cecil even today.

# Carisbrooke Castle, Isle of Wight

The original castle was built by the Normans in the late 11th century and by Elizabeth's reign the curtain wall and circular towers were completely unsuitable for defence purposes against cannon. In Chapter 15 we explain that even though the Armada had been defeated, Spain was still likely to try to invade England again. One obvious landing point would be the Isle of Wight, from which all kinds of attacks could be made on the south of England. So although Elizabeth didn't like spending money, she eventually paid the brilliant Italian architect Federigo Gianibelli to update Carisbrooke just in case.

Gianibelli extended the medieval towers along the south wall and turned them into gun platforms that could take at least two cannon. At the same time he built a series of earthworks called *arrowhead bastions*, which went all the way around the castle and were a death trap for any attackers.

To reach the castle wall you had to drop down a 12-foot ditch (and up the other side!), cross open land, drop down a 6-foot ditch, climb a 12-foot wall, cross more open ground and drop down a third ditch before attempting to climb the 30-foot ramp that led to the wall itself. The attackers couldn't see any of these ditches until it was too late. Oh, and by the way, while you were doing navigating these ditches, you were being fired at by four cannon, angled in such a way as to catch you in a murderous crossfire. As it happened, nobody ever attacked the castle to see how well this would work.

While you're at Carisbrooke, check out the cannon in the museum. It was made by the Owen Brothers of London in the 1540s and was one of several owned by local parishes for self-protection.

# Compton Wynyates, Warwickshire

Edmund Compton redesigned the family home in the 1480s, using a striking red brick. His was one of the first country houses not to have the thick walls and small windows necessary for defence. Compton, like everyone else, was hoping the country wouldn't return to the Wars of the Roses (see Chapter 2).

Compton was on good terms with the Tudors. His son, William, was page to Prince Henry, and the two became friends. In 1515 William started a building programme at Wynyates using windows and other features that Henry gave him from altered or demolished royal houses. He built the great entrance porch, the chapel, the brick-fluted and twisted chimneys and many of the towers that survive. Of all Tudor buildings, the chimneys at Wynyates are impressive; no two are the same.

Henry VIII visited William many times, and the window of the bedroom that he used still shows his arms in stained glass, along with those of Catherine of Aragon. Elizabeth I also stayed at Compton Wynyates in 1572.

A curious feature of the house is the Priest's Room at the top of one of the towers, so called because of five consecration crosses carved in the window-sill. This detail is curious because (as far as historians know) the Comptons were Protestants, who were unlikely to have given refuge to a fugitive priest.

In one respect Compton Wynyates has been fortunate. In 1574 Henry, Lord Compton, began to build Castle Ashby, and so he neglected Wynyates while lavishing money and attention on his new home. Wynyates was therefore spared any efforts to keep it up to date. In the 18th century an order to demolish the house was ignored. It was restored in 1884, and in 1978, when Castle Ashby was opened to the public, Compton Wynyates became the family's principal home.

# Deal Castle, Kent

The most likely place for an attack by the French in Henry VIII's reign was along the south coast of England. In 1539 Henry built a string of castles from St Mawes and Pendennis in the west to Sandown in the east to keep the French out. In 1545 Francis I's troops landed on the Isle of Wight and hand to hand fighting took place at Sandown fort, which hadn't quite been finished in time! Deal Castle is one of the best known of the surviving fortresses built for Henry VIII.

Cannon had improved so much by this time that high medieval walls, as at Carisbrooke, were useless against them. The answer was to build low, squat defences, bristling with guns.

Deal's core was formed by the keep, around which were clustered six semi-circular bastions, all with walls 4 metres (14 feet) thick to withstand the expected bombardment. Four tiers of artillery defended the fortress: one mounted on the roof of the keep, two others in the upper storeys and the fourth in the bastions.

Building work began in April 1538 to specifications by the German architect Stephen Haschnperg, who'd also worked on the fortifications at Carlisle near the Scots border. Due to the project's urgency, 1,400 workers were employed, and Anne of Cleves was entertained at a huge banquet there when she landed at Dover in 1540.

# The Great Court of Trinity College, Cambridge

Cambridge is the second oldest university in the country after Oxford, and the series of colleges were built by the Church or private individuals from the 13th century onwards.

Henry VIII rebuilt the King's Hall and Michaelhouse as Trinity College in 1546. The Great Court dates back to 1428 and was developed by Dr Thomas Neville, master of the college from 1593–1615. The Great Gate was begun about 1490 and completed in the 1530s, and the chapel was built between 1554 and 1561. The Great Hall and the Old Library both date from the end of Elizabeth's reign, as does the Queen's Gate, from 1597. In the centre of the court is an octagonal fountain that was built between 1601 and 1602. Like much Tudor building, it's crumbled, and the one you see there today was rebuilt to the original design in 1716.

The figure of Henry VIII stands over the main gate, carved in stone and surrounded by heraldry. Next time you're at Trinity College, check out the sceptre in the king's hand – it's a wooden chair leg!

# Hampton Court, London

The most famous royal palace didn't start off royal at all. The original building belonged to the Medieval warrior-monks of the Order of St John and Henry VIII's lord chancellor, Thomas Wolsey, bought the place and did it up. Because he was richer than Henry VIII in the 1520s, Wolsey was able to spend a fortune on the palace, creating new kitchens, courtyards, galleries and magnificent rooms for Henry, who was sure to visit.

In 1528 Wolsey gave Hampton Court as a present to Henry VIII because he realised his career was on the way down (see Chapter 4). The king then added the chapel, the Great Hall and a magnificent lavatory with no fewer than 28 seats! Because of the drop of the land from the spring at Kingston the palace had running water from a tank on the roof and Henry's apartments even had hot running water, which must have been unique in England at the time. Eventually, the compound included gardens, a tiltyard (for jousting), tennis courts and a large hunting park.

Hampton Court was one of Henry VIII's favourite homes, and he spent more than 800 nights there – more than at any other palace apart from Greenwich. Many of the Tudor buildings at Hampton Court were demolished in the late 17th century to make way for the present apartments, but the chapel, the Great Watching Chamber (where the king conducted his business) and the Great Hall survive.

Some modern visitors claim to hear the ghost of Catherine Howard screaming as she runs down the corridors to beg Henry VIII to forgive her before her execution (see Chapter 5 for the details of her death).

## Hardwick Hall, Derbyshire

The new Hardwick Hall was built in the 1590s by Elizabeth, dowager countess of Shrewsbury, better known as Bess of Hardwick (see Chapter 17). Bess inherited Hardwick Hall from her father, and with the wealth she gained from the death of her fourth husband, George Talbot, in 1590, she was able to afford to build a much more impressive house, which still stands today.

Glass is one of the standout features of Hardwick Hall. In the late 16th century glass was very expensive and showed the wealth of its owner more effectively than the size of the house. The important rooms had more and bigger windows. These spaces were located on the top levels, where the family lived, to take advantage of the most light. The servants' quarters, in contrast, had small windows.

Hardwick Hall doesn't include a great hall, and so communal dining was clearly not a feature of life at the house. But the Tudor building does have a Great Gallery, which is one of the longest and widest to survive from the period and the only one to retain its original tapestries and pictures. In the 16th century tapestries, mostly imported from France, were extremely expensive and woven with cloth of gold and silver. They brought the rooms alive with colour. In fact, many of the rooms have survived as they were in Bess's time, along with beautiful embroidery stitched by Bess and her ladies.

# Henry VII's Chapel, Westminster Abbey, London

This magnificent chapel is the most superb example of Tudor architecture. If you look up at the roof you can see that it has 15th-century heraldry with ornate fan vaulting and Tudor heraldry of roses and dragons all over the place.

The chapel was originally designed as the final resting place of Henry VI. At the time the dead king was a candidate for sainthood and so this mausoleum would have become another place of pilgrimage, built as it was so close to the shrine of the 11th-century king Edward the Confessor, and would have brought in lots of cash for the church.

Work began in 1502, when the existing 13th-century lady chapel dedicated to the Virgin and the nearby chapel of St Erasmus were demolished to make way for the new structure. Actual building began in January 1503, and by the time Henry VII died in 1509 about £15,000 had been spent and a further £5,000 authorised.

But Henry VIII's priorities were different from those of his father, and Henry VI remained buried at Windsor. Instead, Henry VII and his wife, Elizabeth of York, lie in the chapel, side by side in the magnificent tomb designed for them by the brilliant Italian sculptor Pietro Torrigiano.

If you can get close enough, have a look at the face of Henry VII – we *know* he looked exactly like that. But even better is the nearby tomb of his mother, Margaret Beaufort, which is so lifelike you almost expect the old dear to sit up and smile at you. The chapel also includes the tombs of Elizabeth I, Mary I, James I and Mary Queen of Scots.

# Penshurst Place, Kent

Penshurst, 30 miles south-east of London, was the medieval home of Sir John de Pulteney, who was lord mayor of London four times, and much of his original building survives. In the 15th century it became the home of Henry V's brothers – John, duke of Bedford, and then Humphrey, duke of Gloucester. After Pulteney's death three generations of the Stafford family, dukes of Buckingham, owned the house. Each duke added to the building, and their additions remain to this day.

Edward, the third duke, entertained Henry VIII at Penshurst with a lavish banquet in 1519, but such hospitality didn't prevent Henry from having him executed for high treason two years later, at which point Penshurst returned to the Crown because, in theory, all land in England belonged to the king under the medieval feudal system which had almost, but not quite, disappeared. Although Henry visited Penshurst, he doesn't seem to have undertaken any work there.

In 1552 Edward VI gave the house to Sir William Sidney, whose son, Henry, added the Queen Elizabeth Room. The magnificent Long Gallery, which presently houses a collection of tapestries and portraits, was added by Sidney's younger son, Robert, who was a very wealthy man in his own right. He was the nephew of Robert Dudley, earl of Leicester (Elizabeth's favourite; see Chapter 12) and Ambrose, earl of Warwick. Queen Elizabeth I visited the house many times.

# Chapter 20

# Ten Major Tudor Events

*B*eing confronted by a lot of dates can be offputting, but they're actually pretty handy. When exploring history, try thinking of dates as being like children's clothes pegs. You hang things on them – events, conflicts and actions, – so that you can find them again.

This chapter highlights ten major events and essential dates for the Tudor period. Although some historians may debate our choice of events, the episodes we look at here mark important shifts in the evolution of the Tudor monarchy. Taken together, you get a picture of a dynamic period during which England's self-confidence grew and became increasingly bloody.

## The First Tudor King, Henry VII (1485)

School books often say that 1485 marks the division between *medieval* and *modern* history, with the beginning of a new monarchy. Although the distinction between these periods makes sense today, matters didn't look that way in 1485!

Some people welcomed the death of the unpopular Richard III and hoped that his passing would mark the end of the feud between the Houses of York and Lancaster (which we describe in Chapter 2), especially when Henry Tudor (Henry VII) married Elizabeth of York. Others saw Henry VII as yet another usurper. In a sense both groups were right, because a rebellion occurred in 1486, and within ten years two claimants were pursuing the crown. The rightful Yorkist claimant, Edward, Earl of Warwick was kept in the Tower until his execution in 1499, while Henry VII kept the throne.

Henry VII did indeed establish a new dynasty, but he was a medieval king in his style of governing, relying on traditional methods and institutions to govern. (Flip to Chapter 4 for more about Henry VII.)

# Henry VIII's Coronation (1509)

The young, magnificent and handsome Henry VIII married the beautiful and intelligent Catherine of Aragon soon after he became monarch in 1509, and not long afterwards they were crowned together in Westminster Abbey. The episode was a gorgeously executed piece of political propaganda.

English chronicler and lawyer Edward Hall recorded the coronation scenes in vivid detail, describing the elaborate work of tailors, embroiderers and goldsmiths who dressed both the courtiers and their horses. The King and Queen processed through the City of Westminster along streets hung with tapestries and cloths of gold. Henry was dressed with diamonds and rubies, so many that the actual material of his garments was almost obscured.

They entered the abbey under embroidered canopies and walked along a strip of cloth, which was cut up as soon as they passed, as souvenirs for onlookers. William Warham, Archbishop of Canterbury, carried out the crowning. Afterwards everyone went to Westminster Hall for an enormous and sumptuous banquet with jousting and feasting followed by weeks of celebrations. (Turn to Chapter 4 for more on Henry VIII's early years.)

# Breaking with Rome (1534)

The Act of Supremacy in 1534 ended papal power in England and made Henry VIII Supreme Head of the Church of England, breaking centuries of tradition.

Pope Julius II had given Henry permission to marry Catherine, his brother's wife. But Henry became convinced that his marriage to Catherine of Aragon was against the law of God, which was why she failed to bear him a son. For her part, Catherine was sure that her marriage was legitimate, and she had the support of her nephew, Charles V, the supremely powerful Holy Roman Emperor who had raided Rome and held the Pope Clement VII prisoner.

When Henry's new love Anne Boleyn became pregnant in the autumn of 1532, he was certain that the child would be a boy and married her. The ceremony was performed by Thomas Cranmer, Archbishop of Canterbury who declared the marriage to Catherine null and void, believing that Henry was right and ready to break his oath of allegiance to the pope. (You can read more about the break with Rome in Chapter 7.)

# Anne Boleyn's execution (1536)

Henry VIII moved heaven and earth to marry Anne, a woman whose sexual grip on him didn't relax through six long years of courtship and frustration. However, she was suddenly cast aside because Henry believed that she'd committed both adultery and incest; and adultery by the Queen was always treason because it threatened the legitimate succession.

Anne's fate shows the volatility of Henry's temperament – his gullibility, his ruthlessness and the personal nature of Tudor politics. Anne had given birth to Elizabeth, but she failed to bear a son – just like Catherine. Again, the King had doubts about the lawfulness of his second marriage. Was God punishing him again?

Anne was the leader of a family-based political faction that had attracted Henry's powerful secretary, Thomas Cromwell. Cromwell was allied to the Boleyn family until the end of 1535 because Anne's marriage had been the result of the Act of Supremacy, which Cromwell had drafted and put through the English Parliament.

When Catherine died in 1536, alliances changed. Cromwell played on Henry's doubts about Anne and her flirtatious nature, and Henry ordered her arrest. The evidence against Anne was weak and she was almost certainly innocent, but Henry believed her to be guilty and so she was beheaded at the Tower. (We describe the fate of Anne and all Henry's wives in Chapter 6).

# Dissolution of the Monasteries (1540)

The Dissolution of the Monasteries, also known as the Suppression of the Monasteries, was more than a decree with religious and political overtones; it was an act of vandalism. Great libraries were destroyed or dispersed, works of art confiscated and great buildings left to fall into disrepair and ruin.

The year of 1540 ended a process of dissolution that began in 1523, and closed a part of English religious life that had existed for a thousand years. Monks and nuns were forced to return to the everyday world and their lands returned to the Crown, which acquired property worth many millions of pounds – about 20 per cent of the landed wealth of England. Thomas Cromwell carried out a survey of monastic wealth, published as the *Valor Ecclesiasticus* in 1536. This report showed the vast amount of land the clergy owned and how the inhabitants gave taxes to the papacy, a sum known as *Peter's Pence*.

Henry believed that monks and nuns were living lives of luxury and idleness. He also contended that closing the monasteries was a safe way for the Crown to acquire a lot of money and lands, much of which he later sold. Much of acquired land was sold to Catholics, but when Mary became monarch (flip to Chapter 10), asking them to return the land to the Church was impractical after they'd held it for almost 20 years.

# Elizabeth I's Ascension (1558)

After 1558 the future of the English Church was Protestant rather than Catholic, and its governors were gentlemen rather than nobles or clergy. The future also held friendship with Scotland and hostility to Spain.

Having a woman on the throne was nothing new for England, but unlike her sister Mary, Elizabeth was a remarkable woman. Elizabeth's court was secular, highly educated and Protestant. From her mother Anne Boleyn, she inherited the ability to use gender and sexuality as weapons, which made her a highly original ruler. Indeed, much of Elizabeth's foreign policy through to 1581 was about marriage negotiations as much as security. Her frequent changes of mind allowed her to retain control in the male-dominated world of politics. (Only in relation to Robert Dudley did her desire almost overcome her political sense, as we describe in Chapter 13.)

Her Church Settlement of 1559 was revolutionary and against the advice of her councillors, but it reflected her own tastes and opinions. Few were happy with it. But Elizabeth believed that God had given her the realm of England to rule, and she would allow no interference (Chapter 14 has more on these issues).

Elizabeth was also one of the great image creators of the English monarchy. Many portraits of her survive that show her love of pearls and the elegant hands of which she was so proud. She was Gloriana, the Virgin Queen. Her inviolate body became the symbol of a realm free from invasion and foreign power.

# Birth of William Shakespeare (1564)

William was born to John Shakespeare and Mary Arden in April 1564 and was baptised in Holy Trinity church, Stratford-upon-Avon. He was the eldest of eight children, five of whom survived, but little is known about their upbringing. At 18 he married the pregnant Anne Hathaway. Scholars know little of his religion and even less about his education. But a travelling theatre company, The Queen's Men, visited Stratford in 1587, and William may have joined them at that point. Certainly by 1595 he had joined The Chamberlain's Men company.

Historians don't know when he began to write – or why – but he did write poems dedicated to his patron, the Earl of Southampton. The first authentic dramatic work was a version of *Richard III* debuting in 1595. He was quickly in demand and within two years bought a substantial house in Stratford, where his wife and family continued to live in spite of his many commitments in London.

He was well-known during his lifetime in the world of London theatres and at court. His gift with words and empathy with the human situation ensured that his plays survive as a monument to Elizabethan culture and to the English language in general. He died in 1616, but his work survives as the crowning achievement of the English Renaissance.

# *Conflict with the Papacy (1570)*

In 1570, Pope Pius V issued the papal bull *Regnans in Excelsis*, excommunicating and deposing Elizabeth I. Philip II like many others thought Pius's move was a mistake because it created problems for English Catholics:

- ✔ Before 1570, the English Catholics saw themselves as loyal Englishmen who disagreed with the Elizabethan religious settlement and looked to Mary, Queen of Scots, as the heir to the throne. They wanted Elizabeth to acknowledge Mary but weren't prepared to help Mary, by conspiracy or in any other way.

- ✔ After 1570, in principle the option to help was no longer open to English Catholics. If they accepted the pope's authority, they couldn't accept Elizabeth as monarch, and thus became potential traitors to the English Crown.

Elizabeth had no idea how many Catholics lived in her dominions or how seriously they would take the bull. Most conformed to her conservative Protestant Church Settlement and became an identifiable and manageable problem (as we relate in Chapter 14). But how should she identify individuals who supported the papacy, because for them *Regnans in Excelsis* was a declaration against Elizabeth?

The bull forced the Queen to support the Protestant side in the religious division, which was opening up throughout Europe. Eventually Elizabeth's Protestant support led to war with Spain (check out Chapter 16).

# War with Spain (1585)

The extraordinary thing about the war between England and Spain is that it took so long to happen! Elizabeth had been backing pirates raiding the Spanish colonies since the mid-1560s. English trade with the Low Countries was embargoed, English volunteers were fighting the Spanish alongside the Dutch rebels and Francis Drake had out-paced Philip, King of Spain, in his round-the-world voyage. Elizabeth professed goodwill towards Philip with one hand, but then knighted Francis Drake with the other.

Philip was exasperated but held back because he knew the quality of the English soldiers and seamen. He also had enough to deal with in the Low Countries with North African pirates and with the Turks in the Mediterranean. His acquisition of Portugal in 1580 only added to his problems. Spain's naval power was essentially for the defence of its coastline, but after 1580 Philip's priorities changed: partly due to his success in Portugal, partly to the brazen way in which Elizabeth welcomed Francis Drake and partly to Philip's continued success in getting his silver supplies through from the New World.

When a Catholic assassin killed William the Silent, the Dutch lost their leader and chief inspiration. The English Council was alarmed and feared England would be next on Philip's hit list (as we relate in Chapter 16). The war was finally on!

# England's Defeat of the Spanish Armada (1588)

England was already a great sea power before encountering the Spanish Armada, but 1588 reinforced her supremacy and gave her sea dogs huge confidence (turn to Chapter 16 for more details).

Philip's attack was planned as a glorified raid to conquer southern England and force a regime change, although with Mary Queen of Scots dead, who Philip planned to install in Elizabeth's place is unclear. The Marquis of Santa Cruz, a great sea commander but a poor administrator, was placed in charge of preparations.

In England the preparations were being carefully monitored. The English navy was strengthened, arms stockpiled and arrangements made for musters. A counter-attack was also prepared, and on 19 April 1587, just weeks before the Armada was intended to sail, Drake struck at Cadiz and destroyed supply ships that were loaded and waiting in the harbour for the order to sail north. The surprise and destruction were complete. No Armada was able to sail in 1587.

When Santa Cruz died, he was replaced by the efficient Duke of Medina Sidonia, and soon the Armada was ready to leave Lisbon. The Armada entered the western approaches and then a major flaw was revealed. Medina had instructions where to rendezvous with the Duke of Palma, but he had no idea how he was to do so. Medina received no news from the duke until the ships reached Calais and the news was bad: it would be at least a week before the army of Flanders would be ready. The Armada simply had to stay where it was.

The same night Lord Howard of Effingham sent in fireships at Calais and scattered the Armada along the Flanders banks. The next day Effingham sent in the warships and pounded the Spanish. The ensuing Battle of Gravelines demonstrated the superiority of the English gunners and resulted in a comprehensive defeat of the Spanish and the loss of about 16,000 Spanish men.

# Chapter 21

# Ten Tudor Firsts

**M**any people talk of the Tudor period as being the beginning of the modern world, at least in England. Things aren't quite that clear cut, but the years 1485–1603 did witness a great number of new inventions and discoveries. Many of these weren't just 'firsts' for the Tudor world; they were new arrivals that in some cases are still with us in one form or another, or which changed forever established ways of doing things.

This chapter highlights ten of the most significant and long-lasting Tudor 'firsts'. So grab a coffee, and maybe a few tomatoes to nibble, and read on!

## Sailing into the First Dry Dock, Portsmouth (1495)

The only way to repair ships in the Middle Ages was to *careen*, which meant tilting them by shifting the weight of cargo and/or guns so that the keel was out of the water for long enough to get the work done. This method was very dodgy – when they careened the *Royal George* (the British flagship) in 1782 it sank with a huge loss of life.

You could wait for a very high tide and drag a damaged ship as far onto the foreshore as possible and start work on it, but even then, water would still be present in the bilges and the hold, and carpenters would sometimes have to work waist-deep. The next problem was then to wait for another high tide before you could get the ship afloat again.

In 1495, a man called Robert Brygandine hit upon a solution to this problem. Working with the architect Sir Reginald Bray, Brygandine put the idea of building a *dry dock* to Henry VII. Because Henry was keen to build up his navy and Bray was the designer of the magnificent Henry VII Chapel in Westminster Abbey (see Chapter 2), this was a marriage made in heaven.

The first Portsmouth dry dock isn't there any more, but if you're visiting the *Mary Rose* (see Chapter 3) take a walk along to the *Victory* (Lord Nelson's flagship at the Battle of Trafalgar) and you'll be standing where the dock was built. It was made of wood and stone, with walls packed with earth. A ship could sail in, the gates were shut,and the water was then pumped out, with the gates keeping the sea back. The result? Carpenters and shipwrights could work in peace and in the dry.

Only royal ships could use this brilliant invention and it remained in use until 1623. It set Portsmouth up as *the* shipbuilding heart of the Royal Navy for centuries.

# Building the First Printing Press in England, London (1500)

Setting up the first printing press in England was the brainchild of Jan van Wynkyn of Worth in Alsace, Germany who came to England either in 1476 or 1481. The pronunciation of Worth ended in a 'd' sound, which was handy for a printer, so he came to be known as Wynkyn de Word – cool or what?

Wynkyn worked for the printer William Caxton in Westminster, near the Abbey, and he became a rival to another printer, John Lettou. In 1495, Wynkyn took over Caxton's print shop before moving to Fleet Street five years later.

Wynkyn is famous for more firsts than almost anybody. He was the first to use *italic* type in 1528 and the first to print music with type, working with Ranulf Higdon in the book *Polychronicon* as early as 1495. He was also the first to have a bookstall in St Paul's churchyard, which became the centre of the English book trade.

The Tudor age was an age of patrons – you'd get nowhere without somebody powerful to open career doors for you – and Wynkyn's patron was the clever, intellectual Margaret Beaufort, mother of Henry VII.

The 'father of Fleet Street', as Wynkyn came to be known, printed 500 books that ran to 800 editions in his lifetime, providing cheaper books for the mass market. A lot of these books were religious, as you'd expect from a period full of religious problems, but he also printed poetry and books for kids, with illustrations.

Wynkyn's moveable type set the pattern for centuries of printing and his base in Fleet Street went on to make the place the newspaper capital of the world by the 19th century.

# Publishing the First Cookery Book, London (1500)

One of Wynkyn's rivals in the early London printing trade was Richard Pynson, who became royal printer to Henry VIII (so, successful as he was, eat your heart out Wynkyn de Word, because you didn't get the top job!). All the key documents of Henry's early reign were printed by Pynson.

Centuries later, in 2002, the Marquess of Bath was having a clear out of his huge library at the family home at Longleat, when he came across a book called *The Boke of Cookery*. He nearly threw it out. It turned out that his book is the only known copy of the work in the world, and it tells us a lot about the food of the Tudors.

A lot of Pynson's book is about great feasts that earlier kings – Henry IV, Henry V and so on – enjoyed. This focus is as typical of 'celebrity chefs' then as now – getting as much recognition from the top brass as they can.

In 2006, two of the recipes from *The Boke of Cookery* were made in BBC TV's Breakfast Show. 'Pommes Moled' is Apple Pudding. It's got apples (!), rice, almonds, sugar, saffron, salt, nutmeg, cinnamon and ginger in it, and sounds scrummy! Another dish, 'Saracen Bruet for Ten Messes' (Turkish Stew), may sound a little bit un-PC today, but it's a sort of goulash. Rabbit, partridge, chicken, red wine, cloves, mace, pine nuts, currants, ginger, sugar and cinnamon were thrown in (careful though, 21st century reader – this recipe may contain nuts!).

# Playing the First Lottery in England (1569)

Defending a country was expensive. Navies and armies had to be paid, guns and other weapons made and maintained. And don't get us started on the cost of fortifications! Rulers could raise extra cash from taxation, but people didn't like taxes and might rebel rather than pay them.

So Queen Elizabeth's government came up with a brilliant idea: Print some tickets (400,000 of them, to be precise) and get people to buy them. There was a guaranteed prize every time (bring it on!) that was usually silver plate or tapestry – what every young upwardly-mobile Elizabethan wanted. How could it fail? Adverts appeared all over the place on scrolls that showed the royal coat of arms and line-drawings of the prizes. As a bonus, people who bought tickets could also feel really good about themselves, because the money raised was for the 'reparation of the havens [harbours] and strength of the Realm [country] and towards such other publique good works.' Makes you proud to be an Elizabethan, doesn't it?

And if you couldn't afford a ticket, you could buy a share in one – a third or a sixteenth or whatever – sort of like today's syndicates.

The idea was dreamt up in 1566 and the first draw took place three years later. By 1571, however, the idea was dropped – perhaps the world just wasn't ready for lotteries.

# Navigating with the First County Maps in England (1579)

In the 21st century, many people would struggle to find their way from A to B without their trusty satnavs, or at least without motorists' gazetteers. While you're zooming along in your car, local radio stations warn you of delays on motorways and large, lit signs remind you that 'tiredness can kill' and tell you to take a break.

Tudor travellers had no such gadgets and gizmos to help them on their way. Instead, they trusted to luck for most of the century, relying on appalling track-like roads and wooden sign-posts.

Then along came Christopher Saxton. He was the son of a Yorkshire farmer (or clothier – perhaps both), born about 1540. In 1570 he was commissioned by Thomas Seckford, Master of the Court of Requests, to draw maps of all thirty-four counties in England and Wales.

To create his maps, Saxton used a system of triangulation first used in the Netherlands forty years earlier; a Dutch expert, Remigius Hogenberg, worked with him. Italian technology helped to produce these maps – a new engraving technique had been developed there in the 1560s. Arty bits (which, sadly, we don't use any more) like ships and sea-monsters were added later and each map was hand-coloured. When each map was finished, it was sent to Cecil for approval. On some of these maps, which still exist in the official archive today, Cecil himself has written the number of troops he knew to be available in each area.

The man who paid for all this, though, was Thomas Seckford (the queen was superb at getting other people to fork out for *her* defence) but he did get his coat of arms on the maps, so he was happy. So was Christopher Saxton. The queen gave him a ten-year monopoly on all map-making in England and a nice little manor house at Grigston in Suffolk.

Behind all this activity was William Cecil (see Chapters 12–18), Queen Elizabeth's chief adviser, who needed accurate maps for political reasons: rebels in the north, invading Scots, foreign armies landing on the coast, and other eventualities. Cecil needed to know where, how far, and how long, and where to locate the water supplies, the hills and the marshes.

There was one problem, though. There were no roads on Saxton's maps; nobody thought it was necessary.

# Writing with the First Shorthand System (1588)

In the year of the Armada (see Chapter 15) it was more vital than ever that state secrets were kept secret. Nobody was more aware of that than Francis Walsingham, Elizabeth's spymaster, and it can't be a coincidence that someone who knew him well was a man called Timothy Bright.

Bright was born in about 1551 near Sheffield and he graduated from Trinity College, Cambridge in 1569. He was actually a medical student and was studying in Paris in 1572 when Catherine de Medici launched her massacre of Protestants there (see Chapter 13). Terrified, he ran for safety to the house of the English ambassador, who happened to be Francis Walsingham, and a relationship was born.

As a doctor, Bright wasn't very good. His time at St Bartholomew's Hospital in London was very undistinguished, even though he was one of the first to write about melancholy (depression) and its related medical conditions.

Perhaps because of his links with Walsingham, however, Bright went on to write *Characterie: the Art of Shorte, Swifte and Secret Writing by Character* and presented it to the queen in 1588. Like Pynson's cookery book, only one copy of this books remains in existence – in the Bodleian Library in Oxford.

Bright used a series of lines, circles and half circles as 538 symbols for words. Some letters were omitted from his alphabet, so, for example, his own name, Timothy, would have to be spelt with an 'i' at the end; he'd not included a 'y'!

Bright may have intended to develop an international sign language but it never happened, and it's possible that his shorthand system was used to record church sermons to be printed and published later and perhaps even the plays of Shakespeare and Marlowe.

Bright did better out of his shorthand system than he did in medicine. The queen gave him a monopoly to publish his system for fifteen years.

# Inventing the First Knitting Frame (1589)

Some inventions were delayed because of their effect on existing systems – the knitting frame was one.

The inventor, William Lee, was an Anglican curate born in 1563 in Calverton near Nottingham, one of the most important of the textile areas in England. He graduated from Christ's College, Cambridge, twenty years later, intending to be an ordinary parish priest.

The story goes that Lee became furious with hand-knitting because his fiancée spent all her time making her own clothes and had no time for him! Outraged, he started to think up ways of speeding up the knitting process.

The original machine he came up with had eight needles to the inch. The result of this was coarse cloth, so he made modifications that included twenty needles to enable his machine to make fine cloth. By 1598, Lee was able to knit silk in this way too. He gave up the Church and focussed entirely on his invention, taking the frame (small enough to fit into a country cottage) to London to show to Baron Hunsdon and the court.

Queen Elizabeth was impressed, but in a very far-sighted and wise move, she turned down his application for a patent because she realised the harm his gadget would do to the hand knitters. James I felt the same when Lee tried again in 1603. Only the 18th century didn't care, and by that time, it was all about mechanical power, profit and greed, and Lee's knitting frame of two centuries earlier came into its own. The result? Finely-knit stockings, wide-spread unemployment and a working-class movement – the Luddites of the early 1800s – determined to destroy machinery in the forlorn hope of keeping their livelihoods.

# Flushing the First Water Closet (1596)

Sir John Harington (1561–1612) is best remembered today as a courtier, poet, wit and general pain in the neck. He was born near Bath as the son of a courtier and he was the queen's godson. She called him 'Boy Jacke' for the rest of her life. He went to school at Eton and university at King's College, Cambridge, getting his Master's degree in 1581. He married well and became infamous at court for his risqué poetry and naughty translations of Greek poetry which upset almost everybody.

Harington's most famous gaffe was _A New Discourse of a Stale Subject, called the Metamorphosis of Ajax,_ printed in 1596. Now, you probably don't realise it, but you've just heard an Elizabethan joke (tell it at parties – it'll be a riot!). Ajax was a character in Greek Mythology, but _jakes_ was a Tudor word for a toilet or privy. Good, eh?

Well, the queen didn't think so and sent Harington 'into the country' (in other words, away from her) until he could behave himself. All this nonsense disguised the fact that Harington had indeed changed the privy for ever. His 'device' (he never gave it a name) had a leather valve which opened and closed by levers and a cistern which flushed waste with clean water. It also had a stopper to prevent unpleasant smells from coming up from the cesspit below.

Now the queen was in two minds over this. She hated making decisions and Harington's device gave her a problem. She liked it enough to have one installed in Richmond Palace, but probably didn't use it because there was still no sewerage piping to carry waste away and because she was scared of the gurgling noise it made.

If the queen had approved, of course, flush loos would have become all the rage. Because she didn't, Englishmen and women had to make do with chamber pots and holes in the ground for many years to come.

# Nibbling the First Tomatoes in England (1597)

No, the Tudors didn't invent tomatoes. They weren't even the first people to import them from where they grew in central and south America. In fact, tomatoes in England nearly didn't happen at all.

Tomatoes were found in 1519 by Hernando Cortez, the Spanish conquistador, in the garden of Montezuma (he of the 'revenge'), the Aztec king. From there, tomatoes got back to Spain and then on to Italy. Since they were called *pommi d'oro* (golden apples) it's likely they were the yellow variety.

When botanists gave names to all sorts of plants later on, the tomato was called *Lycopersicon esculentum,* which means 'wolf-peach', and that's a clue to why Englishmen didn't like them. The 2nd-century medical expert Galen had described what appeared to be a tomato fourteen centuries earlier, explaining that it contained a poison to kill wolves – hence the Latin name. Galen wasn't very good but everybody thought he was, so the idea stuck.

One man who thought otherwise was John Gerard, a barber-surgeon who may have been the first man to grow tomatoes in England. In his *Herbal* of 1597 he wrote that tomatoes were grown in Spain and Italy, and this was probably reason enough to consider them poisonous. They were good, he said, for treating gout and ulcers, but other antidotes were better and had no side effects.

Gerard's *Herbal*, like Galen's writings, was highly influential, so it was nearly a century before tomatoes were welcomed with open arms by the English.

# *Drinking the First Coffee in England (1599)*

Queen Elizabeth's England was full of brave, even foolhardy adventurers who were prepared to risk their lives to find new worlds or at least grab the riches they held.

One of these adventurers was Antony Sherley (1595–1630). Sherley sailed on a completely unauthorized mission to Persia (today's Iran and Iraq) to set up English trading posts and to get the *shah* (the Persian king) onside against the Ottoman Turks. William Parry, one of Sherley's men, wrote the first account of coffee drinking in English:

> *'They [the Turks; sit] drinking a certain liquor, which they do call Coffe, which is made of seede much like mustard seede, which will soon intoxicate the braine ...'*

The Turks claimed it warmed them up when the weather was cold and was cleansing because it made them break wind!

A number of Jacobean explorers and travellers mention coffee and the first coffee-house in England was probably opened in Oxford in 1652. Whether Sherley ever actually ever brought any of the beans back for roasting in England is open to doubt – Elizabeth's government made it clear he'd over-stepped the mark with his Persian adventure and he was told not to come back.

He was certainly back by 1603, however, when he annoyed James I in one of the king's many clashes with parliament. Sherley may or may not have been the first English coffee-drinker, but his arrest led to the vital change in the law which set up parliamentary privilege; an MP cannot be arrested just for speaking his mind.

# Index

## • *C* •

## • *G* •

# • *Y* •

# Notes

# FOR DUMMIES®

## Making Everything Easier! ™

# UK editions

## BUSINESS

**Marketing Kit For Dummies**
978-0-470-74490-1

**Business Plans Kit For Dummies**
978-0-470-74381-2

**Consulting For Dummies**
978-0-470-71382-2

## REFERENCE

**British Politics For Dummies**
978-0-470-68637-9

**Football For Dummies**
978-0-470-68837-3

**Researching Your Family History Online For Dummies**
978-0-470-74535-9

## HOBBIES

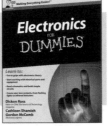

**Growing Your Own Fruit & Veg For Dummies**
978-0-470-69960-7

**Allotment Gardening For Dummies**
978-0-470-68641-6

**Electronics For Dummies**
978-0-470-68178-7

Anger Management For Dummies
978-0-470-68216-6

Boosting Self-Esteem For Dummies
978-0-470-74193-1

British Sign Language
For Dummies
978-0-470-69477-0

Business NLP For Dummies
978-0-470-69757-3

Cricket For Dummies
978-0-470-03454-5

CVs For Dummies, 2nd Edition
978-0-470-74491-8

Divorce For Dummies, 2nd Edition
978-0-470-74128-3

Emotional Freedom Technique
For Dummies
978-0-470-75876-2

Emotional Healing For Dummies
978-0-470-74764-3

English Grammar For Dummies
978-0-470-05752-0

Flirting For Dummies
978-0-470-74259-4

IBS For Dummies
978-0-470-51737-6

Improving Your Relationship For
Dummies
978-0-470-68472-6

Lean Six Sigma For Dummies
978-0-470-75626-3

Life Coaching For Dummies,
2nd Edition
978-0-470-66554-1

# FOR DUMMIES®

## A world of resources to help you grow

## UK editions

### SELF-HELP

978-0-470-66541-1     978-0-470-66543-5     978-0-470-66086-7

### STUDENTS

978-0-470-68820-5     978-0-470-74711-7     978-0-470-74290-7

### HISTORY

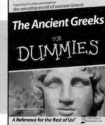

978-0-470-99468-9     978-0-470-74783-4     978-0-470-98787-2

Origami Kit For Dummies
978-0-470-75857-1

Overcoming Depression For Dummies
978-0-470-69430-5

Positive Psychology For Dummies
978-0-470-72136-0

PRINCE2 For Dummies, 2009 Edition
978-0-470-71025-8

Psychometric Tests For Dummies
978-0-470-75366-8

Raising Happy Children
For Dummies
978-0-470-05978-4

Reading the Financial Pages
For Dummies
978-0-470-71432-4

Sage 50 Accounts For Dummies
978-0-470-71558-1

Self-Hypnosis For Dummies
978-0-470-66073-7

Starting a Business For Dummies,
2nd Edition
978-0-470-51806-9

Study Skills For Dummies
978-0-470-74047-7

Teaching English as a Foreign
Language For Dummies
978-0-470-74576-2

Teaching Skills For Dummies
978-0-470-74084-2

Time Management For Dummies
978-0-470-77765-7

Work-Life Balance For Dummies
978-0-470-71380-8

**Available wherever books are sold. For more information or to order direct go to www.wiley.com
or call +44 (0) 1243 843291**

19546 (p2)

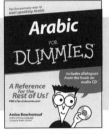

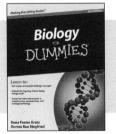

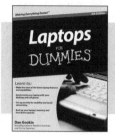

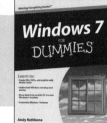